P9-ELH-962

BACKROADS & BYWAYS OF
VERMONT

Drives, Day Trips &
Weekend Excursions

CHRISTINA TREE, LISA HALVORSEN,
AND PAT GOUDEY O'BRIEN

THE COUNTRYMAN PRESS
A division of W. W. Norton & Company
Independent Publishers Since 1923

Copyright © 2018 by Christina Tree

All rights reserved
Printed in the United States of America

For information about permission to reproduce selections from this book,
write to Permissions, The Countryman Press, 500 Fifth Avenue, New York, NY 10110

For information about special discounts for bulk purchases, please contact
W. W. Norton Special Sales at specialsales@wwnorton.com or 800-233-4830

Manufacturing by Versa Press
Series book design by Chris Welch
Production manager: Devon Zahn

The Countryman Press
www.countrymanpress.com

A division of W. W. Norton & Company, Inc.
500 Fifth Avenue, New York, NY 10110
www.wwnorton.com

978-1-68268-164-0 (pbk.)

10 9 8 7 6 5 4 3 2 1

To my Davis family. —CT

To Riley, Melanie, and David for your continued
support throughout the writing of this book. —LH

For Greer, one of my favorite travel companions. —PGOB

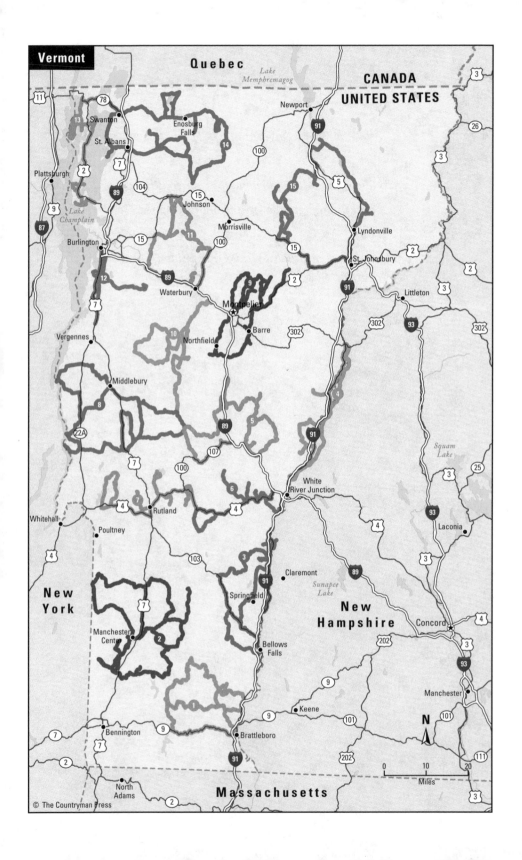

Contents

Introduction

THE LAY OF THE LAND

Vermont is bigger than it looks. This may be one of the country's smallest states, but the more you drive here the more you appreciate the truth of the saying, "Iron Vermont out and it would be as big as Texas."

The Green Mountains constitute one big wrinkle down the spine of this skinny state. While the Ice Age smoothed them considerably, their peaks still rise more than 4,000 feet in places. Several lower ranges and countless rounded hills rumple the flanking landscape.

Forests blanket mountainsides and steep valley walls, but farms and orchards patch hillsides and riverbanks and spread along the floor of the Champlain Valley. The state's distinctive look is a blend of its natural landscape and the beauty of what has been added—the houses, barns, churches, and meetinghouses, a large percentage of which date from 1790 to the 1850s.

THE LAY OF THE ROADS

Most major Vermont highways would be considered backroads in other states.

According to Johnathan Croft of Vermont's Agency of Transportation, "Vermont roads have evolved over the course of the last 250 years or more.... Highways laid out in the late 1700s or early 1800s are still in use today and are the ubiquitous dirt roads that connect farms to villages, and villages to neighboring villages, creating a web across rural Vermont."

The majority of the state's 14,000 miles of road date back to the early nineteenth century, and almost half of these miles remain unpaved. Old highways tend to follow rivers, and backroads—many unpaved—branch off of these like so many veins off the stem of a leaf.

WILLIAMSVILLE BRIDGE

The drives we describe are predominantly paved, and the unpaved stretches can be easily circumvented. But it would be a shame not to explore unpaved roads wherever they appear along our routes. Sun dapples through the canopy of leaves on dirt roads in ways that it doesn't on pavement, and dirt roads lead to a Vermont that you rarely glimpse otherwise. Our favorite roads—paved or dirt—are the "gap" and "notch" roads over the hills and mountains that connect valleys. Look quickly at their crests and you glimpse the valley below and hills beyond, and frequently mountains beyond the hills, rising in waves.

All our routes should be navigable in any vehicle that can comfortably fit through a covered bridge. And while this guide is all about backroad beauty, we also make use of Vermont's two scenic interstates as escape hatches, useful shortcuts, and access routes.

BACKROADS VS. BYWAYS

"Byway" has a better ring to it than "backroad." Across the country, the formal recognition of hundreds of "National Scenic Byways" in recent decades has enabled federal funding for maintenance, signage, pullouts, visitor centers, and such. Vermont shares the **Connecticut River Byway** (ctriverby ways.org) with New Hampshire and promotes its own 410-mile Connecticut River Byway as one of 10 **Vermont Scenic Byways** (vermontvacation.com/byways). We include many of these officially scenic Vermont byways in our drives but as departure points for our roads less traveled. We use "byway" and "backroad" interchangeably.

VERMONT TOURING HISTORY

In contrast to neighboring New Hampshire, Vermont was never known in the nineteenth century for grand resorts. The era of railroads and steamboats spawned a number of lakeside inns, and both Stowe, with a hotel high on Mount Mansfield, and Manchester, with the still grand Equinox Hotel at its center, were summer destinations. More visitors, however, found their way via the wide web of railways to rural farms for extended summer stays. In the late nineteenth century, the state also promoted the sale of farms that had been abandoned by owners who headed West after the Civil War. Many urbanites snapped them up, triggering the state's ongoing second-home industry.

"Tourism" as such began after World War I. "Auto touring" had come into vogue earlier, but Vermont roads were known as the worst in New England. It wasn't until after the flood of 1927—which washed out a number of major highways and more than 100 covered bridges—that the state focused on highway improvement. In the 1930s the state publicity bureau began inviting tourists to explore "Unspoiled Vermont." The federally funded *WPA Guide to Vermont* and *Let Me Show You Vermont* by Charles Edward Crane, the first serious guidebooks to touring Vermont by road, appeared. There was a push to eliminate billboards and improve views from roadsides. Homes and farms throughout the state hung out signs, inviting passing tourists to spend the night.

Clearly, however, Vermonters were only willing to welcome the kind of visitors who took the trouble to navigate their roads. In 1936 a federally funded, 260-mile Green Mountain Parkway was proposed to run the length of the state, passing just below the crests of Pico, Killington, and several other peaks, but it was roundly defeated in a public referendum.

In the years following World War II, Vermont's status as a ski destination grew steadily, adding weight to the obvious need for better year-round access from urban areas. By 1970 I-89, sweeping northwest from the Connecticut River Valley to Burlington and the border, offered access from Montreal and Boston, and I-91 brought visitors from New York City and the southeast. But it took almost another decade for I-91 to creep north from White River Junction to the Canadian border. The link to I-93 came only in 1982, and put even the Northeast Kingdom within three hours of Boston.

The most recent upgrade to many Vermont roads has come in the wake of Tropical Storm Irene, which ripped through southern Vermont on August 28, 2011. It was the state's most devastating natural disaster since "The Great Flood" of 1927. Two iconic wooden covered bridges were destroyed and more than a dozen badly damaged. More than 500 miles of road and 200 bridges required repair. Yet within a month of the storm, 84 of the 118 sections of state roads that had been closed were reopened, along with 28 of the 34 closed state bridges. Traveling backroads, especially those that follow upland streams and river valleys, you notice new bridges and erosion measures as well as miles of new paving.

TOWNS VS. VILLAGES

In northern New England, a town is defined by the territory it included when it was chartered. It can, and almost always does, contain many villages dating from different periods as population shifted over the centuries. Vermont has 251 towns, and with the exception of greater Burlington and several smaller cities, most of these are small in population and relatively large in area. Many towns began as eighteenth-century hilltop settlements that today may be almost deserted but are named on the map as the "center." Some of these, such as Weathersfield Center (because of its exceptional early meetinghouse) and Brownington Center (home to the Stone House Museum), are destinations in this guide.

DIFFERENT REGIONS

Our drives circle through the state, but all of them draw readers deep into the pervasive landscape that's distinctly Vermont. In most states, visitors head just for specific areas: in Massachusetts, it's the Berkshires or Cape Cod; in Maine, it's the coast; and in New Hampshire, the White Mountains and lakes. In Vermont, formal "attractions" remain scarce, but beauty—both natural and man-made—is ubiquitous. Everywhere there are swimming holes, mountain views, covered bridges, galleries, iconic villages, farms, and historic sights and museums.

That said, Vermont's landscape varies substantially from north to south and even more from east to west. The lower Connecticut River Valley, with its eighteenth-century houses and nineteenth-century mill villages, has a different look and feel than the more isolated, even more rural and open Northeast Kingdom, laced with dirt roads and spotted with lakes. On the western side of the state, mountains drop through widely scattered hill towns to a 30-mile-wide, farm-filled valley with views of the Adirondack Mountains in New York. In winter, skiers converge on the self-contained ski resorts spaced along the 250-mile spine of the Green Mountains—from Stratton and Mount Snow in the south to Jay Peak on the Quebec border—all of which increasingly resemble each other. In summer and fall these resort towns provide lodging at off-season prices, but this book is designed to lure visitors away from these hubs and Vermonters themselves out of their corners of this amazingly varied state.

DIFFERENT SEASONS

Driving conditions, as well as the look of this landscape, vary dramatically with the seasons. Vermont is best known for ski and foliage seasons, and lodging prices may be correspondingly high.

SKI SEASON runs from Christmas vacation week through early March, after which the skiing frequently remains fine but prices drop. While Vermont's mountains and valleys are exceptionally beautiful when snow-covered—especially as viewed from ski trails—skiers have to maximize daylight hours on the slopes and probably will not do much backroad exploring.

SUGARING SEASON is usually late February through early April, depending on where in the state the producer is located. A combination of below-freezing nights and warmer days triggers "sap runs," when trees produce the sap that sugarhouses turn to syrup. Many sugarhouses are open to the public, and most maple producers, also known as sugarmakers, welcome visitors to stop by whenever they are boiling. The Vermont Maple Sugar Makers Association also hosts an annual Vermont Maple Open House Weekend, typically the last weekend in March, with more than 90 producers offering tours of their sugarhouses and sugarbushes, tastings featuring "sugar on snow," and sugaring demonstrations. Sugaring marks the start of **mud season**, the well-named time of year when dirt roads can turn impassable and a time for many innkeepers to take a vacation and for restaurants to limit the days and times they are open.

SUMMER is Vermont's best-kept secret, a relatively quiet and ideal time to explore its byways. Many attractions are only open from Memorial Day

Tips for a Successful Road Trip

1. **Beware depending on your GPS**. It's been known to lead users up stream-beds and "thrown up" (disused) roads.
2. **Be aware that cell phone service is spotty**. Take advantage of hot spots and WiFi where you can.
3. **Be prepared for frequent changes in weather** and the predictable drop in temperature between the base and top of a mountain. Even on the hottest day, it's a good idea to have a hoodie, raincoat, or wind jacket in reserve.
4. While all suggested routes are navigable by two-wheel drive, four-wheel drive is recommended during mud season and on some of the rougher dirt roads. Also be aware of height restrictions on covered bridges; signs for winter closings, especially on notch roads; and moose crossing signs. Moose are especially active and difficult to see at dusk and dawn.
5. **Ticks** are an unfortunate worry in meadows and along paths in the woods. Try to avoid bare ankles and check yourself after hikes.

through fall foliage, and many of these only open weekdays after the July Fourth weekend, the unofficial start of summer. Long-established summer resorts, like Manchester and Stowe, are busy. Major ski resorts keep their lodging base filled at prices well below ski season, with golf, mountain biking, programs, and other amenities, but away from ski resorts, visitors scatter to all corners of the state.

FOLIAGE SEASON is said to be a Vermont invention. Its popularity coincided with the widespread availability of color photography after World War II and was first aggressively promoted in the state-published *Vermont Life,* which featured images of hillsides turning crimson and gold. Daily bulletins track "peak color" as it moves from north to south and from higher to lower elevations, beginning in mid-September at higher elevations and throughout the Northeast Kingdom, lasting through Columbus Day weekend in central and southern Vermont.

HOW THIS BOOK WORKS

Backroads & Byways of Vermont is not intended as a guide to the entire state—for that we recommend *Vermont: An Explorer's Guide.* While our drives include resort towns, the focus is on getting away from tourist hubs. It suggests drives through covered bridges to high roads with unexpected vistas, to waterfalls and swimming holes, to crafts studios and farms selling their own eggs or cheese and maybe even prize-winning beer. We hope that you enjoy the same sense of discovery that we did in researching these routes, and we hope this book introduces you to Vermont people as well as places.

BASICS: Each drive includes:

Estimated route length

Estimated time the route takes

Highlights

How to get there

"On the Road" detailed description

DETOURS, SHORTCUTS, AND SIDE TRIPS: Our 15 stem routes vary in length and can be stretched or shortened with the options we offer through sidebars as we go along.

LODGING: *Best Places to Sleep* and *Best Places to Eat* are described at the end of each route. We have attempted, where possible, to highlight inns and bed & breakfasts along quiet byways rather than in resort towns. Note that lodging prices tend to vary with seasons, peaking in foliage season, on weekends in ski season, and summer holiday weekends.

PRICES:

		Lodging	Dinner
$	Inexpensive	Under $125	Under $15
$$	Moderate	$126–199	$16–25
$$$	Expensive	$200–300	$26–35
$$$$	Very Expensive	$300+	$35+

Note: Places to eat along Vermont backroads can be few and far between, so we mention them as we go along. Ranging from general stores to formal restaurants, these are inexpensive ($) unless noted otherwise.

1

THE WEST RIVER AND MOUNT SNOW VALLEYS

ESTIMATED LENGTH: 82 miles

ESTIMATED TIME: 1 to 3 days

HIGHLIGHTS: VT 30 snakes up the **West River Valley** by covered bridges and the handsome villages of **Newfane** and **Townshend**, on to **Jamaica Village**, gateway to **Jamaica State Park**, then south over the hill to Wardsboro, on down to the **Mount Snow** resort area in **West Dover** and on to **Wilmington Village**. A high, winding stretch of the **Molly Stark Scenic Byway** (VT 9) leads back to I-91, with a stop at the **Hogback Mountain Scenic Overlook** and the **Southern Vermont Nature Museum**. We also offer a shortcut between Newfane and West Dover, following the **Williams River** through a covered bridge and over **Cooper Hill** with its splendid view.

SIDE TRIP HIGHLIGHTS: Countless backroads branch off this stem route and we describe a favorite 18-mile loop over the hills, beginning at the covered bridge on VT 30 in West Dummerston. Allow the better part of a day for this trip as you journey down to the Connecticut River, and up US 5 to the village of **Putney**. The way back to Newfane, **Putney Mountain Road**, is beautiful but challenging, with access trails with panoramic views.

GETTING THERE: I-91, Exit 2 at Brattleboro. Note Vermont's largest **Welcome Center** is northbound on I-19 in Guilford, south of Brattleboro.

ON THE ROAD

It's said that Vermont is a state of mind, and in the world's only Brattleboro, the area's hub and gateway, you quickly understand why. Stop for the varied and individually owned shops, galleries, and restaurants, and stay long enough to catch the vibe of this lively community. Turn north on Main Street and follow signs for VT 30.

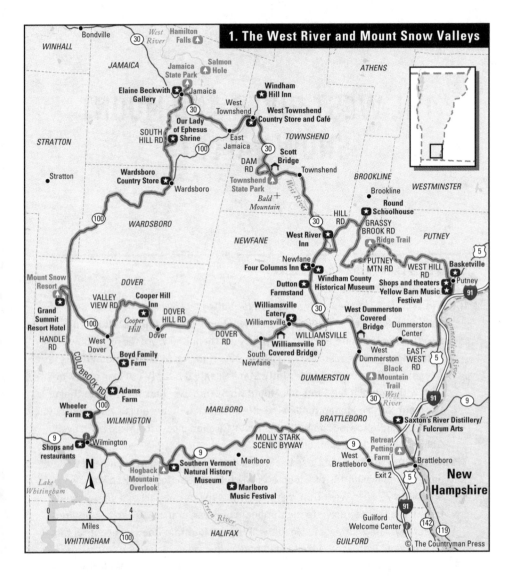

This is one of Vermont's major old high roads, meandering northwest over the mountains and down along rivers, all the way to the New York State border. It begins here at the confluence of the West and the Connecticut Rivers, a spot worth stopping at. Parking is on your right at the Retreat Meadows, a backwater at the mouth of the West River, good for peaceful paddling. On your left is the **Children's Farm & Forest** at **Retreat Farm** (retreatfarm.org) with visitor-friendly farm animals and 9 miles of well-kept, mostly wooded hiking trails maintained by a local non profit organization, which also operates neighboring **Grafton Village Cheese**, a big, red, barnlike outlet for a variety of Vermont products as well as its own nationally distributed cheese. Just up the road on the right, that unpromising metal building houses both

Saxtons River Distillery (802-246-1128) and **Fulcrum Arts** (802-257-2787), featuring glass blown in the adjoining hot shop.

The road curves northwest along with the West River for a half-dozen miles, past the green iron bridge leading to The Nature Conservancy's **Black Mountain Trail** (a half mile down Rice Farm Road on the opposite riverbank). The **West Dummerston Covered Bridge** and its parking lot are a couple minutes beyond. This is a summer swimming hole and the beginning of a 4-mile **scenic shortcut** up through Dummerston Center and down the other side of the hill to US 5, running along the Connecticut River. It marks the beginning of the **side loop to Putney**.

SIDE TRIP
To Putney and Back
VT 30 to Putney via the East-West Road, and Back on the Putney Mountain Road

ESTIMATED LENGTH: 18 miles

Having driven this loop both directions, we suggest beginning at the **Dummerston Covered Bridge**, 4.5 miles south of Newfane Village. Follow East-West Road for 2 steep and wooded miles up to the village of **Dummerston Center**, and 2 more miles down into the Connecticut River Valley. Turn north on US 5 and follow it north through farmland into the village of **Putney**.

Putney's riverside fields have been farmed since the mid-eighteenth century, and its hillsides sustain long-established orchards. It's home to nationally prominent Putney School and Landmark College, geared to "students who learn differently." Putney is also a destination for patrons of the summer chamber music series at the **Yellow Barn Music Festival** (802-387-6637), serious puppetry at **Sandglass Theater** (802-387-4051), and year-round films and live performances at **Next Stage Theater** (802-387-0102). Putney's relatively flat as well as scenic byways are also a mecca for bicyclists. **West Hill Shop** (802-387-5718) offers maps and rentals.

On the northern edge of the village, **Basketville** (802-387-5509) is a long-standing shopping destination, selling woven baskets as well as imports, a trove of wicker furniture, Vermont woodenware, and more while also serving as an outlet and tasting venue for Putney Mountain Winery. **The Gleanery** (802-387-3052) in historic Putney Tavern, overlooking the village green, offers a locally sourced menu Wed.–Sun. for lunch and dinner. Across Main Street (US 5), the beloved **Putney Diner** (802-387-5433) is open 6 AM–3 PM daily (opens at 7 AM Sun.); **Katy's** (802-536-4196; open 12–8 PM except Tues. and Wed.) offers a creative, reasonably priced menu and full bar; and **Curtis' Barbeque** (open seasonally, 10 AM–dusk Wed.–Sun.) is hidden behind the gas station near I-91 Exit 4. The Curtis family's pork ribs and chicken are seasoned with their secret sauce. Order at the blue bus and feast on picnic tables.

Back at the center of the village, the **Putney General Store** (802-387-4692) has marked the junction of US 5 and Kimball Hill Road since 1790, but the building has had a rough past decade, burning twice, once to the ground. Currently owned by the Putney Historical Society, it offers tables and a deli with a blackboard menu.

Turn up Kimball Hill Road, which turns into Westminster Road. Fork left at the sign for West Hill Road and follow it up past **Green Mountain Orchards** (802-587-5851), open daily 8 AM–6 PM from berry to apple season, with PYO. Continue up another mile and turn right (3.3 miles from US 5) at **Putney Mountain Road**. This hard-packed dirt road is narrow, steep, muddy in wet weather, and closed in winter, but on a summer day it can be a heart-stoppingly beautiful drive. There are frequent pullouts at narrow points, but watch for crossing wildlife, from chipmunks to deer. Trees

PUTNEY'S TAVERN AND GENERAL STORE ARE AT THE HEART OF THE VILLAGE

thicken and the sunlight dapples through in a way it doesn't on paved roads. At 2.1 miles, the road crests and there is ample parking on the right for the 0.6-mile **Ridge Trail** to the open crown of **Putney Mountain** and views east across southern New Hampshire to Mount Monadnock and west to the Green Mountains. The road turns to hardtop in less than 2 miles and ends at paved Grassy Brook Road. Fork left and it's just over a mile to VT 30; stay straight and follow Grassy Brook north a few miles through a steep-sided valley to the country's only **Round Schoolhouse**.

The Round Schoolhouse

Sited at the center of Brookline Village, this round brick building was designed in 1821 by schoolmaster "Thunderbolt" Wilson, ostensibly so that he could see in all directions in case he needed to escape. Wilson later practiced as a doctor in Newfane and Brattleboro, but his former life as an infamous Scottish highwayman was revealed at his death; he had been fingered by a fellow felon, and scars on his ankles and neck suggested chains and a rope. The full story and his pistols are on view in the **Windham County Historical Museum** (802-365-4148) in Newfane. Heading south again from Brookline Village, turn right on Hill Road, past **West River Inn**, then right again on Grassy Brook Road to the iron bridge across the river and VT 30.

On the southern edge of Newfane, the barnlike **Dutton Farm Stand** (802-365-4168) features fruit and produce from Paul and Wendy Dutton's local orchards and farms; inquire about PYO strawberries and raspberries in nearby riverside fields. The village of **Newfane** is just ahead, and the magnificent green invites a stroll. Turn left beyond the Newfane Store and park by **Four Columns Inn** (802-365-7713; open seasonally for lunch Wed.–Sun.). This white-pillared mansion was built in 1830 to remind the owner's wife of her girlhood home in the South, and the **Greek Revival Windham County Courthouse** dates from the same era. A Federal-era Congregational church and the matching white clapboard town hall are spaced sedately on this large village green with its Victorian fountain.

When court sessions began meeting in Newfane in 1787, the village was about the same size, but 2 miles up on Newfane Hill. Beams were unpegged and many houses moved down by ox-drawn sleighs in the winter of 1824. Initially the county jail here fed guests in the same rooms as inmates, and the village has long been known for lodging as well as dining. Between 1880 and 1936, this was a busy stop on the narrow-gauge West River Railroad from Brattleboro to Londonderry. It's best remembered as "33 miles of trouble" for its many disasters. Read the story in the **Historical Society of Windham County** (802-365-4148), the brick building that looks like a post office, south of the green. (Open Memorial Day through Columbus Day, Wed., Sat., Sun.; noon–5 PM.)

Beyond Newfane the road rises and dips along above the river for a half-dozen miles on its way to the village of **Townshend**. Here the village

NEWFANE VILLAGE GREEN

PICNIC TABLES OVERLOOK TOWNSHEND DAM

common is a full 2 acres. It's framed by a 1790s white Congregational church, clapboard homes, a former brick tavern, the ghost of a business block, and Leland and Gray Union High School, founded as a Baptist seminary in 1824.

The road winds on between the river and steep, gumdrop-shaped hills.

The **Scott Bridge**, built in 1870 and Vermont's longest single-span covered bridge (closed to traffic), is a few miles up on the left, just before the **Townshend Lake Dam**, a 1961 flood-prevention measure. The narrow **Dam Road** crosses the dam to picnic areas and accesses a rough beach that is open for swimming when water quality permits. A left at the end of Dam Road is the shortest approach to **Townshend State Park** (802-365-7500), with tenting sites and a steep but rewarding 2.7-mile hiking trail to the top of **Bald Mountain**.

Back on VT 30, the **Townshend Dam Diner** (802-874-4107; open 5 AM–8 PM daily except Tues.) is 1.8 miles on the left, a funky local gathering spot for down-home food and prices. At this writing, a P&J sandwich is $2.29, with chips and a pickle. We recommend the hot fudge sundae.

West Townshend, not far beyond, is marked by its vintage 1824 store/post office, now the **West Townshend Country Store and Café** (802-874-4800;

open daily 7 AM–7 PM). There's a thrift store upstairs and a clay oven out back for the pizza served on Fridays, when there's also music and a **farmers' market** on the back lawn (4–7 PM, May through October).

The junction of VT 30 and VT 100 in East Jamaica marks the midpoint of this drive. It's another 3 miles to Jamaica. Here the **Three Mountain Inn** (802-874-4140) has been offering hospitality since the 1790s; the **North Country General** (802-444-0269) is open daily except Wednesday with a

DETOUR

Jamaica State Park, down Depot Street and over the iron bridge, is a popular place for fishing, swimming, hiking, and camping. In warm weather the **Salmon Hole** beckons. This deep, still pocket in a wide bend in the West River was well known to many generations of Native Americans, judging from an archaeological dig that has unearthed 3,000 artifacts. It also figures in history as the site of a 1748 ambush of British and colonial soldiers by Frenchmen and Indians.

Fishermen favor this stretch of the river because of its easy access to both deeps and riffles. On May and September weekends, when water is released from the Ball Mountain Dam just upstream, this is prime viewing ground for white-water paddling races. A recreation trail meanders along the river on the rail bed of the defunct West River Railroad. The park's other popular multiuse trail runs 1.1 miles from the river to the base of **Hamilton Falls**, dropping through pools and shoots for a total 125 feet. Please do not try to climb up along the falls to the inviting pools along this drop. Too many people have died trying.

light but imaginative all-day menu, wine, and craft beers; and the **Elaine Beckwith Gallery** (802-874-7234) is a destination for contemporary art lovers. The heart of the village is **D&K's Jamaica Grocery** (802-874-4151), open 7 AM–8 PM. Pick up hot food or picnic fixings from the deli and one of the maps that owner Karen Amden has had printed, pointing the way to local fishing spots and sights like Pikes Falls.

From **D&K's**, follow the road that branches off VT 30 to the left; it begins directly across from the general store as Pikes Falls Road but almost immediately we bear left on **South Hill Road**, a beautiful, mostly paved shortcut up and over the hill and down to VT 100 in the village of Wardsboro. Two-thirds of the way we recommend turning up (dirt and dead end) Mowrey Road for the minute it takes to reach the most unlikely building in all Vermont: an exact replica of a first-century stone house that sits on a similar hillside in Ephesus, Turkey.

Continue on South Hill Road as it winds down and levels out in Wardsboro Village, a crossroads with the requisite post office, church, and general store; **Cindy's Bittersweet Memories Café** (802-896-1130; open 6 AM–2 PM daily except Thurs.) is a likely breakfast or lunch spot. A sign on the red-and-blue-striped **Wardsboro Country Store** warns PARK HEAD ON. PARALLEL PARKERS WILL BE SHOT, but this too is a friendly oasis, known for house burritos, chicken pot pies, and Matt and Kip's house-made sausage, especially popular during Wardsboro's famous annual July Fourth parade.

Our Lady of Ephesus Shrine

This shrine replicates the stone house, set high on a similar hillside in Turkey, that is a pilgrimage site for both Muslims and Christians because it is believed to have been the final residence of Mary, the mother of Jesus. The door to the chapel is usually open, and there's a sense of peace inside and out. This was part of an extensive horse farm and, a short way up the road, the stables and riding ring have been expanded into **Our Lady of Ephesus House of Prayer** (802-896-6000), with the horse stalls converted to surprisingly comfortable guest rooms. The retreat center is set high with a sweeping view of the surrounding hills. There is a story here, and Mary Tarinelli, who with her husband transformed the property and raised funds to create the shrine, is frequently on hand to tell it.

OUR LADY OF EPHESUS SHRINE

THE MOUNT SNOW VALLEY

The entrance to **Mount Snow Resort** (1-800-245-SNOW) is another dozen miles south on VT 100 in West Dover. Skiing aside, the resort offers extensive mountain biking with lift-serviced trails and an 18-hole golf course. The view from the 3,600-foot-high summit is worth checking to see if the **Bluebird Express Chairlift** (802-464-6640) is running. Weather permitting, it operates late June through Labor Day, 10 AM–5 PM Wed.–Sun., then Fri.–Sun. until mid-October, from the base lodge to and from the summit lodge with its **Bull Wheel Café**.

More than 2,100 guests can bed down at the base of Mount Snow. Aside from the **Grand Summit Resort Hotel** (802-464-8501), this includes mostly condo-style units, an especially good value for families. Restaurants, lodges, and shops line VT 100 as it runs south to Wilmington. There is a wide choice of traditional inns and bed & breakfasts, as well as condo complexes scattered through the valley, representing by far the largest number and widest range of places to stay in the southeastern corner of Vermont.

Mount Snow made its splashy debut as a ski destination in 1954, when Reuben Snow's farm was transformed by ski lifts and trails, lodges, a skating rink, and an immense floodlit geyser. Ski lodges mushroomed and 1960s

VIEW OF THE SOMERSET RESERVOIR FROM MOUNT SNOW

development around the small village of West Dover was intense enough to trigger a pioneering environmental protection law, Act 250, in 1970. The resort area has long since mellowed into a low-key family destination, especially in summer. Attractions still include the multigenerational working farms: **Adams Farm** (802-464-3762), offering a petting barnyard, wagon rides, and "farm-to-table" BBQ; **Boyd Family Farm** (802-464-5618), with long views from its display gardens and offering PYO flowers and blueberries; and **Wheeler Farm** (802-464-5115), producing milk for the **Cabot Cooperative** and featuring its maple syrup and cream at its roadside farm stand. VT 100 follows the North Branch of the Deerfield River for 6 miles south to Wilmington, but you might want to cut over on Crosstown Road in the middle of West Dover Village and follow higher, wooded **Handle Road** (turning into Cold Brook Road), passing the farms that have formed this valley's summer colony since the 1880s.

SCENIC 13-MILE SHORTCUT BACK TO VT 30 SOUTH OF NEWFANE

From VT 100 in the busy heart of West Dover Village (across from Crosstown Road), the well-named **Valley View Road** corkscrews 3 miles up a steep hill, becoming Cooper Hill Road on the way to its 2,500-foot-high crest. Here much of southeastern Vermont seems to roll away at your feet. On a clear day, the White Mountains hover on the horizon to the northeast.

"It's tranquil" up here, observes Charles Wheeler at **Cooper Hill Inn** (802-343-633) across the road. The hospitable, reasonably priced inn fronts on this vista and backs on a view of Mount Snow across the steep Deerfield Valley. The classic, old hilltop village of Dover is just beyond, with a white clapboard church, town hall, and library framing a common. From here Dover Hill Road winds east, descending to the Rock River and following it through the single-lane, 1870s **Williamsville Covered Bridge** to the hamlet of Williamsville, home to an 1828 general store that's now a local dining destination, the **Williamsville Eatery** (802-365-9600). Continue on Williamsville Road and by the swimming hole near the Rock River bridge (look for parked cars) to VT 30.

WILMINGTON

In the middle of the village of Wilmington, the only traffic light between equidistant Brattleboro and Bennington marks the junction of VT 100 and VT 9.

A left leads back to Brattleboro, but we suggest turning right first to

COOPER HILL ROAD

explore Wilmington Village's West Main Street. Parking is sequestered behind shops and restaurants down by the Deerfield River. In 2011 Tropical Storm Irene caused the river to overflow its banks here and swamp iconic **Dot's Restaurant** (802-464-7284; open 5:30 AM–8 PM, until 9 PM Fri. and Sat.); **Quaigh Design Centre** (802-464-2780), a long-established showcase for work by Vermont's top craftsmen and artists; and inviting, independently owned **Bartleby's Books** (802-464-5425). Happily, all three village anchors are back and better than ever.

Lake Whitingham, 8 miles long and set in forested hills, is just west of the village. Also known as Harriman Reservoir, it was created in the 1920s by damming the Deerfield. For directions to its access points for hiking, swimming, and boating, and for area trail maps, stop by the visitor center at 21 West Main Street, maintained by the **Southern Vermont/Deerfield Valley Chamber of Commerce** (802-464-8092).

THE MOLLY STARK TRAIL

VT 9 itself was recognized as one of the region's first tourist routes, formally pronounced a "scenic" road in 1938. It's now the **Molly Stark Scenic Byway,** named for the wife of the general who traveled this route in August 1777 on his way to defeating the British at the Battle of Bennington. One of Vermont's few east/west highways, it's been widened and improved to bear truck traffic, but the 18 miles back to Brattleboro remain a twisty, roller coaster kind of ride. Be sure to stop 5 miles east of the light at the **Hogback Mountain Overlook**, a former ski hill with a view that's said to encompass 100 miles. The adjacent **Southern Vermont Natural History Museum** (802-474-0058; open Mon.–Fri. 10 AM–4 PM, Sat.–Sun. 10 AM–5 PM; $) is secretly below the large gift shop through which you enter. It features 80 dioramas depicting New England birds and mammals but includes many more local and environmentally focused exhibits. The surrounding 600 acres offer hiking trails.

Several miles beyond, a turnoff is marked for Marlboro, a sleepy, mostly white-clapboard village. It's home to Marlboro College, the venue for the **Marlboro Music Festival** (802-254-2394) chamber music concerts, performed mid-July to mid-August weekends by internationally famous artists who congregate here to work together and perform. Continue on 10 more miles through West Brattleboro to I-91 Exit 2.

Best Places to Sleep

FOUR COLUMNS (802-365-7713), 21 West Street, Newfane. This luxurious inn, fronting on Newfane's splendid green and backing on woodland, offers 17 recently renovated rooms with king and queen beds, comfortable, unfussy furnishings, and splendid baths. Facilities include a small gym and spa with a steam bath, treatment room, and outside space. A continental breakfast is included in the rates, and pets are accepted in some rooms. $$–$$$; also see *Best Places to Eat*.

WEST RIVER INN (802-365-7745), 117 Hill Road, Brookline. With its big red barn and white, black-shuttered farmhouse, this is a classic country B&B. It's minutes from Newfane but far enough off the beaten track to feel like the find that it is. Nick and Terry Kaiser offer seven antiques-furnished rooms with beds ranging from twins to kings, with and without private bath. There's a swimming hole, and families, dogs, and horses are all welcome. Rates include full breakfast. $–$$.

WINDHAM HILL INN (802-874-4080 or 800-944-4080), 311 Lawrence Drive, West Townshend. High above the West River Valley, this 1825 brick farmhouse is a luxurious retreat with 21 antiques-furnished rooms divided between the main house and an annex with views down the valley. Facilities include a landscaped pool and tennis court. $$$–$$$$.

THREE MOUNTAIN INN (802-874-4140), 30 Depot Street, Jamaica. Ed and Jennifer Dorta-Duque welcome guests in the 1790s tavern room with its large hearth and a cozy corner bar. Guest rooms are divided between upstairs rooms and garden units in a neighboring house and cottage, all nicely decorated, some with whirlpool tub, gas or wood fireplace or wood stove. A pool and lawn chairs overlook mountains. Dinner is available. $$–$$$ includes a three-course breakfast.

COOPER HILL INN (802-348-6333), 117 Cooper Hill Road, East Dover. High on a hilltop on a quiet country road with panoramic views, this is a spacious inn with bright, tastefully decorated guest rooms (private baths) ranging from king-bedded rooms with fireplaces to family suites. There's a large dining room, game room, and flower gardens with a landscaped hollow for weddings. The house can hold 24 and is frequently rented in its entirety. $$–$$$.

Two Outstanding State Campgrounds

TOWNSHEND STATE PARK (802-365-7500), 2755 State Forest Road, Townshend. This 1930s Civilian Conservation Corps creation offers 30 basic tent sites and four lean-tos. It's a bit of a secret given its seemingly isolated location on a dirt road in a state forest, but it's minutes from VT 30. The steep, 2.7-mile hike up Bald Mountain offers views across the valley. $.

JAMAICA STATE PARK (802-874-4600), 48 Salmon Hole Lane, Jamaica. Open early May through Columbus Day weekend. This is a popular campground with 41 tents/trailers and 18 lean-to sites with easy access to swimming, fishing, and hiking. $.

Best Places to Eat

ARTISAN RESTAURANT AND TAVERN AT THE FOUR COLUMNS INN (802-365-7713; dinner daily except Mon.; lunch seasonally Wed.–Sat.; Sun. brunch), 21 West Street, Newfane. The dining room is rustically elegant (no tablecloths) and the menu is locally, seasonally sourced. A moderately priced pub menu is available in the tavern and, weather permitting, on the pleasant patio. $$–$$$.

WILLIAMSVILLE EATERY (802-365-9600; dinner Thurs.–Sun. from 5 PM), 26 Dover Road, Williamsville. This former village store has an open kitchen and features craft beers and ciders, wood-fired pizzas Thursday and Sunday, and a mix of starters and entrées the remaining evenings. Reservations recommended. $–$$.

TWO TANNERY ROAD (802-464-2707; twotannery.com), 2 Tannery Road, off VT 100, West Dover. Open for dinner Tues.–Sun. The building itself is said to date in part from the late 1700s and the bar began service in the original Waldorf-Astoria. The food is consistently flavorful, and creative. Nightly specials, reservations encouraged. Entrées $$–$$$.

THE GLEANERY (802-387-3052; open for dinner Wed.–Sun; lunch Wed.–Sat; Sun. brunch; specially priced three-course Sunday night menus), 133 Main Street, Putney. The open, timbered dining room has a hearth and the feel of the old tavern it occupies. In warm weather there's also seating on the porch. The menu changes daily, depending on what's available at local farms. Lunch is light: flatbreads, burgers. The dinner menu offers a half-dozen entrées, including several vegetarian options. Dinner reservations suggested. $$.

2

MANCHESTER AND THE MOUNTAINS ROUTE

ESTIMATED LENGTH: 100 miles

ESTIMATED TIME: 2 to 3 days

HIGHLIGHTS: The region, peppered with cozy villages with centuries-old churches and homes, is reminiscent of a Norman Rockwell painting. And that's not far from the truth, as America's favorite artist made his home in **West Arlington** for 14 years, drawing inspiration from the surrounding countryside. Opportunities for outdoor recreation abound, although there's also a thriving arts scene anchored by the **Southern Vermont Arts Center**. Locavores won't be disappointed, as many farm-to-table restaurants use locally sourced foods, and farms throughout the region offer artisanal cheeses, maple syrup, and other farm-grown products for sale.

GETTING THERE: If traveling from the north, US 7 to VT 7A is the most direct route. From Boston, take I-91 to Exit 2, then VT 30 north to **Manchester**. From Albany, New York (the closest major airport if renting a car), take I-90 east to NY 787, then north to US 7 to VT 279 (Bennington Bypass), which turns into US 7. Get off at Exit 4.

ON THE ROAD

While Manchester may be synonymous with **Orvis** (802-362-3750), the outdoor gear retail giant, and designer outlet stores, this southwestern Vermont town has much more to offer visitors. Take some time to explore this community, which encompasses both **Manchester Center** and **Manchester Village**, before you hit the road.

Manchester Center is where you will find the stores, a mix of name-brand

LEFT: CHISELVILLE BRIDGE, SUNDERLAND

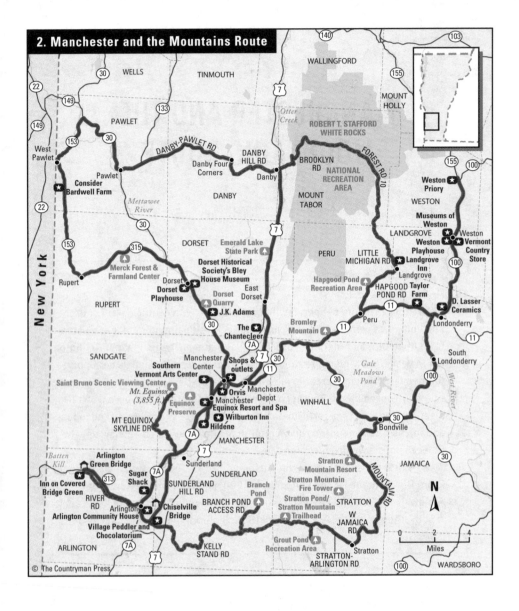

2. Manchester and the Mountains Route

outlets, and local shops, including **Manchester Woodcraft** (802-362-5770), seller of Vermont-made wood products since 1950, and **Mother Myrick's Confectionery** (802-362-1560), famous for its buttercrunch toffee, chocolates, and Lemon Lulu cake. The **Northshire Bookstore** (802-362-2200), a well-stocked independent bookstore with a knowledgeable staff, sells both new and used books along with audiotapes, CDs, and gift items.

If outlet shopping is in your plans, it's worth a stop at the **Manchester Visitor Center**, located at 4802 Main Street at the roundabout, to pick up the

Manchester Designer Outlet Coupon Savings booklet. It's also available at some of the outlets and online.

Orvis was founded by Charles Orvis in Manchester in 1856 to sell fly-fishing equipment, and today it still carries a wide selection along with sportswear, home furnishings, luggage and travel accessories, and an assortment of products for dogs. You can learn the fine art of casting at one of its fly-fishing schools, or visit the **American Museum of Fly Fishing** (802-362-3300), adjacent to the Orvis flagship store, to view displays of fishing rods and reels, flies, photos, and paintings. Some items in the vast collection date back to the 1700s.

Manchester Village is more genteel with its stately mansions and inns, including the famous **Equinox Resort and Spa** (802-362-4700), which has hosted a number of U.S. presidents, among them Ulysses S. Grant and Theodore Roosevelt. The 1822 **Bennington County Courthouse** is here, as is **Hildene** (802-362-1788), the Lincoln family home.

After exploring Manchester, jump on VT 30 North at the roundabout. Allow time to stray off the main route, as many noteworthy attractions can be found on secondary roads. The first is the **Southern Vermont Arts Center** (802-362-1405), a left on West Road for 2.5 miles. As you head up the 0.8-mile curvy drive to the center, you'll pass a small pond and several large sculptures displayed in the fields and woods. Picnic on the grounds or have lunch at **Café Sora** (802-367-1028), which serves Japanese home-style cuisine Thursday through Sunday. Except for special exhibitions, admittance to the **Yester House Galleries** and the **Elizabeth de C. Wilson Museum and Galleries** is free.

Zip back to VT 30 to continue to Dorset. Stop at **J. K. Adams** (866-362-4422), a kitchen supply store that was founded in 1944 and today is world renowned for its handcrafted cutting boards. These and other wooden products are made in Vermont from sustainably harvested hardwoods. In winter, the local farmers' market moves from **Adams Park** in Manchester Center to this location, with a number of food and craft vendors setting up booths in the store's warehouse.

Soon after the store, look for a parking area on the right for **Dorset Quarry**. In summer it will be packed with cars, as this is a popular swimming hole. It is the oldest marble quarry in the country, founded in 1785 by Isaac Underhill, and was in operation for 130 years. Marble from this and other area quarries was used for the Supreme Court Building in Washington, D.C., the New York Public Library, and the Montreal Museum of Fine Arts, among other notable buildings. Today the property is privately owned, although the owners allow locals and visitors to swim in the quarry.

Continue your local history lesson at the **Dorset Historical Society's Bley House Museum** (802-867-0331) at the corner of VT 30 and Kent Hill Road.

Visiting Hildene

Hildene (802-362-1788; open 9:30 AM–4:30 PM daily), 1005 Hildene Road, Manchester. As a boy, Robert Lincoln, oldest son of President Abraham Lincoln and Mary Todd Lincoln, summered at the Equinox Hotel in Manchester with his mother and brother Tad. His fond memories of exploring the Battenkill Valley came into play when he decided that he wanted a summer home in the country where he could escape from his demanding schedule as president of the Pullman Palace Car Company. So in 1903 he hired Shepley, Rutan, and Coolidge, a prestigious Boston architectural firm, to build a 24-room Georgian Revival mansion that he called **Hildene** for "hill" and "valley." Construction was completed in 1905. He would spend the next 21 summers here with his wife, Mary.

HILDENE, ROBERT TODD LINCOLN'S SUMMER ESTATE

Today his 412-acre estate is open to the public. Start at the welcome center and museum store in the historic Carriage Barn for an introduction to the family and its history, the estate, and the restoration of Sunbeam, a 1903 Pullman car. You can tour the home and its elegant formal garden of European-influenced parterre design that Jessie Lincoln, Robert's daughter, created for her mother—as well as other gardens, the observatory, and the farms. The 1,000-pipe Aeolian organ in the front entrance hall was a gift from Robert to his wife and is played daily for visitors. In summer, Jessie's restored 1928 Franklin roadster is on display at the house.

Sunbeam was used by President Theodore Roosevelt's press corps in 1912 during his presidential campaign. You can walk through the car and learn about the African American Pullman porters, their day-to-day work schedule, and the challenges they faced. The exhibit includes a timeline spanning the century from President Lincoln's Emancipation Proclamation in 1863 to the Civil Rights Movement and March on Washington in 1963.

Transportation is provided to these attractions and the farms. **Hildene Farm** is a solar-powered goat dairy and cheese-making operation where you can watch as artisan cheeses are made. **The Dene** includes a greenhouse, composting facility, apple orchard, vegetable gardens, and songbird sanctuary with a floating boardwalk that crosses a wetlands area. Hildene also has 12 miles of walking trails, with interpretative signs along the Farm Loop Trail.

Artist, educator, and longtime resident Elsa Bley willed her house to the museum. Exhibits provide an insight into the area's many long-gone industries, including the marble and iron industries, Harmon Mint (Republic of Vermont coins), and Fenton Potteries, an early nineteenth-century business.

The museum's collections also focus on everyday life with artifacts, photos, and memorabilia from schools and generations of area families. Playbills and photographs from the **Dorset Playhouse** (802-867-5777), located on nearby Cheney Road, are on display along with artwork created by Dorset artists between 1885 and 1950, a period when the town's pastoral setting was a magnet for creative individuals.

Just past the museum, turn left on Church Street, which loops around the historic Dorset Town Green, which is ringed with uniformly white clapboard

OUTDOOR SCULPTURES AT THE SOUTHERN VERMONT ARTS CENTER

DORSET PLAYHOUSE

homes sporting dark green or black shutters, all on the National Register of Historic Places. Stop by the **Dorset Union Store** (802-867-4400) for deli sandwiches, homemade cookies, fresh-brewed coffee or iced tea, and other snacks, then settle in at one of the picnic tables on the small green for lunch. Another option, though pricier, is the **Dorset Inn** (802-867-5500) across the green. Ask to be seated outside, weather permitting.

Before jumping back in your car, visit **3 Pears Art Gallery** (802-770-8820) adjacent to the store. This beautifully curated gallery offers a mix of works by local and regional artists ranging from fine art to ceramics, artisan jewelry, and garden art. Back on VT 30, continue north for 2 miles to VT 315 West, which leads to the **Merck Forest & Farmland Center** (802-394-7836). It's 2.5 miles to the entrance road and another 0.3 mile to the visitor center, where you can get a map and purchase farm-raised meats and produce, maple syrup, and Vermont-made gifts. The center has a number of rustic wood-heated cabins to rent throughout the year, as well as lean-tos and tent sites, but its primary focus is to educate visitors about the sustainable management of woods and farmland through workshops, demonstrations, and other activities.

Visit the 62-acre working farm to see the sheep, pigs, and other livestock or pick berries in season. More than 30 miles of recreational trails are open for hiking, horseback riding, snowshoeing, and cross-country skiing. In early spring stop by the sugarhouse to learn how maple sap becomes syrup as part of the farm's certified-organic sugaring operation. The center also manages a 3,100-acre forest.

As you leave, turn left, then follow VT 153 for 5.5 miles to the **Consider Bardwell Farm** (802-645-9928) in West Pawlet, where you can purchase raw-milk artisan cheeses made from both goat's and cow's milk.

The 300-acre farm has a most fascinating history. It was started near the end of the Civil War by Consider Stebbins Bardwell, who established a cheese-making co-op in 1864, the first in Vermont, on his farm near the New York border. The idea of collecting milk from area dairies to make cheese at one central location was considered a novel concept at the time. The farmer-members of the West Pawlet Dairy Association, as it was known, later began sending their cheese by rail to Boston, New York City, and other out-of-state markets.

Today owners Angela Miller and Russell Glover make all their cheeses by hand, using milk from their herd of Oberhasli goats and from Jersey cows on neighboring farms. Many of these award-winning cheeses are named after local places—Dorset, Rupert, Mettawee—with one of their newest offerings, a tangy cow's-milk cheese called Experience, named for Bardwell's grand-

ENTRANCE TO THE MERCK FOREST & FARMLAND CENTER

Mount Equinox

No one is quite sure how **Mount Equinox** got its name, although a common belief is that "Equinox" is derived from a Native American word, *akwanok* or *ekwanok*. Another story links it to a scientific expedition led by Captain Alden Partridge, director of the American Literary Scientific and Military Academy, which later became **Norwich University** (802-485-2000). Partridge believed that outdoor experiences were integral to education, and so, with a troop of cadets, he climbed the mountain to make some barometric observations. The date was Sept. 19, 1823, around the time of the autumnal equinox.

But whatever its origin, there's no question that experiencing the 3,855-foot mountain, which towers over the village of Manchester, is an absolute must when visiting the area. The 914-acre **Equinox Preserve** (802-366-1400) on its eastern slope has more than 11 miles of well-maintained trails that cut through different forest habitats, home to a variety of bird and wildlife species. Although many of the trails traverse the lower elevations, the 3.1-mile Blue Summit Trail will take you to the top of Mount Equinox and its endless panoramic vistas.

Pick up the "Trail Map and Guide" at the **Equinox Resort and Spa** (802-362-4700), which owns much of the preserve's conserved land. Parking is available behind the resort. The trail system also may be accessed from the **Southern Vermont Arts Center** (802-362-1405) when open.

Instead of hiking, you can drive to the summit on the **Mount Equinox Skyline Drive** (802-362-1114). The tollhouse is on VT 7A in Sunderland. The 5.2-mile road twists its way to the top, with picnic areas and pull-offs for the views along the way. At the top of the **Saint Bruno Scenic Viewing Center**, you can learn about the history of Mount Equinox, the Carthusian Monks who own the mountaintop, the Sky Line Inn that once stood here, and the **Mount Equinox Annual Hill Climb** sports car race. Be sure to heed the instructions given when you pay the toll to prevent an overheated engine or smoking brakes on the way down.

mother. You can buy cheese at the self-serve farm store and are welcome to take a self-guided walking tour of the farm, visit the pastured animals, or enjoy a picnic on the grounds.

After your farm visit, continue on VT 153 to VT 30 and then head south to Pawlet, where you'll take VT 133 (off to the left). Follow this until you come to a Y, where you'll go right on Danby-Pawlet Road for 6 miles. Turn right again on Brook Road, take the next left onto Danby Hill, and then a slight left to return to Brook Road. When you get to the T in Danby, take a right, then a quick left on Mount Tabor Avenue, which will bring you to US 7. Head north to Brooklyn Road, the first right-hand turn.

This is Green Mountain National Forest Road 10, a 14-mile seasonal road that winds through the scenic **Robert T. Stafford White Rocks National Recreation Area** (802-362-2307). Deer and other wildlife are often spotted along this road, which was built by the Civilian Conservation Corps in the 1930s.

At the end—the first stop sign on this entire route—turn onto Little Michigan Road. You'll pass by the **Landgrove Inn** (802-824-6673; see *Best Places to Sleep*) before reaching the **Landgrove Town Hall**. Take a right on Hapgood Pond Road. Follow this for 2 miles to the **Hapgood Pond Recreation Area** (802-362-2307), a Green Mountain National Forest site where you can picnic, swim, and camp. Returning to the main road, turn right and continue to the village of Landgrove, then go 6 miles east on VT 11 to Londonderry.

Although an interesting drive, note that this road is closed in winter. Your alternate route to Hapgood Pond would be to head south from Danby on US 7 with a stop at **Emerald Lake State Park** (802-362-1655) in East Dorset. Once back in Manchester, travel east on VT 30/11 for 9 miles, and then take a left into Peru. Turn left on Hapgood Pond Road to access the recreation area.

Or skip this side trip to the pond and just continue on VT 11 through Peru to Londonderry to visit the **Taylor Farm** (802-824-5690). This working dairy farm is open for tours and wagon rides (sleigh rides in winter). The farmers make artisanal cheeses that are for sale through mail order and at the farm. Try their Maple-Smoked Farmstead Gouda, Chipotle Gouda, or Green Mountain Nettle, the last made with dried nettle leaves.

From Londonderry you have two options to return to Manchester. VT 11 travels through Peru past **Bromley Mountain** (802-824-5522), which is as well known for its summer **Mountain Adventure Park** as it is for its family-friendly winter skiing. Or take the longer route, heading south on VT 100 for about 7 miles through South Londonderry. At the intersection of VT 100 and VT 30, go right on VT 30 through Bondville to connect with VT 11 to return to Manchester, where you can continue south on VT 7A to Arlington past Mount Equinox.

NORMAN ROCKWELL COUNTRY

Not long after you cross the Arlington town line you will come to the **Sugar Shack** (802-375-6747), a gift shop and bakery that houses the Norman Rockwell Exhibition. This impressive exhibit showcases many of the illustrations and paintings the artist did when he lived here from 1939 to 1953, including his *Saturday Evening Post* covers. What makes this exhibit stand out is that many of the artworks are paired with the photos from which Rockwell

At Londonderry, take VT 100 north for 5 miles to Weston. On the way you will pass **D. Lasser Ceramics** (802-824-6183), worth a stop to watch artisans at work turning out brilliantly colored vases, dishware, and other pottery pieces in more than 30 different color patterns.

Weston is home to the world-famous **Vermont Country Store** (802-824-3184), begun in 1946 by Vrest Orton and still run by the family today. The sprawling store, which includes four buildings, has an eclectic inventory of household goods, health products, clothing, bedding, and more, with many products that evoke nostalgia. The founder's creed that every product sold must "work, be useful, and make sense" still holds true today. **Bryant House Restaurant** (802-824-6287), in a historic 1827 building adjacent to the store, caters to the traveler interested in traditional New England fare, including Yankee pot roast, cod cakes, clam chowder, and chicken potpie. **Mildred's Dairy Bar**, open summers only at the back of the restaurant, offers lighter take-out fare. Across the street, the **Weston Village Store** (802-824-5477), in operation since 1891, sells Vermont products, from cheese and homemade fudge to maple syrup and specialty foods, along with puzzles, games, and souvenirs.

VERMONT COUNTRY STORE, WESTON

The **Weston Playhouse** (802-824-5288), the state's oldest professional theater, is located on the Weston Village Green. Its first summer stock production was in 1937, featuring a then-unknown actor named Lloyd Bridges. Today several shows are produced each summer season. Patrons can dine before the performance at the playhouse, which has partnered with the **Hartness House Inn and Tavern** (802-885-2115) in Springfield to provide farm-to-table cuisine with a different menu for each production.

Before leaving Weston, check out the trio of museums—the **Old Mill Museum** and dam, the **Craft Building**, and the **Farrar-Mansur House**—that constitute the **Museums of Weston** (802-824-3119). Each depicts life in eighteenth- and nineteenth-century Weston. The **Craft Building**, the town's first firehouse, houses a Concord coach that the Weston Cornet Band used as a bandwagon from 1880 to 1930.

For a spiritual experience, visit the **Weston Priory** (802-824-5409) 4 miles north of the village. Stay on VT 100 until you come to VT 155. Just after you turn onto this route, look for a small sign for the priory. The Benedictine monks invite visitors to walk the trails and the labyrinth by the barn chapel. The public also may attend daily worship services.

If you miss the turn for VT 155, you will end up in Ludlow, home to the **Okemo Mountain Resort** (802-828-1600), offering year-round outdoor adventure.

painted and the written remembrances of the neighbors and townspeople who modeled for him. The exhibit also includes memorabilia and an interesting film about his life.

After visiting the **Sugar Shack**, head south into the village and turn right onto VT 313 West (opposite the Arlington Inn). The road winds through a pleasant residential area before hitting the countryside. Continue for 4.4 miles to Covered Bridge Road. You can't miss it, as the barn-red covered bridge, known as the **Arlington Green Covered Bridge**—or the **West Arlington Bridge**, depending on whom you ask—is situated right on the road. Take a left through the 80-foot lattice truss bridge, constructed in 1852, one of the oldest surviving covered bridges in Vermont.

On the other side you will pass by the **Chapel on the Green (West Arlington United Methodist Church)**, built in 1804. Directly ahead are two white farmhouses. The one on the right was Norman Rockwell's home for the 14 years he lived in Arlington and is now the **Inn at Covered Bridge Green** (802-375-9489; see *Best Places to Sleep*). The roadside historic plaque shares information on the renowned artist and illustrator and some of his famous works.

Take a left on River Road, a well-maintained dirt road that follows the **Batten Kill**—*kill* being the Dutch word for "river." You can cut back to the main road on Benedict's Crossing or take this road back to VT 313. You may see anglers casting for trout or kayakers lazily paddling down the river. In the meadows it's not uncommon to spot a flock of wild turkeys.

The **Arlington Community House**, built in 1829, is just past the turn-

TOP: ARLINGTON GREEN COVERED BRIDGE
BOTTOM: INN ON COVERED BRIDGE GREEN, FORMER HOME OF NORMAN ROCKWELL

off for VT 313 West. This Federal-style brick building was deeded to the **Arlington Community Club** by children's author and former resident Dorothy Canfield Fisher, who inherited it from her Aunt Martha Canfield. It originally served as the town library. Fisher is buried in the **St. James Episcopal Church Cemetery** directly across the street.

East Arlington Road, your first left-hand turn, will take you to Sunderland

Hill Road, where you can drive through the **Chiselville Bridge** that spans Roaring Branch Brook. The lattice truss bridge was built in 1870. Continue along this road until you see Hill Farm Road on your left, which will take you past the **Hill Farm Inn** (802-375-2269) and an old church and cemetery. A left at the end of the road connects you with VT 7A again.

Or, after going through the bridge, retrace your route to Old Mill Road. Take a left and follow this a short distance to the **Village Peddler and Chocolatorium** (802-375-6037), where you can learn about the history of chocolate and how it's made, sample chocolate, and view exhibits of old-fashioned metal molds and chocolate sculptures. You can make your own chocolate bar or choose from the display cases of chocolates and homemade fudge.

DETOUR

Continue past the **Chocolatorium** on Old Mill Road to Kansas Road, then Kelly Stand Road, a right-hand turn. Note that this unpaved road, also known as the Stratton-Arlington Road, is closed in winter and only maintained from June 1 to November 1. It's the main gateway to the southern end of **Green Mountain National Forest** and spectacular in autumn for leaf peeping.

Outdoor enthusiasts especially will enjoy this 16-mile route, as it follows the **Roaring Branch River** (great fly-fishing!) and provides access to two picturesque ponds. To reach the secluded **Branch Pond**, look for the Branch Pond Access Road and be prepared for a short portage from parking area to water. **Grout Pond** (802-362-2307), a 1,600-acre year-round Green Mountain National Forest recreation area, offers fishing, swimming, picnicking, and camping. Eleven of the 17 sites are walk-ins, with some accessible by boat. Hiking is excellent here, with 10 miles of multipurpose trails that link to another trail system. For a pleasant, flat-terrain hike that you can complete in one to two hours, take the 2.6-mile **Pond Loop Trail**.

Just before the entrance to the **Grout Pond Recreation Area**, you will find the **Stratton Pond/Stratton Mountain Trailhead**. Hike the 3.6-mile trail to the historic fire tower for 360-degree views. On a clear day you can see mountain ranges in four states. Continue for another 3.5 miles to Stratton Pond, where you can swim or camp. The entire loop is about 10.6 miles. Note that you also can access the summit and fire tower via the scenic **Stratton Gondola** from **Stratton Mountain Resort** (802-297-4000).

After Grout Pond the road turns back to pavement. Travel 4 miles and take a left at the **Stratton Meeting House**. Follow this until you get to VT 30, where a left-hand turn will take you to the **Stratton Mountain Resort**. Popular in winter, the resort also offers a number of fun activities in summer, including golf, yoga at the summit, and an outdoor concert series featuring world-class musicians. Continuing past the ski area, you can take a left onto VT 30 at Bondville and head back to Manchester.

In winter, or if you'd rather stick to paved roads, after visiting the **Choco-latorium**, return to VT 7A and take a left. Follow this to VT 313 East to pick up US 7, heading north to Manchester Depot, where you can catch VT 30 into Manchester.

Best Places to Sleep

WILBURTON INN (802-362-2500), 257 Wilburton Drive, Manchester Center. Guests are greeted by Jetson, a friendly cavalier King Charles spaniel, and innkeeper Melissa Levis, who runs this historic, dog-friendly hilltop inn with brother Max. The Tudor-style mansion has 11 spacious bedrooms with additional guest rooms in several outlying buildings scattered about the 30-acre property. Guests can visit the **Museum of the Creative Process** (802-379-6350) on the grounds or play tennis, swim, or follow the **Sculpture Trail** to view the massive art installations. Every Wednesday in summer is Farm Night, featuring outside dining with music and artisanal vegetarian cuisine from **Earth Sky Time Community Farm** (802-384-1400), owned by another brother, Oliver Levis. The inn also hosts several special events throughout the year, from murder-mystery weekends to doggie slumber parties. $$–$$$.

LANDGROVE INN (802-824-6673), 132 Landgrove Road, Landgrove. This 18-room inn on a quiet backcountry road is the perfect place to unplug. In fact, there is no cell service here but no shortage of activities either, as the 32-acre property has tennis courts, an outdoor pool, and hiking and cross-country skiing trails. Innkeepers Tom and Maureen Checchia established the **InView Center for the Arts** (802-824-6673), in a studio behind the inn, which offers multiday art workshops. The early nineteenth-century inn has rooms to fit every budget, from deluxe with king-sized bed, fireplace, and Jacuzzi tub, to economy with double bed and shared bath. Special lodging and meal packages are offered for workshop attendees. A full country breakfast is included, although coffee, cold cereal, and fresh fruit are available on a self-serve basis for guests who want to get an early start on their day. $–$$$.

INN ON COVERED BRIDGE GREEN (802-375-9489), 3587 River Road, Arlington. The inn, run by Clint and Julia Dickens, has seven nicely appointed guest rooms, each with private bath, in the main house, once the home of Norman Rockwell. Pets are allowed in the two housekeeping cottages, one that was converted to a small art studio for Rockwell's son, Jarvis, and the other the artist-illustrator's studio. The latter, which sleeps four, has two bedrooms and baths, a full kitchen, and a living room with a wood-burning fireplace. In the fall the cottages have a three-night minimum stay. The inn has sweeping views of quintessential New England—a covered bridge, white church, and dairy farm—as well as easy access to the Batten Kill for fishing and canoeing. $$–$$$.

Best Places to Eat

YE OLDE TAVERN (802-362-0611), 5183 Main Street, Manchester Center. The taproom, serving classic cocktails and its signature 1790 draft ale, opens at 4:30 PM. Restaurant hours are 5–9 PM. The inn, which dates back to when Vermont was still an independent republic, embraces its centuries-old heritage with stenciled walls, period-perfect furnishings, and a "bill of fare" that includes Yankee pot roast, chicken potpie, and other regional dishes. Steak, fish, and pasta also are on the menu. Portions are generous, and all entrées come with cranberry fritters with Vermont maple butter. An early-bird menu is available before 6 PM. $$–$$$.

THE CHANTECLEER (802-362-1616), 8 Read Farm Lane, East Dorset. Open Wed.–Sun. 5:30–9 PM. Considered one of the standout restaurants in southern Vermont, this eatery, with its European-influenced American cuisine, won't disappoint. The setting in a renovated dairy barn gives it a casual-chic ambience, but the food is the star attraction here, with creatively prepared meat and fish entrées on the menu. Desserts are equally exquisite. Try the Bananas Chantecleer, premium vanilla ice cream covered with warm bananas and caramel-rum sauce. Reservations recommended. $$$–$$$$.

3

RIVER TOWNS

CORE ROUTE ESTIMATED LENGTH: 55 miles

ESTIMATED TIME: 1 to 2 days

HIGHLIGHTS: The **Rockingham** and **Weathersfield meetinghouses**, both hauntingly beautiful, mark the center of vanished eighteenth-century villages. We follow backroads through covered bridges and over hills from Rockingham to Weathersfield Center, then dip down to the Connecticut River Valley and drive almost to the 3,100-foot summit of **Mount Ascutney**. Downtown **Windsor**, a few miles north, is studded with historic buildings, including the eighteenth-century tavern in which Vermont's constitution as an independent republic was drawn up. Across the **Windsor-Cornish Covered Bridge** in New Hampshire, the **Saint-Gaudens National Historic Site** is a must stop.

SIDE TRIP HIGHLIGHTS: 52 miles (1 to 2 days) follows river roads from Windsor to **Chester** with a short detour south from Chester to the time-frozen village of **Grafton**.

GETTING THERE: From north and south, I-91 to Exit 6 and west on VT 103.

ON THE ROAD

A mile west of I-91, turn off VT 103 onto Meeting House Road, then up the steep driveway to the **Rockingham Meeting House** (802-463-3964). The wonder is that this lonely white clapboard building, dating from 1790, is open (thanks to dedicated volunteers) from Memorial Day to Columbus Day, 10 AM–4 PM. It is set in an extensive burial ground, with thin, mostly slate headstones spreading out over a green plateau. Contrasting with the simple white exterior, the beauty of the interior comes as a surprise. Light streams

LEFT: WEATHERSFIELD CENTER MEETINGHOUSE

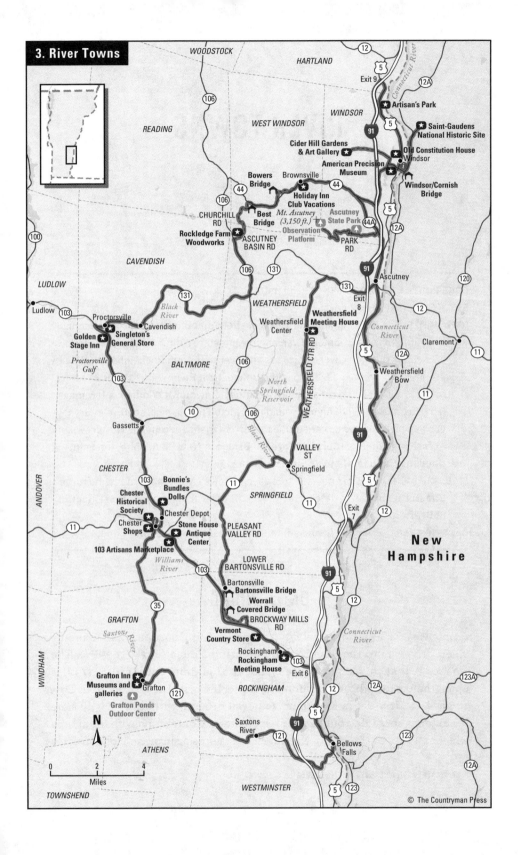

WOODSTOCK

HARTLAND

WINDSOR

WEST WINDSOR

READING

★ Artisan's Park

Exit 9

★ Saint-Gaudens National Historic Site

Cider Hill Gardens & Art Gallery ★

Old Constitution House
Windsor

American Precision Museum

Brownsville

Bowers Bridge ★

Windsor/Cornish Bridge

Holiday Inn Club Vacations

CHURCHILL RD

Best Bridge ★

Mt. Ascutney (3,150 ft.)

Ascutney State Park

Observation Platform

PARK RD

CAVENDISH

Rockledge Farm Woodworks ★

ASCUTNEY BASIN RD

Ascutney

LUDLOW

Black River

WEATHERSFIELD

Weathersfield Meeting House ★

Claremont

Ludlow

Proctorsville

Cavendish

Weathersfield Center

Connecticut River

Golden Stage Inn ★

Singleton's General Store ★

Weathersfield Bow

Proctorsville Gulf

BALTIMORE

North Springfield Reservoir

Gassetts

Black River

VALLEY ST

CHESTER

Springfield

Bonnie's Bundles Dolls ★

SPRINGFIELD

Chester Historical Society ★

Chester Depot

Exit 7

Chester Shops ★

Stone House Antique Center ★

PLEASANT VALLEY RD

103 Artisans Marketplace ★

LOWER BARTONSVILLE RD

Williams River

New Hampshire

ANDOVER

Bartonsville
Bartonsville Bridge ★

GRAFTON

Worrall Covered Bridge

Saxtons River

BROCKWAY MILLS RD

Vermont Country Store ★

Rockingham
Rockingham Meeting House ★

Grafton Inn ★
Museums and ★
galleries

Grafton

ROCKINGHAM

Exit 6

Grafton Ponds Outdoor Center

N

Saxtons River

WINDHAM

Bellows Falls

ATHENS

0   2   4
Miles

TOWNSHEND

WESTMINSTER

© The Countryman Press

ROCKINGHAM MEETINGHOUSE

in through two tiers of outsized windows, each with 20-over-20 panes. The natural wooden interior seems to glow. Box pews fill the floor and more pews line the gallery, all with seats and backs worn shiny from centuries of use.

"My family paid to have a box pew," volunteer Lee Reed tells us, explaining that her connection with this place runs back 13 generations to an ancestor buried here in 1743. "The building was originally barn red because white paint was too expensive," she says.

A church until 1839 and a town hall for three more decades, this was the original center of the town of Rockingham, Lee explains, but by the mid-nineteenth century population shifted, creating new villages—Bellows Falls and Saxtons River—to take advantage of water power. Bellows Falls, sited at one of the largest drops in the entire Connecticut River, boomed into a manufacturing and rail center.

In 1907 more than a dozen buildings surrounding this one burned down. Relieved that the meetinghouse had survived, area residents rallied to restore it, one of Vermont's earliest preservation efforts.

Luckily it was a light-handed restoration. The building was painted white, but the eighteenth-century king post framing and the "pig pen" pews remain intact, as do many of the glass panes, and the plaster is original, said to be made with cattle hair rather than horsehair. Thanks to the outstanding acoustics created by the original sounding board above the pulpit, this remains a popular venue for concerts, weddings, and events, but only June through September, given the continued lack of heat and electricity.

Recognized as "the oldest building in Vermont that still exists in a condition close to its original state," the meetinghouse is a National Historic Landmark, owned and maintained by the town for which it remains the geographical center. (Bellows Falls, home to the current town hall and 3,000 of Rockingham's 5,000 residents, is 4 miles south.)

"It's not spooky," Lee Reed insists, explaining that she was baptized and married here and that it is filled with warm family memories. Funny thing though, just then she asks if I saw someone come in. "I felt someone there behind me," she explains.

The surrounding burial ground contains more than a thousand headstones, many with clear, eerily illustrated epitaphs, some of the finest gravestone art to be found in New England. Unfortunately, rubbings are not permitted.

Meeting House Road loops back to VT 103; turn left for Rockingham's better-known attraction, **The Vermont Country Store** (802-463-2224), an offshoot of the Weston store known for its catalog featuring hard-to-find old-timey gadgets.

The license plates on cars, trucks, and RVs parked by this big red barn of a place are from all over the country. Walls and aisles inside are filled with a wild and wonderful mix of products from the past: cotton sleepwear and nature-based tonics, Vermont Common Crackers, American-made lawn chairs, weather sticks, and cat clocks with moving eyes. In a corner beyond the free cheese samples, women make sandwiches to take to the shaded picnic tables outside near the dairy bar.

Back again on VT 103, take the next right turn (after a truck depot) on Brockway Mills Road, another left on Williams Road just beyond the railroad tracks, and follow it along a narrow shelf of land above the Williams River. The weathered **Worrall Covered Bridge** (1870) marks a bend in the river and, too soon, the road rejoins VT 103, but just for a fraction of a mile. Turn onto Lower Bartonsville Road (the tip-off is a sign for the local vet), and the new **Bartonsville Bridge** comes up quickly. Rebuilt in 2012 after Tropical Storm Irene wiped out its predecessor, this is one of the state's longest covered bridges, and the fact that it's here at all is a tribute to residents of tiny Bartonsville (another Rockingham village), which spearheaded $2.6 million in fundraising to replicate rather than replace it. This road passes vintage stone and brick homes, turns to dirt just beyond the vet's house, becomes Pleasant Valley Road, turns back to pavement at the Windham/Windsor County line, and climbs over a shoulder of Whitney Hill to join VT 11, a major east-west connector.

Turn east (right) and stay with VT 11 another half-dozen miles into down-

WORRALL COVERED BRIDGE

town **Springfield**, turning north (left) beyond the Springfield Theater onto Valley Street, which turns into Brook Road as it climbs over Pudding Hill and past the Springfield Country Club before crossing the Weathersfield Town line. It's here that you begin to see **Mount Ascutney** rising above a roll of farm-patched hills. This is now the **Weathersfield Center Road**, and the hilltop village clustered around the proud, brick meetinghouse appears suddenly to the right; there's an entrance from the side road just beyond.

Completed in 1821, the **Weathersfield Center Meeting House** (802-263-9497) is one of Vermont's most elegant Federal-era public buildings. The façade includes fanlights above its three entrances, a second-story Palladian window, and a graceful double-tiered bell tower capped by a weathervane. It's open regularly only for Congregational Church services at 10 AM Sundays, late June through Labor Day weekend.

A grove of tall maples, planted in the 1860s, shades a long green leading to the meetinghouse. A tall granite shaft commemorates the MEN WHO HAVE VOLUNTEERED TO SERVE THEIR COUNTRY IN THE LATE WAR OF THE GREAT REBELLION, BEGUN IN 1862 AND SUPPRESSED IN 1865. Farther along, an eighteenth-century millstone memorializes ALL THOSE WHO HAVE SERVED OUR COUNTRY IN TIME OF STRESS IN ITS FIRST 200 YEARS.

MOUNT ASCUTNEY

Two miles north of the meetinghouse we reach VT 131. Turn east (right), then north (left) at the junction with US 5 in Ascutney. From here it's 5 miles to Windsor, but on a beautiful day it would be a shame not to detour along the way to **Ascutney State Park** (open mid-May–mid-Oct; $ day-use fee). The entrance is a mile up VT 44A, and a well-surfaced, 3.8-mile "parkway," built in the 1930s by the Civilian Conservation Corps, spirals gently up through hardwoods. Note the pullout with picnic facilities and a great view up the valley. A parking lot in the saddle between the mountain's south peak and summit accesses a steep, 0.8-mile foot trail that takes you the additional 344 vertical feet to the summit. A former fire tower has been shortened and transformed into an observation platform. It's well worth the climb for a 360-degree panorama, sweeping from the White Mountains to the northeast and west across Vermont farms and forests rolling into the Green Mountains. The park is also good for camping and hiking, and it's a popular launch spot for hang gliders.

WINDSOR

There's more to Windsor Village than meets the eye of passers-through. On the northern end of town on US 5, the **Old Constitution House** (802-674-6628; open Memorial Day–Columbus Day, Sat.–Sun. 11 AM–5 PM) is the tavern in which delegates from both sides of the Connecticut River and the Green Mountains met on July 2, 1777, to found the Republic of Vermont. The constitution they adopted was the first in America to prohibit slavery and establish voting rights for all males. Even if the building is closed, it's worth stopping to walk the path behind that leads to **Lake Runnemede**. This hidden gem is a destination for birders and walkers. A painting by early twentieth-century artist Maxfield Parrish depicts the scene here: a mountain resembling Ascutney towering above still water. It hangs in the nearby People's United Bank. Parrish lived across the river in Cornish, New Hampshire. The painting was his gift to the bank tellers in thanks for "keeping my account balanced."

Back down US 5 in the middle of town, work by current local artists can be viewed along the balcony inside **Windsor House**. Built in the 1830s, this stately brick, white-columned building was one of Vermont's proudest inns for some 130 years. The handsome U.S. post office across the street was designed by well-known early nineteenth-century architect Ammi Young, and its upstairs courtroom served as Woodrow Wilson's summer White House during the years he vacationed in Cornish (1913 to 1915).

Windsor remains an Amtrak stop, and its early rail connections to New York City and Washington fueled the town's prosperity and its evolution as the area's prestigious summer colony. In Cornish, hillside farms with splendid views of Mount Ascutney were selling cheap in the late nineteenth century. The summer home of prominent sculptor Augustus Saint-Gaudens,

Saint-Gaudens National Historic Site (603-675-2175), 139 Saint Gaudens Road, off NH 12A; open Memorial Day–Columbus Day, 9 AM–4:30 PM daily; $. The centerpiece of the 195-acre grounds (open dawn to dusk) is **Aspet**, the summer home of Augustus Saint-Gaudens from 1885 until his death in 1907. It also includes the sculptor's studio, galleries, and formal gardens. Copies of his most famous sculptures, cast from the original molds, are displayed around the beautifully landscaped grounds. An excellent film in the visitor center describes the sculptor's life and work. Saint-Gaudens is best remembered for his public pieces: the Shaw Memorial on Boston Common, the statue of Admiral Farragut in New York's Madison Park, the equestrian statue of General William T. Sherman at the Fifth Avenue entrance to Central Park, and the Abraham Lincoln sculpture in Chicago's Lincoln Park.

Bring a picnic lunch for Sunday afternoon chamber music concerts at 2 PM in July and August.

CARITAS SCULPTURE BY AUGUSTUS SAINT-GAUDENS GREGORY SCHWARTZ FOR THE NATIONAL PARK SERVICE

now a national historic site, became the nucleus of this "Cornish Colony," the name for the group of well-known writers, artists, and otherwise creative urbanites who bought surrounding properties.

The Cornish Colony flourished from 1885 to 1935, and its spirit lingers. Cornish was the home of Maxfield Parrish until his death in 1966, and writer J. D. Salinger lived quietly by the river here until his death in 2010. Maxwell Perkins, the editor remembered for discovering authors Thomas Wolfe, Ernest Hemingway, and F. Scott Fitzgerald, commuted from Windsor to his office at Scribner's in Manhattan. His graceful vintage 1815 brick mansion is now the **Snapdragon Inn** (802-227-0008), and you can sleep in guest rooms once occupied by famous authors.

The 460-foot-long Windsor/Cornish bridge, linking US 5 and NH 12A, was the longest covered bridge in the country until a new Ohio bridge outdistanced it in 2008. This is still arguably the most photogenic, set against

A VIEW OF MOUNT ASCUTNEY AND THE WINDSOR-CORNISH COVERED BRIDGE

American Precision Museum (802-674-5781), 196 Main Street, Windsor; open Memorial Day weekend–Oct., daily 10 AM–5 PM; $. The 1846 Robbins & Lawrence Armory, a National Historic Landmark, is said to hold the largest collection of historically significant machine tools in the nation. At the 1851 Great Exposition in London's Crystal Palace, the firm demonstrated rifles made with interchangeable parts, a concept perfected here. Based on that presentation, the British government ordered 25,000 rifles and 141 metal-working machines and coined the term American System for this revolutionary approach to guns and other machines. Special exhibits feature machine tools from the collection and their impact on today's world.

Mount Ascutney's isolated hump. The **American Precision Museum** (see sidebar), is south of the bridge on US 5.

One of our favorite stops in Windsor is **Cider Hill Gardens & Art Gallery** (802-674-5293; open May–Oct., Thurs.–Sun. 10 AM–5 PM). Sarah Milek's extensive display gardens are 2.5 miles up a dirt road from its junction with US 5, State Street. It becomes Hunt Road, turning to dirt as it climbs. The nursery is also the setting for Gary Milek's gallery, featuring his striking Vermont landscapes and botanically correct floral prints and greeting cards.

Windsor's vintage 1901 brick railroad station down on Depot Avenue houses **Windsor Station Restaurant and Barroom** (802-674-4130; open for lunch Thurs.–Sat., dinner Tues.–Sun.; $–$$) and the neighboring **Windsor Welcome Center** (802-674-5910), which is housed in a former baggage building and manned by volunteers.

In recent years tourist traffic has, however, shifted to **Artisans Park**, several miles north of downtown and a mile south of I-91 Exit 9. Enterprising local therapist Terry McDonnell bought a former farm on the Connecticut here in the 1990s, envisioning its commercial development as the visitor-friendly campus that's been evolving ever since. McDonnell has retained 14 riverside acres, creating the **Path of Life Garden** ($), with 18 distinct landscaped and sculpted areas, each designed to convey a step in the cycle of human life. Patterned on a vintage garden in Ireland, it includes a maze lined with 800 hemlock trees and a 90-foot rock labyrinth. Access is through **Great River Outfitters** (802-674-9933; open daily year-round), which offers 3-mile kayaking, canoeing, and tubing on a placid and popular paddling stretch of the river, ending here. Camping and a variety of other ways of experiencing the garden are also offered. The commercial anchors of Artisans Park are **Simon Pearce Glass** (802-674-6280; open daily 10 AM–5 PM) and the **Harpoon Brewery** (802-674-4591). At the Simon Pearce, visitors can watch glass being blown and shaped from a catwalk

SARAH MILEK AT CIDER HILL GARDENS

above the factory floor; the shop includes seconds and there's also a pottery barn. The Harpoon Brewery offers tours, but its big draw is the **River Taps and Beer Garden** (802-674-4591), the town's liveliest gathering place/informal restaurant. Brews on tap change with the season, and in the summer, it expands with outside tables, frequent music, and special events. The park also includes **Silo Distillery** (802-674-4220), with tours and tastings of its vodka, whiskey, and bourbon and several shops selling Vermont-made cheese, preserves, and more.

From I-91 Exit 9 it's a quick run back down the interstate to Exit 6, but we suggest exiting at Weathersfield, 10 minutes south, and following US 5 south along the river through Weathersfield Bow, a sleepy hamlet with a historic marker commemorating one-time resident William Jarvis. During his tenure as U.S. consul in Lisbon, Jarvis managed to smuggle 4,000 Merino sheep out of Spain and into the United States, transporting them to his Weathersfield Bow estate and employing a Spanish shepherd to tend them. Spain had closely guarded its herds of Merinos, a more productive breed with water-shedding wool and longer fibers than other sheep. That was 1811, and the War of 1812 sent prices for domestic wool soaring.

New England's burgeoning textile mills gobbled up the wool, and by 1830 Merino sheep had become the state's main livestock; by 1840 there were upward of 2 million Merino sheep in Vermont. Jarvis can be credited with much of the prosperity we still see preserved in brick and clapboard. Merino sheep transformed the Vermont landscape, expanding open pasture land, much of which was subsequently preserved by the dairy farms.

From Weathersfield Bow, it's another 7 miles south on US 5 to I-91 Exit 7, much of it along the river. Our core route ends here.

Best Places to Sleep

SNAPDRAGON INN (802-227-0008), 26 Main Street, Windsor. This 1815 mansion, set on spacious grounds, was home for many years to Max Perkins, legendary editor to Thomas Wolfe, Ernest Hemingway, and F. Scott Fitzgerald, whose works are found in the inn library. The nine second- and third-floor guest rooms vary in size, but all are artistically furnished with an eye to light and comfort; Wolfe and Hemingway are said to have slept in #8. A path leads from the garden to Lake Runnemede. A buffet breakfast is included in the $$–$$$ rates.

WINDSOR MANSION INN (802-674-4112), 153 Pembroke Road, Windsor. Set high on a hill above town with a view of Mount Ascutney, this former mansion is a longtime inn, recently renovated and renamed. With 17 guest rooms, spacious living and dining rooms, and landscaped grounds, it lends itself to weddings and meetings but welcomes overnight guests. $$

Best Places to Eat

WINDSOR STATION RESTAURANT AND BARROOM (802-674-4130; open for lunch Thurs.–Sat., dinner Tues.–Sun.). The interior of this 1902 railroad station is darkly paneled, brightened with art, and divided among the Lounge Car with pub food and the more formal Dining and Parlor Cars with an Italian-accented menu. Produce is locally sourced; locally crafted beers are a specialty and dinner reservations are advisable. $–$$.

SIDE TRIP

Windsor to Chester
With a 7-Mile Detour to Grafton

ESTIMATED LENGTH: 52 miles

From Windsor VT 44 runs west to the sleepy village of Brownsville, the former gateway to the ski resort at Mount Ascutney that operated from the 1950s until 2010. The ski condo complex at its base survives as time-share **Holiday Inn Club Vacations** (1-888-HOLIDAY; from $) and a local mountain bike club, **Sport Trails of Ascutney Basin** (stabvt.org) maintains an extensive trail system here. A short distance beyond the village, right turn on Ely Road and follow it 0.6 mile to the vintage **Bowers Covered Bridge** (1919). Back on VT 44, turn onto Churchill Road and follow it through the **Best Covered Bridge** (1889), then continue as it turns into Ascutney Basin Road. Turn in at the sign for **Rockledge Farm Woodworks** (800-653-2700; open Tues.–Sat. 9 AM–5 PM, Sun. 12–4 PM), a 200-year-old farm with a long family woodworking tradition. Visitors are welcome to watch as Vermont hardwoods and burls are crafted into nationally distributed furniture and woodenware that's also sold here. Bring a picnic for the tables under the apple trees.

Turn onto VT 106 and follow it south, turning west on VT 131, along the Black River to the old mill village of Cavendish, then on another couple miles to Proctorsville. Continue a minute beyond the green to **Singleton's General Store** (802-226-7666). Best known for its smoked meats and sauces, this much-expanded, family-run general store is a source of fishing and hunting licenses, rods and reels, sporting goods, craft beers, sturdy outdoor wear, and more. Back at the green, turn on Depot Street where **Crows Bakery and Opera House Café** (802-226-7007; open 6:30 AM–6 PM Tues.–Sat., 7 AM–5 PM Sun.) offers from-scratch daily-baked pies, cakes, and cookies, as well as tempting sandwiches and wraps. Daily blackboard specials too.

At the end of Depot Street, turn left on VT 103 and follow it south through Proctorsville Gulf along the Williams River, passing old farms on your way to Chester and its Stone Village, a double line of early nineteenth-century houses built from locally quarried granite. If her flag is out, you might want to stop at **Bonnie's Bundles Dolls** (802-875-2114). Bonnie Watters doesn't like to sell her handmade cloth dolls to retail shops, preferring to meet the people who buy them. She specializes in portrait dolls (you supply a photo of a child or friend).

Continue on through Chester Depot, a village cluster around the Victorian railroad depot, a destination for **Green Mountain Railroad** (800-707-3530) foliage excursions from Bellows Falls. At the junction with VT 11, turn right into Chester Village, the heart of this hospitable town. Shops and restaurants line the common, flanking the **Fullerton Inn** (802-875-2444). Across Main Street, the information center offers a restroom as well as brochures describing places to stay. The neighboring **Chester Historical Society** (802-875-5459; open seasonally, weekends 2–4 PM) tells the town's unusually colorful history. Distinctive shops include **Phoenix Books Misty Valley** (802-875-3400); **Six Loose Ladies** (802-226-7373), a volunteer-run outlet for locally spun yarns as well knitting and crocheting supplies; and **DaVallia Arts & Accents** (802-875-8900), with Vermont-made jewelry, pottery, and gifts.

Turn south on VT 103 for the **Stone House Antiques Center** (802-875-7373), with 90-plus dealers, and **103 Artisans Marketplace** (802-875-4477), showcasing fanciful wrought-iron and metal work by owners Elise and Payne Junker as well as a wide variety of crafted work. At the neighboring **Heritage Deli & Bakery** (802-875-3550; open daily 7 AM–6 PM), soups and pastries are made from scratch and signature sandwiches are named for famous Vermonters; take-out or eat in the cheerful café with its Provençal print tablecloths. The **Free Range Restaurant** (802-875-3346; open Tues.–Sat. for dinner, also for Sat. lunch and Sun. brunch) offers an appealing atmosphere and menu. From Chester it's 10 miles down VT 103 to I-91 Exit 6, or you can loop back to I-91 via Grafton (see *Detour*). $–$$.

SHOPS AND RESTAURANTS FLANK THE FULLERTON INN ALONG CHESTER'S COMMON

Best Places to Sleep

GOLDEN STAGE INN (802-226-7744), 399 Depot Street, Proctorsville. Centrally air-conditioned and handicapped accessible, this charming inn dates in part to 1788 as a stagecoach stop. Michael and Julie-Lynn offer six bright, comfortable guest rooms and two suites. A swimming pool is set in gardens, and the 5 acres are home to hens, sheep, and sheep. A full breakfast with eggs from the house chickens and honey from the house hives (giving new meaning to the word *golden*) as well as afternoon treats and a bottomless cookie jar are included in the rates. Inquire about inn-to-inn walking tours (vermontinntoinnwalking.com). $$.

HENRY FARM INN (802-875-26740), 2206 Green Mountain Turnpike., Chester. Minutes from the village center, there's an out-in-the-country feel to the old tavern built in 1760, set on 56 rolling acres. It retains its pine floors, beehive oven, paneling, and sense of pleasant, uncluttered comfort. The nine rooms are large, with private bath; two are suites with kitchen. What you notice are the quilts and the views. A path leads to the spring-fed pond up the hill, and a swimming hole in the Williams River is across the road. Rates include a full country breakfast. $$.

Best Place to Eat

FULLERTON INN (802-875-2444), 40 The Common, Chester. Open for lunch Wed.–Sat., dinner Mon.–Sat. This middle-of-town landmark features reasonably priced, dependably good food. The dinner menu, available on the front porch (weather permitting) and in the tavern as well as the dining room, includes a roasted half duck and locally raised steak. There's also a wide choice of reasonably priced comfort food. $–$$.

DETOUR

7 Miles South from Chester to Grafton

Despite its population of less than 700, Grafton looms large on Vermont's touring maps, thanks to the Windham Foundation, which preserves the village's classic looks. Prior to the Civil War, Grafton was home to upward of 1,500 residents and 10,000 sheep. Wool was turned into 75,000 yards of Grafton cloth annually; soapstone from 13 local quarries left town in the shape of sinks, stoves, inkwells, and foot warmers. But then one in three of Grafton's men marched off to the Civil War, and few returned. Sheep farming, too, "went west." An 1869 flood destroyed the town's six dams and its road. The new highway bypassed Grafton. The town's tavern, however, built in 1801,

ROCKING CHAIRS LINE THE PORCH AT THE GRAFTON INN

entered a golden era. Innkeeper Harlan Phelps invested his entire California gold rush fortune in adding a third floor and double porches, and his brother Francis organized a still-extant cornet band. Guests included Emerson, Thoreau, and Kipling; later both Woodrow Wilson and Teddy Roosevelt visited. By the mid-nineteenth century, however, the tavern was sagging and nearly all the 80-some houses in town were selling cheap with plenty of acreage. Then, in the 1960s, the Windham Foundation, funded by a resident summer family, bought much of the town and set about restoring it. The **Grafton Inn** (802-843-2248) was renovated, cheese making was revived, the village wiring was buried, and **Grafton Trails & Outdoor Center** (802-843-2400) was established, with swimming and trails for cross-country skiing and mountain biking, along with a **Nature Museum** (802-843-2111) and the **Vermont Museum of Mining & Minerals** (802-875-3562). Clustered within the village's few streets are the **Grafton Forge Blacksmith** (802-843-1029), a working blacksmith shop; the **Gallery North Star** (802-843-2465), a destination for fine art lovers; and the **Jud Hartmann Gallery** (802-843-2018; open mid-Sept.–Christmas), showcasing the sculptor's nationally acclaimed bronze portrayals of Native Americans. The old general store has been reimagined as **MKT: Grafton** (802-843-2255), featuring a café with a lunch and brunch menu. The way back to I-91 is down VT 121 through Saxtons River to Bellows Falls.

Best Place to Sleep and Eat

GRAFTON INN (802-843-2248), 92 Main Street, Grafton. Comfortable, antiques-furnished rooms are divided between the inn and neighboring cottage, and there are also four rental houses. In total the inn can accommodate 90. Candlelit dining is in **The Old Tavern Restaurant**, and the **Phelps Barn Pub** offers a pub menu. $$–$$$.

4

THE UPPER CONNECTICUT RIVER VALLEY

ESTIMATED LENGTH: 73 miles

ESTIMATED TIME: 5 hours to 2 days

HIGHLIGHTS: This is an exceptionally beautiful stretch of the bistate **Connecticut River National Scenic Byway**. I-91, set high above the Vermont bank of the river, has turned the old highways—US 5 in Vermont and NH 10—into lightly trafficked backroads, alternately hugging the river and threading through farmland. Bridges link villages on opposite riverbanks. The **Montshire Museum** in Norwich, incorporating both states in its name, is a major science museum, but otherwise formal attractions are few. Instead there are farm stands, river landings, swim beaches, and unexpected discoveries like the *Vermontasaurus* dinosaur in a grassy airfield in Post Mills and **Farm-Way**, a vast and varied emporium hidden away near the river in Bradford. Local bicyclists loop back and forth across the bridges, and their well-known advice is, "Take 5 (north) and hang 10 (back south)," which is what this route does, following US 5 north and NH 10 along our favorite reaches of the river.

GETTING THERE: I-89 to I-91, Exit 13 to US 5 in Norwich.

ON THE ROAD

Especially along these 30 miles or so north of Norwich, Vermont, and Hanover, New Hampshire, the Connecticut River forms more of a bond than a border between the two states. Several towns on opposite sides of the river share school districts, and locals identify themselves as residents of the "Upper Valley" almost as often as New Hampshire or Vermont.

LEFT: IN THE UPPER VALLEY, THE CONNECTICUT RIVER CONNECTS TWO STATES TO CREATE ONE REGION
KINDRA CLINEFF

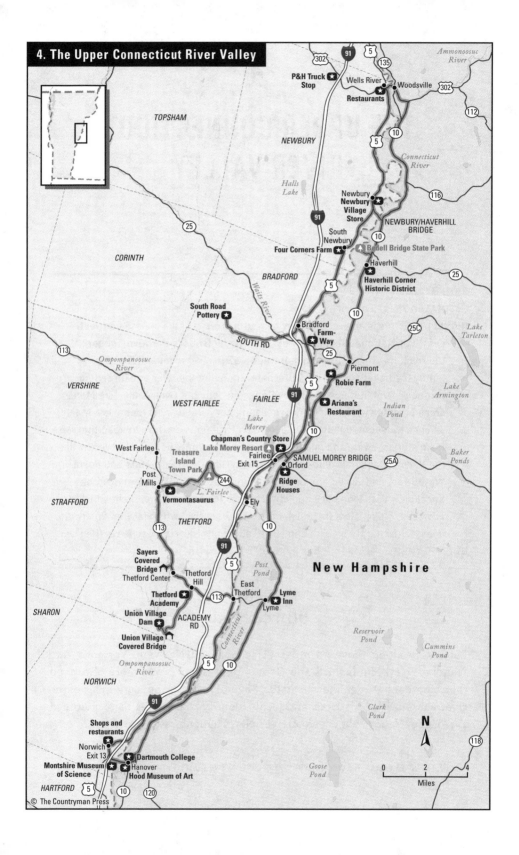

4. The Upper Connecticut River Valley

TOPSHAM

NEWBURY

P&H Truck Stop ⭐

Wells River
Woodsville

Restaurants ⭐

Ammonoosuc River

Connecticut River

Halls Lake

CORINTH

BRADFORD

Newbury
Newbury Village Store ⭐

South Newbury

Four Corners Farm ⭐

NEWBURY/HAVERHILL BRIDGE

Bedell Bridge State Park

Haverhill ⭐

Haverhill Corner Historic District

Waits River

South Road Pottery ⭐

SOUTH RD

Bradford Farm-Way ⭐

Lake Tarleton

VERSHIRE

Ompompanoosuc River

Piermont

Robie Farm ⭐

Lake Armington

WEST FAIRLEE

FAIRLEE

Ariana's Restaurant ⭐

Indian Pond

Lake Morey

West Fairlee

Chapman's Country Store
Lake Morey Resort ⭐

Fairlee
Exit 15

SAMUEL MOREY BRIDGE

Orford

Baker Ponds

Treasure Island Town Park

Post Mills

STRAFFORD

Vermontasaurus ⭐

Ely

Ridge Houses ⭐

L. Fairlee

THETFORD

New Hampshire

Post Pond

Sayers Covered Bridge
Thetford Center

Thetford Hill

East Thetford

Lyme Inn ⭐

Lyme

SHARON

Thetford Academy ⭐

Union Village Dam ⭐

ACADEMY RD

Union Village Covered Bridge

Ompompanoosuc River

Reservoir Pond

Cummins Pond

Connecticut River

NORWICH

Clark Pond

Shops and restaurants ⭐

Norwich
Exit 13

Dartmouth College ⭐

Montshire Museum of Science ⭐

Hanover

Hood Museum of Art ⭐

HARTFORD

Goose Pond

N

0   2   4
Miles

© The Countryman Press

Off the I-91 exit ramp, turn right to find the **Montshire Museum** (802-649-2000) set in 110 trailside acres on the Vermont riverbank. This science center is fit for a city and geared to curious minds of all ages. A left off the I-91 exit ramp leads to the village of **Norwich**.

The historic district of this old river town is a showcase for graceful, early nineteenth-century Federal architecture. At its heart is **Dan & Whit's General Store** (802-649-1602), a trove of hardware, stationery, and garden supplies as well as groceries, gas, and the area's biggest community bulletin board. At the neighboring Victorian-style **Norwich Inn** (802-649-1143), **Jasper Murdock's Alehouse** is a popular stop for lunch and dinner. Down the street, behind the **Norwich Bookstore** (802-649-1114), the **Norwich Square Café** (802-649-1500; open Mon.–Fri. 8 AM–3:30 PM) is a hidden gem, a source of freshly baked croissants, panini, and quiche. Norwich is nationally known to serious bakers as home to **King Arthur Flour**. Its landscaped headquar-

MONTSHIRE MUSEUM TOWER IMAGE COURTESY OF THE MONTSHIRE MUSEUM OF SCIENCE

ters, south of the village on US 5, includes **The Baker's Store and Café** (802-649-6365; open 7:30 AM–6 PM) and a **Baking School** with programs that draw fans from around the country.

We follow US 5 north as it hugs the river for the 10 miles to East Thetford, but then branch off up VT 113. It's less than a mile to **Thetford Hill**, an aristocratic village set high enough to command a view of New Hampshire hills across the river. An elegant Congregational church, a library, and handsome early brick and clapboard homes surround the green. **Thetford Academy**, a short way down Academy Street, was founded in 1819 and enrolls international students as well those from towns on both sides of the river. **Union Village Dam** (802-649-1606), maintained by the Army Corps of Engineers, is less than a mile down Academy Street and through the vintage 1867 **covered bridge** across the Ompompanoosuc River. The recreation area offers a sandy swim beach and shaded picnic facilities.

A mile or so north of Thetford Hill, VT 113 dips down to **Thetford Center**, where there's a general store, brick Methodist church, and the **Sayers Covered Bridge** (left on Tucker Hill Road). In several more miles the small village of **Post Mills** marks the junction with VT 244. Turn right here, then veer right again on Robinson Road by the graveyard across from the cupola-topped white church. Turn in at the sign for the **Post Mills Airport**.

The long, nondescript building and outbuildings here beside the field house one of the world's largest collections of hot-air balloons, airships, and contraptions that were never meant to fly but do. *Vermontasaurus*, a 122-foot-long, 25-foot-high dinosaur, stands in the grassy airfield beyond. The sculpture has been cobbled together with wood from a collapsed barn roof, and several smaller dinosaur sculptures, born from a similar blow-down, are also on hand. Their creator (with the help of students and volunteers) is Brian Boland, who has also created many of the flying machines on view here.

Few people were offering hot-air balloon rides in the 1970s, when Boland began making his own balloons and flying them. He is now known internationally as a hot-air balloon designer and locally as the Willy Wonka of the Upper Valley. Contact **Boland Balloon** (802-333-9254) to schedule an early morning or evening balloon ride; **Silver Maple Lodge & Cottages** (802-333-4326) in Fairlee offers ballooning packages.

Beyond the airfield, VT 244 winds along crystal clear **Lake Fairlee**, past long-established children's camps. There's a Vermont Fish & Wildlife boat ramp, great for launching that kayak on your car roof, but the better place to swim here is a bit farther along at **Treasure Island Town Park** (802-333-9615; open seasonally 9 AM–8 PM; $). There's a sand beach with changing facilities, a picnic area, and playground. VT 244 ends too soon at US 5 in Ely.

The second large lake in Fairlee is less than 3 miles north, just west

VERMONTASAURUS SCULPTURE IN POST MILLS

of Fairlee Village. **Lake Morey** (turn left at the sign for I-91) is named for Samuel Morey, a local inventor who is locally credited with inventing the country's first steam-powered paddle-wheeler in 1793. Robert Fulton, whom history credits with inventing the steamboat, having encouraged Morey to talk freely with him and to demonstrate the invention, patented a boat clearly patterned on his in 1797. Legend has it that an embittered Morey sunk his vessel at the bottom of Lake Morey, where it remains. The lake is lined with vintage summer cottages and is home to family-owned **Lake Morey Resort** (802-333-4311), known for its 18-hole golf course. There's boat access to both Lake Morey and this placid stretch of the Connecticut River; **Fairlee Marine** (802-383-9745) rents paddleboats, kayaks, and canoes as well as motorboats.

Fairlee Village, strung between the river and US 5, is a likely lunch stop, either at the **Whippi Dip** (802-333-3730), a take-out well known for BBQ, or the **Fairlee Diner** (802-333-3569; closed Tues., otherwise open 5:30 AM–2 PM), a 1930s classic with wooden booths and worn-shiny wooden stool tops. The area's current dining sensation is **Samurai Soul Food** (802-331-1041; open

Tues.–Sun. 3–9 PM), blending locally sourced ingredients into an unlikely but successful fusion of Asian, Tex-Mex, and basic comfort food.

Chapman's Store (802-333-9709), opposite the bridge to Orford, New Hampshire, is a must-stop. Since 1924 members of the Chapman family have expanded the stock of this old pharmacy to include 10,000 hand-tied fishing flies, crawlers, Mexican and Indian jewelry, USGS maps, wine, toys, crafted furniture and pottery, paddleboards, and more. Behind the Fairlee Motel on the northern fringe of the village is the **Fairlee Drive-In** (802-333-91920; open seasonally). This '50s classic has been upgraded to screen current blockbusters. Gates open at 7 PM, films begin at dusk, and the snack bar features burgers made with Angus beef from the motel owner's farm.

North of the village, US 5 squeezes between the river and a steep cliff face known as "The Palisades," but beyond this the valley opens wide, running between cornfields and the river for a half-dozen miles. A traffic light marks the junction with US 25; a left here takes you to I-91, and a right leads to **Farm-Way** (800-222-9316; open Mon.–Sat. 8:30 AM–5:30 PM, Fri. until 8 PM),

BOAT LAUNCH ON LAKE FAIRLEE

CHAPMAN'S STORE IN FAIRLEE IS A MUST STOP

Vermont's answer to L. L. Bean. There's no missing this rambling, barn-red store with a line of kayaks out front and annexes spread over 17 acres. It's run by three generations of a family and bills itself as a Vermont "cultural experience." Boots and shoes, more than 20,000 pairs, are a specialty, but there is also a wide selection of clothing, hunting gear, furniture, kayaks, a saddlery, and more.

The village of **Bradford** is on US 5 north of the light. It's built on terraces of land at the confluence of the Waits and Connecticut Rivers. A picturesque, old, stone gristmill is sited across from an impressive waterfall at the entrance to downtown. The mill now houses **Alexander's Restaurant** (802-222-5505; open Tues.–Sat. 11:30 AM–9 PM), which offers seating along the mill raceway and Lebanese as well as standard dishes. In a neighboring mill building, **Copeland Furniture** (802-222-5300) showcases its contemporary furniture crafted from native hardwoods in a factory down the street (check out the seconds).

Bradford's business block has seen better days, but at its center is **Colatina Exit** (802-222-9008; open daily from 11 AM), an expansive trattoria. It

FOUR CORNERS FARMSTAND, SOUTH NEWBURY

specializes in wood-fired pizza but offers a full menu. Rear windows here and at tables in the back of the neighboring **Bliss Village Store** (802-222-4617) offer a view of the golf course below and across the floodplain and river to Mount Moosilauke, easternmost of New Hampshire's White Mountains.

Backroads in the hills west of Bradford link the photogenic villages of East Corinth, Topsham Four Corners, and Waits River, and are home to an unusual number of artists and craftspeople who welcome visitors during the Vermont Craft Council's Memorial Day **Open Studios Weekend** (vermont crafts.com) and the first weekend in October for **Vermont North by Hand** (vermontnorthbyhand.org). **South Road Pottery** (802-222-5798) is generally open May–Oct., daily 10 AM–5 PM, but it's wise to call before heading up South Road (off VT 25 West). Bruce Murray's nationally known pottery studio/showroom is a timber-framed eighteenth-century barn.

Bradford and the quiet end of the valley beyond is an area billed by the local chamber of commerce as "Cohase" (802-757-2549; cohase.org). Pronounced "co-hâs," this is an Abenaki word for "wide valley," and it aptly fits the lay of the land here: rich intervale farmland reaching seemingly to the New Hampshire mountains. Keep an eye peeled for the sign for **Four Corners Farm** (802-855-3342) on the left; it's just up Doe Hill Road in South Newbury. The Grays maintain this 50-acre farm with its Jersey milk cows, Highland beef cows, greenhouses, and acres of vegetables and fruit, including sweet corn, raspberries, snap peas, and the best tomatoes we can remember.

On to Newbury, believed to be the site of a Native American village for many thousands of years. The current town was founded in 1761 by General Jacob Bayley, who is remembered for his role in constructing a military road during the Revolution. It was meant to be an invasion route to Canada, and while that never worked out, it later served as a settlement route from the Connecticut River Valley into the hills of northern Vermont.

The village of Newbury is a beauty, with several eighteenth-century

NEWBURY VILLAGE STORE

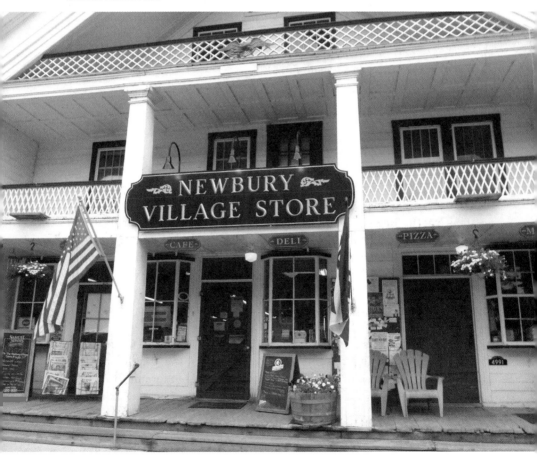

Continue north on US 5 North 6 miles to Wells River. The road shadows the river until it wanders off below and curves back on itself in a double bow. Wells River marked the head of navigation on the Connecticut for the flat-bottomed boats that formed the means of long-distance transport up this valley before the advent of railroads. By contrast, Woodsville, New Hampshire, across the river, boomed as a late nineteenth-century railroad hub, as evidenced by its Opera House block and a three-story rail station. Together the two villages form an up-country breaking point at the junction of East/West US 302—connecting the White Mountains and central Vermont—and North/South I-91. The **P&H Truck Stop** (802-429-2141; open 6 AM–10 PM for hot meals but 24 hours for to-go premade sandwiches, pies, and the like) is just off I-91 at Exit 17 in Wells River. It's a classic truck stop with speedy service, friendly waitresses, homemade bread, an ATM, and a pay phone (cell service is spotty).

On US 5 in Wells River, the **Happy Hour Restaurant** (802-757-3466; open 11:30 AM–8 PM Sun. and Tues.–Thurs., 11:30 AM–9 PM Fri.–Sat.) is a dependable standby. In Woodsville the **Saltwater Bar & Bistro** (603-747-2365; open 11 AM–9 PM Tues.–Sat., 12–7 PM Sun.) features fresh fish, from lobster rolls to blackened swordfish, and **The Little Grille's Comida Mexicana** (603-747-2777) can hit the spot with loaded tacos, nachos, and salads. The return to our stem route is south via NH 10.

homes along its long green and the hospitable **Newbury Village Store** (802-866-5681; open 6 AM–8 PM most days), with comfortable seating near the periodicals, daily baked muffins and cookies, and a café in back overlooking the river. Cross the bridge here to Haverhill to continue our stem route or consider a side trip a bit farther on up the river.

South of the Newbury-Haverhill Bridge, NH 10 runs through a beautiful stretch of this seemingly remote, upper end of the valley. A mile or so south, turn at the sign for **Bedell Bridge State Park**. This is a big name for a quiet, grassy spot by a boat launch, but it's a magical spot with a view of two massive stone piles in the river, all that remains of the two-span covered bridge, the fifth to stand here before it was blown down in 1979, having been rebuilt after a similar storm in the previous year.

Be sure to stop a bit farther south on NH 10 at the **Haverhill Corner Historic District**. This is a time-frozen village, sited at the junction of river route and NH 25, the old Coos Turnpike through the mountains. It was the seat of New Hampshire's Grafton Country from 1791 to 1891, and its former nineteenth-century courthouse is now **Court Street Arts** (603-989-5500), a performance center with frequent programs and exhibits. Take a moment to stroll by the fine late eighteenth- and early nineteenth-century buildings around the common and breathe in the peace of the place. Across the road, Susie Klein and Marty Cohen welcome guests to **Gibson House** (603-989-3125; open June–Oct.), built in 1850 and commanding a view of its gardens below and across the river to Vermont. There are eight imaginatively decorated rooms, and the couple takes pride in tuning guests into this special place; they also host weddings and artist workshops. $$.

NH 10 runs south to Piermont through cornfields that seem to roll back to the Vermont hills, by farmhouses and barns, including one of New England's rare round barns. Stop by the **Robie Farm** (603-272-4872) for raw milk, ice cream, the farm's own aged cheese, eggs, and meat. This 140-year-old dairy farm, which has been in the family for six generations, also offers hiking trails (the Appalachian Trail passes through) and access to the river.

South of the Orford line, **Bunten Farm** is a strikingly handsome 1835

THIS WELL-PRESERVED 16-SIDED ROUND BARN IS ON NH 10 IN PIERMONT

DETOUR

Alternatively, NH 10 runs south through the inviting village of Lyme and on back to Hanover. South of the village but still in Orford, **Peyton Place** (see *Best Places to Eat*) is housed in a 1773 tavern. It's named for its owners, Jim and Heidi Peyton.

Continuing south, NH 10 keeps its distance from the Connecticut, but River Road angles off, dipping beneath a covered bridge and Federal-era farmsteads along the way to Lyme. The village of Lyme is another beauty, with an elegant white 1812 Congregational church and the four-story **Lyme Inn** (603-795-4824) at its head. Below the general store and the post office, **Stella's Italian Kitchen & Market** (603-795-4302; open 10 AM–10 PM; $$) is a popular stop.

Hanover, 10 miles south, is home of prestigious **Dartmouth College** and a cultural hub of the Upper Valley. The Dartmouth Green doubles as the town common, and the village's people-watching place is a rocker on the porch of the college-owned, 108-room **Hanover Inn** (603-643-4300; $$–$$$). The neighboring **Hopkins Center for the Performing Arts** (603-646-2422) stages frequent concerts, theater, and film, and the neighboring **Hood Museum of Art** (603-646-2808; temporarily closed for renovation as of this writing). South of the Green, a scant few blocks are filled with shops and restaurants, more than in the rest of this stretch of the Upper Valley combined.

house, built with bricks made on the property. If it's fall, Chris Bunten Balch is probably out front selling pumpkins. **Ariana's Restaurant** (603-353-4405; open Mon., Wed., Thurs.–Sat. 5–9:30 PM; Sun. brunch 10 AM–1 PM), housed in the adjacent barn, is a dining destination for much of the valley and neighboring hills. (See *Best Places to Eat*.)

Continue south to **Orford Village**, with a lineup above NH 10 of seven handsome homes built between 1773 and 1839 and known as the **Ridge Houses**. Long credited erroneously to architect Charles Bulfinch, they were built instead by local craftsmen using designs from a do-it-yourself guide to Federal styles, *The Country Builder's Apprentice* by Connecticut Valley architect Asher Benjamin. The most elaborate was owned by inventor Samuel Morey, who heated and lighted his house with gas and in 1826 patented a gas-powered internal combustion engine.

This ends the stem of our driving route. We cross the iron Samuel Morey Bridge back to Fairlee and I-91 Exit 15.

Montshire Museum of Science (802-649-2200; montshire.org), Exit 13, I-91, Montshire Road, Norwich. Open daily 10 AM–5 PM except Thanksgiving and Christmas. Few cities have a science museum of this quality. This award-winning, hands-on science center with more than 140 exhibits is sited on 110 trail-webbed acres beside the Connecticut River. The focus is on demystifying scientific phenomena, engaging your senses, and learning about the world around you. The elaborate 3-acre Science Park features water bubbling from a 7-foot Barre granite boulder, and from this "headwater" a 250-foot "rill" flows downhill, snaking over a series of terraces, inviting you to manipulate dams and sluices to change its flow and direction (visitors are advised to bring bathing suits and towels). You can also shape fountains, cast shadows to tell time, and push a button to identify the call of birds and insects. Note Ed Kahn's *Wind Wall*, an outdoor sculpture attached to the museum's tower and composed of thousands of silver discs that shimmer in the breeze, resembling patterns on a pond riffled by wind. In the Hughes Pavilion overlooking Science Park, visitors may enjoy their picnic lunch or purchase lunch and snacks at the outdoor café (summer only).

Some of our favorite exhibits inside the museum include the fog machine up in the tower, the see-through beehive, leaf-cutter ants, the physics of bubbles, the planet walk, and the giant moose. There's also a Solve It exhibit with 20 puzzles and games. Most exhibits are hands-on, and there's a corner for toddlers and many demonstrations geared to youngsters. The Museum Store alone is worth a stop. Check the website for events, programs, and special exhibits. Mid-June–Labor Day, admission: $14 for children, $17 for adults, under 2 are free).

Best Places to Sleep

Listed as they appear along the route

THE NORWICH INN (802-649-1143; norwichinn.com), 325 Main Street, Norwich. The present three-story, tower-topped inn dates from 1889. Joe and Jill Lavin are hands-on owners with the right touch. The 38 guest rooms are divided among the main inn and two clapboard annexes in the rear. The 17 rooms in the inn retain the antiques and charm of an old inn. Those in the annexes are individually, tastefully, and traditionally decorated but with gas fireplaces, spacious baths, and central air. Walker House, with 18 rooms, has an elevator to access the second floor. In Ivy Lodge, two of the four luxurious suites are pet friendly. $$.

LAKE MOREY INN (802-333-4311), Club House Road, Fairlee. On the shore of Lake Morey, this sprawling landmark is a destination for ice skaters as well as golfers. The 130 rooms and suites vary from cozy and old-fashioned in the original building to spacious and balconied in the newest wing. The lake view remains key, along with a player-friendly 18-hole golf course. Facilities include an indoor swimming pool, Jacuzzi, sauna, fitness center, and tennis courts. All three meals are served, and in summer the per-person rates include a children's program as well as breakfast and dinner. $$–$$$.

THE GIBSON HOUSE (603-989-3125; open June–Oct.), 341 Dartmouth College Highway (NH 10), Haverhill, NH. This Greek Revival home, built in 1850 on the green in Haverhill Corner, is a great spot from which to explore the quiet upper end of the valley. Innkeepers Susie Klein and Marty Cohen delight in directing guests to its special places. The eight guest rooms, especially the four big second-floor rooms, are artistic creations, each very different from the next. While the house fronts on NH 10, the 50-foot-long sunny back porch with wicker seats and swing takes full advantage of the splendid view west across the terraced garden and the Connecticut River. A full breakfast is included in the reasonable rates. $$.

Best Places to Eat

CARPENTER AND MAIN (802-649-2922), 326 Main Street, Norwich. Open for dinner Wed.–Sun. Reservations suggested. An 1820s building at the heart of this village is the venue for chef-owner Bruce MacLeod's long-celebrated, locally sourced fare. $$.

JASPER MURDOCK'S ALEHOUSE AT THE NORWICH INN (802-649-1143), 225 Main Street, Norwich. Open for dinner nightly; breakfast Wed.–Sun.; lunch Fri.; brunch Sat.–Sun. The same menu is available in the inn's formal dining room, bright terrace room, and green-walled, comfortable pub, with seating that expands seasonally onto the flowery patio. The dinner ranges from burgers and wings to substantial entrées incorporating the house brews. Long before the current craft brewery craze, this was a source of stouts and ales available nowhere else. $–$$.

ARIANA'S RESTAURANT AT BUNTEN FARM (603-353-4405; arianas restaurant.com), 1322 NH 10, Orford, NH. Reservations suggested, a must on weekends, but chef-owner Martin Murphy tries to keep a table and sit-up bar at the open kitchen open for walk-ins. This is a small restaurant in the barn attached to one of the early brick farmhouses you see spaced along the Connecticut. The menu might range from shepherd's pie (with local veal and cheddar), vegan curried rice, and a choice of pastas to veal cassoulet (local veal osso buco and sausage), roasted dry sea scallops, and sirloin steak. $–$$.

PEYTON PLACE RESTAURANT (603-353-9100), 454 Main Street (NH 10), Orford. Open Wed.–Sun. 5:30–10:30; closed Sun. in the off-season. Reservations a must. Destination dining, this restaurant (named for owners Jim and Heidi Peyton) is housed in a 1773 tavern with a genuine old pub room as well as more formal dining rooms. Dinner entrées might range from house-made vegetarian ravioli to rack of lamb with wild mushrooms. Ice creams and sorbets are handmade in house. Inquire about cooking classes. $–$$.

5

WHITE RIVER VALLEYS

ESTIMATED LENGTH: 94 miles

ESTIMATED TIME: 1 to 3 days

HIGHLIGHTS: I-89 sweeps in a grand arc northwest from the Connecticut River, following the White River and its tributaries into the mountains, in the process backroading the rural heart of Vermont with its classic old villages of **South Royalton, Tunbridge, Strafford, Chelsea, Brookfield, Randolph,** and **Rochester**. Roads run north-south through lush valley farmland and by multiple covered bridges. East-west roads connect the valleys, climbing over steep hills with long views at their crests. Attractions consist mainly of river swimming holes and tubing stretches, and of farms to visit and stay.

GETTING THERE: I-89 from points north and south to Exit 2.

Coming from the south, the **Sharon Welcome Center and Vermont Vietnam Veterans Memorial** (open 7 AM–11 PM) between Exits 1 and 2 is worth a stop. Vietnam War exhibits include a timeline and film clips, and the building features a walk-in "living greenhouse" filled with plants that recycle waste. The coffee is free, the desk is manned, and the bathrooms are outstanding.

ON THE ROAD

Turn left off the exit ramp and then right on VT 14 into the village of Sharon, a crossroads cluster around the white-columned **Sharon Trading Post** (802-763-7404; open 9 AM–9 PM), good for gas, staples, and rental inner tubes. This stretch of White River is especially popular for tubing. The road west follows the river's twists and curves, passing a number of likely put-in spots.

Soon after crossing the Royalton town line, a sign for the **Joseph Smith**

LEFT: THE VINTAGE 1799 TOWN HOUSE, STRAFFORD

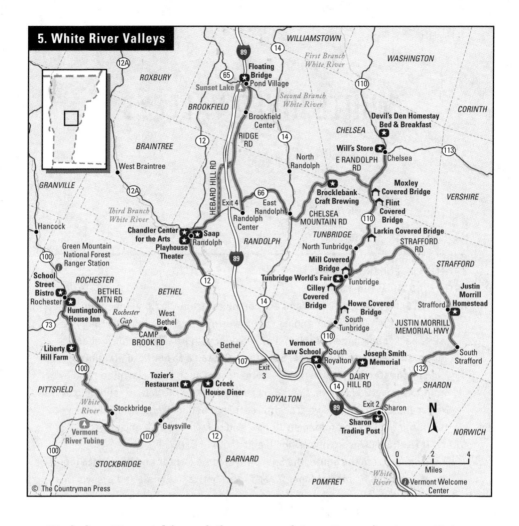

Birthplace Memorial (open daily year-round; 802-763-7742) points up Dairy Hill Road. It's a steep, 2-mile drive up to the hilltop complex that marks the 1805 birthplace of the founder of the Church of Jesus Christ of Latter-Day Saints. The property includes picnic grounds and a visitor center (open daily until 7 PM May–Oct., otherwise until 5 PM) with paintings, sculpture, and films. A memorial shaft measures 38.5 feet high, each foot marking a year in the life of the Mormon prophet.

South Royalton is another mile down VT 14 and a left across the bridge. Since the 1970s this village (population 600) has been home to the **Vermont Law School**. Widely known for environmental law, the school fills many of the nineteenth-century buildings around the outsized common and supports a range of places to eat. Along one side of the common, a block of Victorian brick shops and restaurants evokes the village's past status as a major rail stop; the depot is now a bank. Hidden away across the tracks—accessed through an underpass—a former railroad freight house is now **Worthy Burger** (802-763-2575; open Fri.–Sat. 11:30 AM–10 PM, Sun. 11:30 AM–9 PM, Mon., Wed., Thurs. 4–9 PM), a gathering place specializing in local beers on tap and pub food. **Five Olde Tavern & Grill** (802-763-8685; 192 Chelsea Street; open Sun. 11:30 AM–10 PM, Mon.–Thurs. 11 AM–10 PM, Fri. 11 AM–11 PM, Sat. 11:30 AM–11 PM), a sleek coffeehouse/pub, is another one.

We usually settle in for lunch on one of the six counter stools or slide into a deep booth at the **Chelsea Station Restaurant** (802-763-8685; 108 Chelsea Street; open Mon.–Sat. 6 AM–3 PM, Sun. 8 AM–12 PM). Sandwiches come on house-baked bread, soups are from scratch, and in-season veggies are local. Everyone knows each other but visitors feel welcome (no credit cards accepted).

ALONG THE FIRST BRANCH

Back over the bridge, we follow Chelsea Street (VT 110) north along the first branch of the White River. At a pullout a short way up, a historic marker tells of a 1720 "Indian raid" that all but wiped out Royalton's first settlers. It's clear why others soon replaced them, drawn by rich farmland along the river's curves, cradled between gentle hills.

THE MILL COVERED BRIDGE, TUNBRIDGE

North of South Tunbridge, the photogenic **Howe Covered Bridge** (1897) on the east side of VT 110 leads to a handsome farmstead; another 1.3 miles north, the **Cilley Covered Bridge** is off to the west of the road 0.2 miles up Ward Hill Road, just before the cemetery.

Tunbridge is known far and wide for its annual mid-September **World's Fair** (tunbridgefair.com), held every year since 1867, except in 1918 due to a flu epidemic and during World War II. The fairgrounds fill a grassy, natural riverside bowl in the center of Tunbridge Village. The fair was once known for its girly tent shows and dubbed the "Old Drunks Convention," but the four-day event now draws families from throughout New England. It features a children's barnyard and entertainment as well as a midway, livestock displays and oxen pulls, swine, sheep, goat and cattle contests, as well as plenty of live music. Otherwise, this tiny village is quiet. You might want to stop by the 1830 **Tunbridge General Store** (802-889-5525) and walk a few hundred feet north to take in the view of the picturesque **Mill Covered Bridge** (1883) set in the hollow below.

Back in Turnbridge, VT 110 continues to snake north along the river to Chelsea. These 7 miles cover farms and three more covered bridges walled by more lush, rounded hills. The **Larkin Bridge** (1902) is a mile north of the village of North Tunbridge, and then comes the **Flint Bridge** (1845) east of

DETOUR

This 12-mile detour begins at the concrete bridge beyond the general store. Turn off VT 110 onto Strafford Road and follow it uphill through woods and fields. It crests and then dips through farms tidy enough to suggest that their owners make a living elsewhere. Within an easy commute of Dartmouth College, **Strafford** has always been an upscale town, judging from its elegant, much-photographed Town House, built in 1799 on a rise above the sloping village green. The **Justin Smith Morrill Homestead** (802-828-3051; open Memorial Day to Columbus Day, Wed.–Sun. 11 AM–5 PM) is a short way down the road. Morrill, son of a Strafford blacksmith, became one of the country's most effective lawmakers. He built this fanciful, pink Gothic Revival mansion as his retirement home, but he never managed to spend much time here. He kept getting reelected, serving first as Vermont's congressman and then senator from 1855 until 1898. He is best remembered as the sponsor of the Land-Grant Colleges Acts, the first passed in 1862 and another in 1890, creating a total of 76 current state colleges and universities across the country. The 17-room mansion is fascinating in its own right and for the man and era it evokes. We suggest this side trip as a way to either shorten this route—it's 8 miles back to I-89, Exit 2 in Sharon via VT 132 in South Strafford—or, alternatively, continue the few miles east on VT 132 to Thetford Hill and link with our *The Upper Connecticut River Valley* route (page 65).

BETWEEN TUNBRIDGE AND CHELSEA, VT 110 SNAKES THROUGH LUSH HILLS AND FARMLAND, ALONG THE FIRST BRANCH OF THE WHITE RIVER

the road, and in another 0.7 miles, there's the **Moxley Bridge** (1883), also on the east side.

Chelsea Village, the county seat of Orange County, has not one but two handsome commons, both framed by mostly Federal-era buildings.

Across from North Common, check out **Will's Store** (802-685-33368), a genuine backcountry store with its own house-made ice cream (it's not the soft serve up front). A mile north of the village, Rhoda and Bill Ackerman, both rooted six generations deep in Chelsea, welcome guests to their rambling farmhouse is **Devil's Den Homestay Bed & Breakfast** (802-685-4582), named for a cave on their surrounding 65 acres. The couple have built themselves an annex, leaving the farmstead entirely to guests, but they still serve breakfast.

While Chelsea feels far off the beaten track, it loomed large in the past as a major rural crossroads. From the village, VT 113 runs east to the Connecticut River Valley, connecting in a scenic 15 miles through the hills to

Post Mills (see our *The Upper Connecticut River Valley* route on page 65). VT 110 runs north through farm country toward Barre and Montpelier.

Our route backtracks 2 miles to the **East Randolph Road** and 7 scenic and twisty miles up and over Chelsea Mountain, then down and down to another narrow valley, this one carved by the Second Branch of the White River. Beer lovers might want to turn onto Dickerman Hill Road and **Brocklebank Craft Brewing** (802-685-4838) about halfway down. Brewer Ben Linehan specializes in American pale ales and German and Czech styles; four beers are generally on draft in the taproom (open Fri. 3–7 PM, Sat. noon–6 PM) at this former dairy farm.

Down in **East Randolph**, turn north (right) into the village center and immediately west on VT 66 for another scenic 3 miles up to a top-of-the-world view, then another 3 miles on into **Randolph Center**. This village—composed mainly of brick and clapboard Federal-era homes—lines a Main Street that was cut unusually wide with the idea that it might be the state capital. Instead it is now a quiet village, home to the Vermont Technical College. According to a historical marker, musician and schoolmaster Justin Morgan brought a young stallion from Massachusetts to his home here in 1789; Morgan the man lies buried in the nearby cemetery.

Randolph remains a horsey community, but with the arrival of the railroad in the mid-nineteenth century, population shifted from the center down

IN CHELSEA TWIN BRICK STORES SURVIVE FROM THE FEDERAL ERA

THE BARN AT DEVIL'S DEN HOMESTAY, CHELSEA

to the valley, 3 miles west (now the other side of I-89). Our route heads north instead, up aptly named 7-mile **Ridge Road** with views across a wide valley to the Braintree Range. At VT 65, beyond Brookfield Center, turn west (left) to **Pond Village**, about as picturesque as a four corners can be, clustered beside **Sunset Lake** and its **Floating Bridge**.

Too deep to support the usual pillars, the 330-foot Floating Bridge on Sunset Lake was initially floated on logs in 1820s; then barrels, first wooden and eventually oil drums; then plastic barrels, always with limited success. The current bridge—the eighth, completed in 2015—rests on 10 pontoons and remains the only floating bridge east of the Mississippi. There's almost always someone fishing here, and the phone wires above it are festooned with fishing lines and sinkers from too-high castings. Kids jump off the bridge rails, but you can swim from the small grassy park by the bridge entrance, a tempting place to linger. Spread a blanket and picnic under the willow, beside the sinuous statue of a hippo with its chin resting on a smaller hippo, worn shiny by the stroking of many hands. Sunset Lake has long been known for its crystal-clear water, and in the late nineteenth century its ice was highly valued; harvesting ice was big business, and ice

THE FLOATING BRIDGE ON SUNSET LAKE, POND VILLAGE, BROOKFIELD

blocks were stored in sawdust in the big (long-gone) icehouse by the bridge, kept through summer. The **Brookfield Ice Harvest Festival** (802-276-3959), staged here the last Saturday in January, demonstrates the process with antique ice-harvesting tools and snow sculptures.

At **Green Trails Inn** (802-276-3412) across the road from the lake, Jane Doerfer offers a genuine welcome. Check the website for **Floating Bridge Food and Farms** (floatingbridgefoodandfarms.com) for descriptions of local farms welcoming visitors, an excuse to follow backroads through high pastures to places like **Brookfield Bees** (802-276-3808), selling raw honey from their apiary and turning it into candles and soap; **Fat Toad Farm** (802-279-0098), crafting caramel sauces from their goat's milk; **Green Mountain Girls Farm** (802-505-1767), offering lodging as well as organic meat from the animals they raise; **Plant Spirit Farm & Fibers** (802-276-3839), growing a wide selection of medicinal and culinary herbs, dye plants, flowers, and vegetables; and **Pagoda Pond Gardens** (802-728-6652), with display gardens showcasing hundreds of varieties of daylilies. Off Ridge Road, **Neighborly Farms of Vermont** (802-728-4700; open Mon.–Thurs. 8 AM–2 PM), a family-owned dairy farm, features varieties of their own cheese and also sells products from other local farms. Needless to say, everything around here is organic.

From Pond Village this route turns back down Ridge Road, but after about a mile, we like to veer off onto parallel Hebard Hill Road, commanding awesome vistas as the valley view and mountains end at VT 66 on its downward slope to **Randolph.**

At the confluence of two branches of the White River, two old highways, and I-91 (Exit 4), Randolph's ornate Victorian railroad station is an Amtrak stop and its downtown is the commercial hub of the region. Still, with a population of fewer than 4,800, the feel is small town. The junction of VT 66 and VT 12 is a stop sign, no longer a traffic light, and parking is usually not a problem.

Turn left over the bridge on VT 12 for downtown. Shops along North Main Street are anchored by **Belmains** (802-728-3781), a cross between a five-and-ten and an old-style, small-town department store—worth a stop even if you don't need anything. Its stock of 38,000 items ranges from cards to home furnishings and soft-serve ice cream. A few doors up, **One Main Tap & Grill** (802-431-3772; open for lunch and dinner in summer, otherwise varying hours) is an appealing, casual space specializing in local brews.

Chandler Center for the Arts (802-728-6464; chandler-arts.org) marks the center of town, with a **music hall** (1907) with a 575-seat theater known for its acoustics and frequent live performances, and a **gallery** (802-431-0204) with changing exhibits, open Fri.–Sat. 12–6 PM and during performances. Down the street, the **Playhouse Theater** (802-728-4012), showing current films, is one of Vermont's oldest movie houses (1919).

Worth finding on Pleasant Street (left off North Main Street), **Three Bean Café** (802-728-3533; open Mon.–Fri. 6:30 AM–5 PM, Sat. until 2 PM) is a welcoming space with from-scratch croissants, house-made veggie and meat soups, pizzas and quiche, as well as wraps, coffees, and teas. The next left, Randolph Street, leads to hilltop Kimball House, home to **Saap** (802-565-8292; open Mon.–Sat. 12–9 PM; $), not your ordinary Thai restaurant.

OVER ROCHESTER GAP AND DOWN THE WHITE RIVER

Follow VT 12 and the river south from Randolph, and in about 6 miles turn west (right) onto Camp Brook Road. On a beautiful day, this is a glorious 10-mile drive up, up, and over the Braintree Range and Rochester Gap, then down with views of the Green Mountains ahead. It ends in the middle of Rochester Village at a large, classic green bordering VT 100. Turn right for the lineup of mismatched nineteenth-century clapboard buildings that form the center of Rochester Village, which is full of surprises.

Sandy's Bakery & Bookery (802-767-4258; open 7:30 AM–6 PM) is just north of the gas pumps. Good in the morning for espresso, fresh-made whole-grain breads, and muffins, and at lunch for soups, salads, sandwiches, and vegetarian choices. Cookies all day, beer and wine. The neighboring Bookery is a serious, full-service book store.

The Rochester Café & Country Store (802-767-4302; open 7 AM–5 PM) is across the road. Featuring the 1940s soda fountain, installed when this was a pharmacy, the space has housed various enterprises, from a pool hall to a funeral parlor. This is a popular VT 100 stop for breakfast and lunch with espresso, freshly made soups and juice, and daily specials among its varied menu. Try the maple cream pie. Stroll down to the **BigTown Gallery** (802-767-9670; open Wed.–Sat. 10 AM–5 PM, Sun. 11 AM–4 PM). Anni Mackay designs and makes wearable art, but her studio showcases an eclectic mix of paintings and sculpture, many by local artists. It's also a setting for piano rehearsals and plays performed in the backyard amphitheater. Neighboring **Green Mountain Bikes** (802-767-4464) is a destination for serious bicyclists. Aside from selling, renting, and repairing mountain bikes and bicycles of all kinds, owner Doon Hinderyckx is a font of information about local trails in and beyond the national forest. For detailed information about camping, hiking, and swimming as well as biking in the Green Mountain National Forest, drive several miles north of Rochester Village to the **Green Mountain National Forest Ranger District Office and Visitor Center** (802-767-4261; open 8 AM–4:30 PM daily except Sun. Memorial Day–Columbus Day, weekdays only off-season).

BACK DOWN THE WHITE RIVER

South of the village, note the turnoff for VT 73, a high, 14-mile drive over the Brandon Gap and down into the Champlain Valley. A little way south on VT 100, keep an eye out for **Liberty Hill Farm** (802-767-3926; see *Best Places to Sleep*), with its iconic red barn set off by meadowland. We follow the main stem of the White River on VT 100 for another half-dozen miles to Stockbridge and then turn east with the river on VT 107. In summer the 20-mile stretch of the river from Rochester to Stockbridge and on to Bethel is particularly popular with tubers. Just south of the VT 100/107 junction, **Vermont River Tubing** (802-746-8106) offers rentals and shuttle service upriver to a Rochester put-in (call for river conditions). In 2011 this area was hit hard by Tropical Storm Irene; much of the road along here has been substantially rebuilt since and now offers pullouts and river access.

A bit over the Bethel town line, riverside **Tozier's Restaurant** (802-234-9400; open May–Oct.; $–$$) seems little changed since the 1930s. Seafood is the specialty—lobster or fried clams and sweet potato fries seem to taste

BARNS AT LIBERTY HILL FARM IN ROCHESTER, WHICH IS AN OUTSTANDING, FAMILY-GEARED FARMSTAY
LIBERTY HILL FARMS

best outside (there's a take-out window), but there's also a pine-paneled inside dining room. In Bethel Village, both **Cockadoodle Pizza Café** (802-234-9666) and the **Bethel Village Sandwich Shop** (802-234-9910) come as a pleasant surprise. This drive ends at the I-89 access (Exit 3). Before you hit the interstate, however, you might want to check out **Eaton's Sugarhouse Restaurant and Country Store** (802-763-8809; open daily 7 AM–3 PM) at the junction of VT 107 and 14. The exterior is undeniably funky, but the restaurant is about as good as it gets for puffy pancakes with the house maple syrup, or fresh-carved turkey sandwiches with house-made bread. This is also a good place to pick up maple syrup.

Best Places to Sleep

GREEN TRAILS INN AND FORK SHOP (802-276-3412), 24 Stone Road, Brookfield. Open May–Jan. Sited across from Sunset Lake at the heart of Pond Village, this genuinely hospitable country inn offers eight attractive rooms, including three that work as a family suite with its own entrance. Beds have quality mattresses and linens, and rooms all have well-chosen antiques and books. Innkeeper Jane Doerfer is an accomplished cook and cookbook author; her buffet-style breakfast might include smoked salmon, local cheeses, fresh fruit, and a hot dish such as sausage apple cobbler. By the Floating Bridge on the lake itself, her three-story Fork Shop, built in the eighteenth century as a pitchfork factory, has been nicely renovated as a fully equipped rental (two-night minimum), sleeping 18. Inn rooms $.

HUNTINGTON HOUSE INN (802-767-9140), 19 Huntington Place, Rochester. Sited on Rochester's large, leafy park and dating from 1806, this is an inviting inn. There are six comfortable guest rooms (private baths) in the inn itself, and a former general store next door houses three luxurious two-bedroom condo-style units, each with a full kitchen, dining area, and living room. Doc's Tavern in the renovated barn (open from 4 PM, except Tues.) is an informal sports bar with a pub menu and a dozen local beers on tap, while the 1806 Cocoa Pub (open for dinner Fri.–Sun.) has a more formal feel and a seriously sweet menu, from cocoa-rubbed tenderloin to chocolate fondue. $–$$ for inn rooms, $$ for condos.

GREEN TRAILS INN OFFERS BEDS AND BREAKFAST IN POND VILLAGE, BROOKFIELD

LIBERTY HILL FARM (802-767-3926), 511 Liberty Hill, Rochester. This is the real thing: a working dairy farm with more than 100 Holsteins, set in a broad meadow, backed by mountains. Its much-photographed 1890s red barn, one of the most photographed in Vermont, was built by Dr. Charles Wesley Emerson, founder of Boston's Emerson College. There's a capacious white-clapboard 1825 farmhouse and, best of all, there is hostess par excellence Beth Kennett. Since 1984 Beth and her husband Bob have been welcoming guests of all ages. Kids quickly get to know the cows, each with a name tag in her ear. They can help milk, bottle-feed the calves, and collect eggs. Meals are served family-style, and dinner is as delicious as it is prodigious, much of it sourced from the garden and/or baked from scratch; ice cream is homemade. There are seven guest rooms (five with queen beds, one with two single beds, and a room with four single beds) and four shared baths; families can spread into two rooms, sharing a sitting room and bath. In summer you can hear the gurgle of the White River, good for trout fishing as well as swimming and tubing. Added to these options is Harvest House, a walk across the meadow. Built in 1782, it retains its eighteenth-century feel and four hearths but offers three comfortable bedrooms, a new kitchen, and gracious common space. It accommodates overflow from the farm and can be rented as a whole. $$.

Best Places to Eat

SAAP (802-565-8292), 50 Randolph Avenue, Randolph. Open Mon.–Sat., 12–9 PM. Vermont chef Steve Morgan has a long-standing interest in wild, fresh, and fiery flavors of northeastern Thailand, and his wife Rung, also an experienced chef, is a native of this Issan region. Both are sticklers for using local as well as authentic Thai ingredients, and the results are exceptional. Try an Issan salad of fire-charred pork with toasted rice powder, fish sauce, lime juice, and shallot finished with mint and cilantro, served on sticky rice. $–$$.

SCHOOL STREET BISTRO (802-767-3126), 13 School Street, corner of Main Street (VT 100), Rochester. Open Tues.–Sat. 5–9 PM. This small bistro is a winner with a constantly changing, imaginative, and reasonably priced menu. It includes burgers served with root veggies and a variety of vegetarian and meat dishes. $–$$.

WILD ROOTS RESTAURANT (802-763-0440), 5615 VT 14, South Royalton. Reservations suggested. The dining room in this 1818 brick tavern seats just 20 for farm-to-table dining that includes starters "to share," tantalizing fish, meat, and vegetarian entrée choices, and sides, local beers and spirits. $$–$$$.

CALVIN COOLIDGE
1872-1933

Born July 4, 1872 in a house ba[ck]
of store, Calvin Coolidge from [?]
years of age lived in the Homest[ead]
across the road, now owned by [the]
State of Vermont. Here on Aug. [?]
1923 he was inaugurated Preside[nt]
and here he spent many vacatio[ns]
In the Notch Cemetery he res[ts]
beside his wife & son and 4
generations of forebears.

VERMONT HISTORIC SITES COMMISSION

6

WOODSTOCK/QUECHEE LOOP

ESTIMATED LENGTH: 80 miles

ESTIMATED TIME: 1 to 2 days

HIGHLIGHTS: This drive follows US 4 and the Ottauquechee River over splendid **Quechee Gorge** to the village of **Woodstock**, a famous melding of manufactured and natural beauty, home to the **Billings Farm & Museum** and the **Marsh-Billings-Rockefeller National Historic Park**. Our route winds around Woodstock's exquisite green and continues along the river to Bridgewater Corners, then loops south to the **Calvin Coolidge National Historic Site in Plymouth Notch**, a peaceful village that looks much the way it did when President Coolidge took the oath of office here in 1924. We return north up VT 100 past **Woodward Reservoir** and back along US 4 to Woodstock, veering onto Old River Road to **Quechee Village** and back to I-89. US 4 is a busy, winding east/west highway, but there are hidden gems—places to swim and farms to visit—just off the tourist trail, and we find them following backroads.

GETTING THERE: Exit 1 on I-89 in White River Junction is accessible from Burlington and Montreal on I-89, from urban areas to the south via I-91, and from the Boston area and points southeast via I-93 to I-89. Turn west on US 4 off the exit ramps toward Woodstock.

ON THE ROAD

US 4 is now officially "The Crossroad of Vermont Byway," and while it is unquestionably scenic in places, this is one of the most heavily trafficked roads in the state, the shortest way across "Vermont's waist." We veer off the main drag less than a mile west of the I-89 exit, bearing right onto **Quechee Main Street**. It's just after the **Fat Hat Clothing Company** (802-296-6646)

LEFT: THE CALVIN COOLIDGE NATIONAL HISTORIC SITE

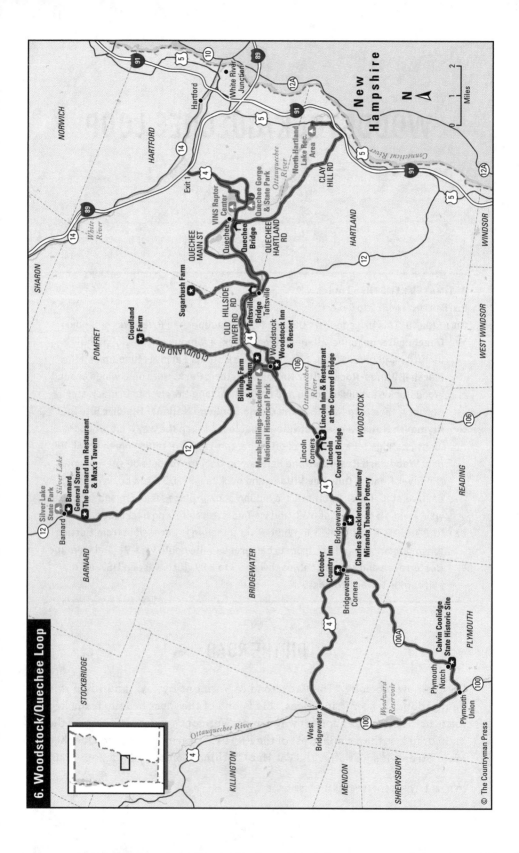

6. Woodstock/Quechee Loop

on the corner, known locally for the floppy hats and clothing made here. Follow this pleasant, wooded road another 0.7 mile and turn left onto **Dewey's Mills Road** (the Strong House Spa is on this corner) and continue around **Dewey's Mill Pond**, a great local fishing spot. Look for picnic tables under the pines, a boat launch, and the trailhead at **Dewey's Landing**. A hiking trail leads from the parking lot and runs along a berm that separates the pond from the river, continuing past the bridge and on down to the bottom of the **Quechee Gorge**, about a mile and a half walk.

By the mid-nineteenth century, water from the millpond and the nearby falls powered the Dewey Company woolen mill, which, at its height, employed some 500 people. In the 1930s its fabric went into Boston Red Sox and New York Yankee baseball uniforms as well as blankets for the U.S. Army and Navy. In 1952 the mills closed and the entire mill village disappeared beneath a U.S. Army Corps of Engineers flood-control project. Dewey's Mill Pond is all that is left of that era. The property surrounding the gorge is now **Quechee State Park** (888-409-7579 for information and camping reservations). Dewey's Mills Road rejoins US 4, Woodstock Road, just east of the gorge.

Across US 4, there is ample parking at the **Quechee Gorge Visitor Center** (802-295-6852) and access to an easy family hike through deep green forest glades to the edge of the gorge, then down to the river. The rugged streambed offers rocky purchase to sit and dip your feet in the water. Members of a party who don't want to hike can find a cup of coffee and comfortable place to relax in the well-stocked visitor center. Even if you have already explored the floor of the gorge, be sure to take in the view from the bridge, 165 feet down.

MINNESOTA, A RESCUE OWL THAT LIVED OUT HER LIFE AT VINS, NOW PRESERVED IN THE VISITOR CENTER

Heading west of the gorge on US 4, the **Vermont Institute of Natural Science/Raptor Center** (802-359-5000; open daily, $) is on the left. At **VINS**, you can view the resident hawks, snowy owls, peregrine falcons, eagles, and other birds of prey who have been rehabilitated here and are living on view in large outdoor flight enclosures. There are hands-on activities for kids and trails to explore on 47 acres of rolling forestland; the hard-packed McNight Trail is wheelchair accessible.

US 4 continues to wind between hills and the river and through the village of Taftsville, marked by a cov-

DETOUR

North Hartland Lake, Dam, and Reservoir

Just west of VINS on US 4, take **Quechee Hartland Road** and follow it for 1.5 miles. Continue on to **Quechee Road/State Aid 4 Road** for 0.3 mile and bear left onto **Clay Hill Road**. Follow 4 miles and turn left onto US 5 N to the flood control dam and **North Hartland Lake Recreation Area** (802-295-2855). There are restrooms, a boat launch, picnic facilities, swimming areas, hiking trails, and fishing holes (the lake is stocked). Inquire about ranger-conducted programs. $.

ered bridge and the tumbling falls beneath it (where it's still generating electricity) and, across the way, the 1840s brick **Taftsville Country Store** (802-457-1135), which includes a village post office and specializes in Vermont food products.

WOODSTOCK

Rounding a few last corners into Woodstock, it's wise to slow; a police car is frequently lurking. Gracious old homes, many now inns or bed & breakfasts, line Pleasant Street, and following US 4 onto Central Street will bring you into the middle of downtown Woodstock. This is a walk-around town, and the first thing you want to do is park, which isn't always that easy. Note the sign for parking off Central Street at the **Woodstock Area Chamber of Commerce Welcome Center** (802-457-3555; with restrooms). Stroll by shops to the legendary green bordered by well-preserved late eighteenth- and early nineteenth-century mansions and the imposing, tower-topped Windsor County Courthouse. Note the covered bridge across the green that leads to River Street, then head on to Mountain Avenue and Faulkner Park. There is parking at the base, and a 1.6-mile path zigzags up to benches high on Mount Tom overlooking the village, valley, and surrounding hills.

Set back away from the green, the **Woodstock Inn and Resort** (802-332-6853) is the lineal descendant of the eighteenth-century Eagle Tavern and a subsequent Victorian clapboard inn that flourished between the 1890s and 1960s, putting Woodstock on the resort map. Today's 142-room resort, created by Laurance and Mary Rockefeller in 1969, makes up in creature comforts what it lacks in patina. Its massive stone hearth in the lobby remains a popular village rendezvous spot.

West of Woodstock Green, US 4 continues to follow the Ottauquechee River as it winds through a narrow valley. Hills slope down to meet the river, but they don't crowd the road. Tropical Storm Irene was rough on two local landmarks west of town, but both bounced back better than ever. **White Cottage Snack Bar** (802-457-3455; open May–Oct., daily 11 AM–10 PM) is a classic 1950s riverside take-out, and **Woodstock Farmers' Market** (802-457-3658; open Tues.–Sun. 7:30 AM–7 PM) remains the area's standout place for locally sourced organic produce as well as soups, sandwiches, and veggie options to go.

Billings Farm & Museum and the Marsh-Billings-Rockefeller National Historic Park

Three residents in particular have affected Woodstock's current look. The first was George Perkins Marsh, a pioneering ecologist who wrote *Man and Nature*, published in 1864, acknowledging man's effect on the environment and suggesting solutions. The work influenced many of the country's movers and shakers, including Woodstock native Frederick Billings, who returned home from the California gold rush to notice how logging and grazing had denuded the local hills. Billings bought the old Marsh farm, transforming the house into a mansion, creating a model dairy farm, and planting more than 100,000 trees on Mount Tom. In 1934, Billings's granddaughter, Mary French, married Laurance Rockefeller, whose father, John D. Rockefeller Jr., had been largely responsible for creating more than 20 state and national parks and historic sites. Laurance had inherited his father's commitment to conservation, creating environmentally sensitive resorts. He replaced the Woodstock Inn, upgraded its golf course and ski trails, and created an umbrella nonprofit, The Woodstock Foundation, for such projects as acquiring and restoring historic homes, burying power lines, building a new covered bridge near the green, and opening and maintaining the **Billings Farm & Museum** in 1983 and the **Marsh-Billings-Rockefeller National Historic Park** in 1998. The visitor center at Billings Farm, which offers parking areas for both sites, features "A Place in the Land," Charles Guggenheim's award-winning film that dramatizes the story of all three men.

Billings Farm & Museum (802-457-2355; $) is open Apr.–Oct., daily 10 AM–5 PM. Visitors can visit barns that house a dairy herd, draft horses, and other livestock. The museum includes exhibits on traditional farm lore and rural living, housed in four barns on the property. Families can observe dairy operations, visit cows and horses, and learn about farming at the turn of the nineteenth and twentieth centuries. Marsh-Billings-Rockefeller National Historic Park (802-457-3368; $) includes the neighboring **Rockefeller Mansion** and the 550 surrounding forested acres on Mount Tom, which is webbed with walking trails. Its **Carriage Barn** (open Apr.–Oct., daily 10 AM–5 PM; free), an inviting space with dark beadboard walls and the feel of a library, features exhibits placing Marsh, Billings, and Rockefeller in the timeline of American conservation history.

US 4 continues through **Lincoln Corners**, with its **covered bridge** built in 1865, and on through the mill village of **Bridgewater**, with a three-story wooden mill building still standing at its center. Tenants change here, but the former woolen mill has been preserved as a low-key shopping center, anchored by **Charles Shackleton Furniture** and **Miranda Thomas Pottery** (802-672-5175; open daily 10 AM–5 PM). Charles works here with fellow crafters to produce exquisite furniture. It's made to order, but models are displayed (along with seconds at the mill), complemented by Miranda's distinctive pottery, hand thrown and carved with traditional designs. A little farther along, the **Bridgewater Corners Store** (802-672-6241) at the junction of US 4 and VT 100A, is a source of local brews, deli sandwiches, and fishing licenses.

PLYMOUTH NOTCH

Turn off onto quieter VT 100A south and follow it about 6 miles to the **Calvin Coolidge State Historic Site** (802-672-3773; open Memorial Day weekend–mid-October, 9:30 AM–5 PM; $). Calvin Coolidge (1872–1933) is best remembered for the famously Vermont virtues of dry wit, thrift, and common sense. The village of Plymouth Notch, in which Coolidge was born, assumed the presidency, and from which he briefly governed the country in the summer of 1924, remains low key. The former president is also buried here. The museum and education center offer a sense of the president, using his own (famously few) words. The **Plymouth Artisan Cheese Factory**, built by the president's father in 1890 and still in business, uses traditional methods to produce its exceptional granular cheddar and a variety of other flavors (plymouthartisancheese.com).

The general store sells, among other things, cold cans of Moxie, the president's favorite soft drink. Its upstairs hall is restored to look just as it did when it served as the office of the Summer White House. The square-steepled Union Christian Church, with its acoustically superb interior, is the setting for frequent concerts and lectures. The general store also sells maple syrup, penny candy, and Coolidge memorabilia. "Colonel" John Coolidge became storekeeper here in 1868, and his son Calvin was born on the Fourth of July, 1872, in the modest attached house. The family moved across the street to the larger Coolidge Homestead when Calvin was 4 years old, and it was there, because he happened to be home helping with the haying, that Vice President Calvin Coolidge learned of President Warren Harding's unexpected death. At 2:47 AM on August 3, 1923, he was sworn in by his father as 30th president of the United States. The historic site currently encompasses 25 buildings, including the 1870s **Wilder Barn**, housing farm implements, horse-drawn vehicles, and the **Wilder House Restaurant** (802-672-4313; open daily 9 AM–4:30 PM for breakfast and lunch), a pine-walled café with

THE CALVIN COOLIDGE STATE HISTORIC SITE VISITOR CENTER

exposed beams in what was once the home of Calvin Coolidge's mother. Power lines have been buried and roads have been paved, but the village looks about as it did in the 1920s, sitting quietly at the foot of East Mountain.

From the Coolidge site, continue on VT 100A for a mile to connect with VT 100. Turn right and travel north about 7 miles through forests and past fields along Woodward Reservoir, reconnecting with US 4 in West Bridgewater. The return trip to Woodstock is a 14-mile stretch back along the Ottauquechee.

ON AND OFF OLD RIVER ROAD

Just after crossing the river on the western edge of Woodstock Village, turn left off US 4 onto **River Street**, following it to VT 12. Stay left on VT 12 past the Billings Farm, then bear right onto **Old River Road**. This will take you east right along the Ottauquechee.

Whether or not you detour off Old River Road into the hills, follow it east along the river, past the vintage 1836 **Taftsville Covered Bridge**, and through the Quechee Country Club golf course and grounds back to Quechee Village. In the mid- and late-nineteenth century, life revolved here around the **J. C. Parker and Co. mill**, which produced a soft baby flannel made from "shoddy" (reworked rags). The mill produced fabrics until its closure in the 1950s. Some 6,000 surrounding acres were subsequently acquired by the **Quechee Lakes Corporation**, the largest second-home and condominium development in the state. Thanks in good part to Act 250, Vermont's land-use statute, the end result is unobtrusive. Most homes are sequestered in woods; open space includes two private 18-hole golf courses. The brick mill building remains the center of Quechee Village, now the original factory and restaurant for **Simon Pearce Glass** (802-295-2711; open daily 10 AM–9 PM). The former mill owner's mansion is now the **Parker House Inn** (802-295-6077).

Irish-born glassblower Simon Pearce converted the old woolen mill to a glass factory in 1981, harnessing the milldam's hydropower for his furnaces. He soon established a national reputation for his distinctive production pieces: tableware, vases, lamps, candlesticks, and more. The factory has since moved to far larger, visitor-friendly quarters in Artisans Park, Windsor (see Drive 3), but a glass-blowing viewing area remains here along

DETOUR

Detour to Cloudland Farm and Sugarbush Farm

There are two interesting side trips here. First up, from Billings Farm, head north on Old River road about 0.75 mile. Follow to Cloudland Road and continue about 4 miles up a steep, twisty dirt road to **Cloudland Farm** (802-457-2599; Thurs.–Sat. by reservation). Many restaurants bill their fare as "farm-to-table," but this isn't exactly a restaurant; instead the tables are at the farm. Guests are seated together at long, common tables in a many-windowed post-and-beam building constructed from white pine harvested on the farm. The set menu features the farm's meat and produce. $$$ but includes multiple courses, $$ on BBQ nights (BYOB). In busy seasons, reservations are advised a week or so ahead. The farm store is open Wed. 10 AM–3 PM, Thurs.–Sat. 10 AM–5 PM. Both the farm and road down afford fabulous views.

If you are up for a short but steep and rewarding detour, take US 4 to Taftsville and go over the covered bridge, up the hill, and turn left onto Hillside Road. It's a dirt road and a steep climb, but it's worth it. Beware in mud season, though. At the top, follow signs to **Sugarbush Farm** (802-457-1757; open daily 9 AM–5 PM). This hilltop farm is widely known for its waxed artisan cheeses and maple syrup, which it ships nationally. But even if you don't buy anything, there's a nature trail to walk and animals to see. This is a beautiful spot with great views of the surrounding hills and valley. It changes moment to moment in front of you as you drive back down.

DETOUR

Detour to Barnard

From the heart of Woodstock, take Elm Street north out of town as it becomes VT 12, passing Billings Farm. Follow for more than a dozen miles through lush green hills to the village of **Barnard** at the tip of **Silver Lake**. This is an aristocratic little village with its share of bed & breakfasts; a vintage 1796 brick inn, now the **Barnard Inn Restaurant & Max's Tavern** (802-234-9961); and the **Barnard General Store** (802-234-9688; open 7 AM–7 PM). The store closed during a down time in the economy, but was rescued by a cooperative of involved residents and is again a thriving hub of local life. It boasts a café area good for breakfast and lunch, as well as milkshakes and sandwiches to take across the street to the lake. It's also a source of groceries and ethanol-free gas. From here, continue straight on North Road to the entrance to **Silver Lake State Park** (802-234-9451), which offers camping (tent and RV sites and lean-tos), boating, swimming, picnics, fishing, and hiking. Note that, from here, North Road continues along a ridge, a beautiful drive ending at VT 107 in Bethel, a few miles west of I-89 Exit 3 (see Drive #6).

To return to US 4, turn south on North Road to VT 12 and follow it back to Woodstock; you do not want to follow Old River Road to Quechee. Or keep right along US 4 through the village and continue 7 miles east, turning through the **Quechee Covered Bridge** to the **Simon Pearce Factory**.

with an expansive store that includes seconds. **Simon Pearce Restaurant** (802-295-1470), overlooking the covered bridge and waterfall, is open for lunch, dinner (reservations suggested), and Sunday brunch. It's one of the best places to eat in the area.

Cross over the covered bridge to return to I-89 along US 4.

Best Places to Sleep

THE QUECHEE INN AT MARSHLAND FARM (802-295-3133), 1119 Quechee Main Street, Quechee. Comfortable, well-appointed rooms at reasonable rates. It's off the beaten path but close to attractions in the Quechee area. $$.

WOODSTOCK INN & RESORT (802-332-6853), 14 The Green, Woodstock. This luxurious inn offers 142 rooms that vary substantially in look and feel but are all fitted with marble baths and furnished tastefully by some of Vermont's craftspeople. Some rooms have fireplaces. Amenities include a landscaped swimming pool; a full-service, LEED-certified spa; a fitness center with indoor pool; and an 18-hole golf course. $$$–$$$$.

THE VILLAGE INN OF WOODSTOCK (802-457-1255), 41 Pleasant Street, Woodstock. This stately B&B includes rooms furnished with antiques, some with their own fireplaces. A full breakfast and an afternoon glass of wine are included in the price of the room. It's within walking distance of Woodstock shops and restaurants. $$.

THE SHIRE RIVERVIEW MOTEL (802-457-2211), 46 Pleasant Street, Woodstock. This independently owned 42-unit motel is on the edge of Woodstock Village. The building spreads out along the banks of the Ottauquechee. Most rooms have river views, and many have porches or deck access; they vary from comfortably furnished, reasonably priced standard units to upscale suites. $–$$$.

THE ARDMORE B&B (802-457-3887), 23 Pleasant Street, Woodstock. Within easy walking distance of shops and the green, this grand clapboard 1867 Greek Revival building has five spacious guest rooms, each with private marble bath. The rooms are named for Vermont authors and illustrators and are stocked with appropriate volumes. A multicourse breakfast is served at the dining room table, and afternoon refreshments are offered. $$–$$$.

OCTOBER COUNTRY INN (802-672-3412; octobercountryinn.com), a short drive off the main road at the junction of US 4 and VT 100A, Bridgewater Corners. This old farmhouse has a large, comfortable living room with inviting places to sit around the hearth and at the big round table in the dining room. A path leads to a hilltop swimming pool. Seasoned innkeepers Edie and Chuck Janisse cater to bicyclists and maintain the website for more than a dozen well-researched bike tours from the inn (bring a bike or rent up the road). The 10 guest rooms, each with private bath, vary in size; most have queen-sized bed, many with Edie's handmade quilts. Rates include a full breakfast; dinner can be arranged. $$.

Best Places to Eat

THE MILL AT SIMON PEARCE RESTAURANT (802-295-1470), 1760 Quechee Main Street, Quechee. Open for lunch (11:30 AM–2:45 PM), dinner (5:30–9 PM; reservations advised), and Sunday brunch (10:30 AM–2:45 PM). This is a cheerful, contemporary place for consistently superior food, served on Simon Pearce's own pottery and glass and with a view of the waterfall and covered bridge. Ballymaloe brown bread alone is worth a lunch visit, especially savored with Vermont cheddar soup or Guinness stew on a fall day. Dinner $$–$$$; lunch: $–$$.

DANA'S BY THE GORGE (802-295-6066), 5945 Woodstock Road, Quechee. Open spring to fall, the restaurant serves breakfast and lunch to travelers along US 4 in a pleasant, bright café atmosphere. $–$$.

THE WOODSTOCK INN (802-332-6853), 14 The Green, Woodstock. Open daily noon–10 PM. The brightly decorated, casually elegant **Red Rooster** is divided nicely into sections around a central fountain, from its sleek bar area to tables by a wall of windows overlooking the inner garden. The menu stresses locally sourced products and produce, from specialty salads and sandwiches at lunch to dinner menus that range from pastas to filet mignon. There's a reasonably priced children's menu too. (Dinner $$$.) The inn's book-lined **Richardson's Tavern**, open evenings, offers moderately priced pub food options. ($$.) Its **Fairways Grille** (802-457-6672) on the adjoining golf course (VT 106 South), open seasonally noon–dusk, is a hidden gem, with salads, sandwiches, and the like served on a spacious terrace, weather permitting. (Lunch $.)

LINCOLN INN AND RESTAURANT AT THE COVERED BRIDGE (802-457-7052), 2709 West Woodstock Road, Woodstock. A fine-dining experience with European touches. Meals are served by reservation only, with one seating per evening, the time depending on the season. Menus are four-course, fixed-priced gourmet events. $$$$.

BENTLEY'S RESTAURANT (802-457-3232), 3 Elm Street, Woodstock. The bar and grill, located at Central and Elm Streets, serves traditional pub fare in a family-friendly atmosphere. The restaurant is open for lunch and dinner with a cozy, relaxing ambience. The walls display local art and memorabilia, and live music and dancing are a staple of the establishment. $$.

VISTA LOOKING SOUTH PAST THE MONUMENT AT THE HUBBARDTON BATTLEFIELD STATE HISTORIC SITE

KILLINGTON/RUTLAND

ESTIMATED LENGTH: 120 miles

ESTIMATED TIME: 2 days

HIGHLIGHTS: Killington is Vermont's second-highest peak, and it's shouldered by a half-dozen more of the highest Green Mountains, forming a destination for hikers and mountain bikers as well as skiers. Lucky for the rest of us, the spectacular view from glass-walled **Peak Lodge**, at more than 4,200 feet in elevation, is part of **Killington Resort** and accessible by gondola. This is said to be the 1763 spot on which the Reverend Samuel Peters described all that he could see as "Verd Monts," thus christening the future Green Mountain state. The 2,170-mile-long **Appalachian Trail** from Georgia to Maine and Vermont's 272-mile **Long Trail** keep company from the Massachusetts border to a point just north of US 4, the old east-west highway that crests here in **Sherburne Pass**. There's also access to many local trails here, including the totally handicapped-accessible trail to **Thundering Brook Falls**.

Continuing west, US 4 drops in less than a dozen miles from this high country to bustling Rutland, Vermont's second-largest city and the gateway to the gentle, open landscape that rolls to the majestic **Taconic Mountains** toward the New York State line. At the gracious old village of **Castleton**, this drive heads north with VT 30 along **Lake Bomoseen**, the largest lake completely within Vermont's borders, offering ample access to swimming, boating, and fishing. At Hubbardton we veer off into rolling, wooded hills to the **Hubbardton Battlefield**, site of a 1777 Revolutionary War battle in which the Green Mountain Boys held off an invasion from Canada. It's an unusually peaceful as well as beautiful spot. Our route winds back to Rutland, from which we also visit the **Vermont Marble Museum** in Proctor.

GETTING THERE: Killington and Rutland are accessible along the US 7 corridor from Burlington and Middlebury to the north and from Bennington and the Massachusetts Berkshires to the south. From the west US 4 is a divided,

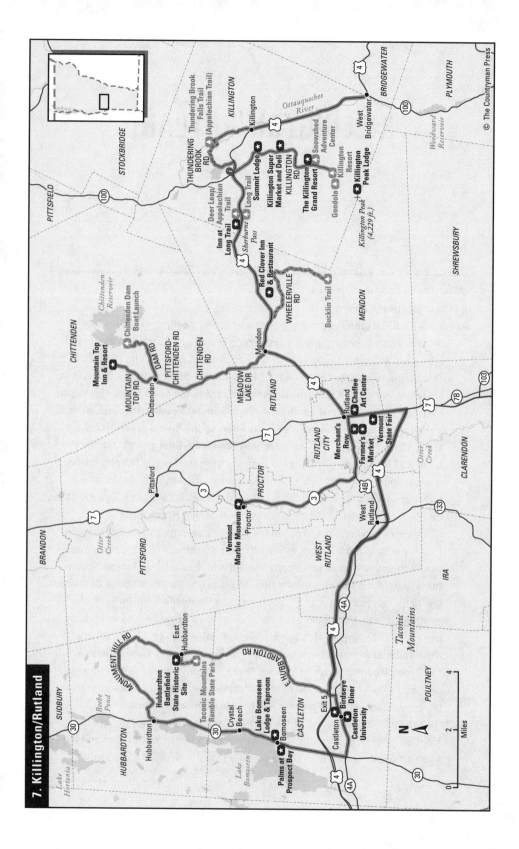

7. Killington/Rutland

© The Countryman Press

limited-access highway for 16 miles from the New York State border at Fair Haven to Rutland. This drive begins at the junction of US 4 and VT 100 in West Bridgewater 14 miles west of Woodstock.

ON THE ROAD

US 4 and VT 100 wind west together from West Bridgewater, leaving the Ottauquechee River valley behind and climbing steadily up into the heavily forested Green Mountains. In about 4.5 miles, River Road comes up on the right. Turn here, and in a little over 1.5 miles, a pleasant drive through the tiny hamlet of Killington leads to the **Thundering Brook Falls Trail**. This is the first universally accessible portion of the **Appalachian Trail** and was built with help from the Green Mountain Club, the Green Mountain National Forest, the National Park Service, and the Appalachian Trail Conservancy. It has fully accessible parking, and the level terrain on the packed-surface trail is suitable for wheelchairs. The trail leads to Vermont's sixth-highest waterfall on the Ottauquechee, whose headwaters are up in these hills. Return to River Road and then take a right on **Thundering Brook Road** to rejoin US 4 farther along.

The access road to Killington Resort is a short way ahead on the left, but before taking this turn, you might want to stop in at the **Killington Pico Area Association** (802-773-4181) on your right, near the junction at which VT 100 heads off to the north. The visitor center is manned, a source of information about the area's myriad trails and events as well as lodging and restaurants.

Turn up Killington Road (Killington Sports is on the corner) to the 4-mile access road to **Killington Resort** (802-422-3333; killington.com). The road is lined with shops, restaurants, and lodges pretty much all the way up to the resort's base area, from which there's a clear view of Killington's peak, crisscrossed with ski trails. The big summer/fall attractions here are the **Mountain Bike Park**, with lift-assisted access to more than 30 miles of trails, and the championship 18-hole golf course. The **Snowshed Adventure Center**, ($–$$) accessed in the main base lodge, offers attractions such as zip lines, a jump tower, slides, aerial lifts, and an alpine coaster; there's also a food court. The enclosed **gondola** ride ($$) to Killington's summit also begins here, ending near the resort's surprisingly luxurious, glass-walled **Killington Peak Lodge**, good for breakfast, lunch, and drinks; check the main information number as well as the website to make sure that the lift is running and the lodge isn't closed for a special event. On a clear day the view sweeps northwest to the Adirondacks and east to the White Mountains.

Detour to Chittenden Reservoir

This isolated, man-made lake, circled almost completely by the Green Mountain National Forest, offers boat access. From US 4 in Mendon, about halfway down the 9 miles between Killington and Rutland, turn right onto Meadow Lake Drive and follow it to Chittenden Road (eventually becoming East Pittsford-Chittenden Road) as it winds through forest and field and by the village of Chittenden. Turn in at forested Dam Road and follow it to the reservoir, where there is an access for small boats and kayaks near the dam. Some rough camping is available along the shore (carry-in/carry-out). The 750-acre reservoir was created by the Chittenden Power Company and completed in 1909. It's now operated by Green Mountain Power.

Another overview of the lake is available from **Mountain Top Inn and Resort** (802-483-2311), a long-established resort with a national following. Both the rustically elegant **Highlands Dining Room** and the **Mountain Top Tavern** (pub menu) are open to non-guests and offer views of the mountain-backed lake. The resort's 40 miles of equestrian trails are also open to non-guests for one- or two-hour trail rides, and there are 15-minute-long pony rides for kids. To reach Mountain Top, turn left on Holden Road at the Civil War statue in Chittenden Village.

Head back down Killington Road to US 4, passing **Killington Supermarket and Deli** (802-422-7736, 2023 Killington Road), a long-standing stop for hungry travelers. Turn left onto US 4 and follow it up to Sherburne Pass, the 2,150-foot height of land for this old highway. Not far over the crest, look for the **Deer Leap** trails on your right. The **Deer Leap**, itself part of the **Appalachian Trail**, is a 4.5-mile loop through the forest, rated difficult. The easier **Deer Leap Overlook Trail** is a 2-mile rocky trek that kids can handle, accessing impressive views of the lowlands. This is a popular place for dedicated **Appalachian Trail** through-hikers to begin; the AT veers west here on its way into the White Mountains and on to its terminus at Mount Katahdin, Maine's highest mountain. Access to both the AT and the Long Trail is also available from US 4, 2.4 miles west of Killington, 0.2 mile before the entrance to Pico Peak Ski Area, which is part of Killington. **The Long Trail** runs 272 miles along the Green Mountains up the length of the state. Built by the Green Mountain Club (greenmountainclub.org) between 1910 and 1930, this is the oldest long-distance hiking trail in the United States.

For a different trek up Killington Peak on the side of the mountain opposite the resort, keep an eye out for Wheelerville Road about 3 miles farther down on US 4 West. Turn left and follow the road to the parking area for

Bucklin Trail. This is a walk in the woods for the initial 2 miles, but at a waterfall it begins to climb steeply up the back side of Killington Peak, offering splendid views across the valley to the Adirondacks. Hikers do complain, however, that after all that work, the summit is crowded with "gondola people" who have taken the easy way up from the Killington base area.

Back on US 4, the highway continues its descent, lined with restaurants and lodging as it winds through the town of Mendon to its junction with US 7 in Rutland. At the traffic light, turn south on US 4&7 and drive through

---

DETOUR

Detour to Rutland

From US 4&7, turn right onto West Street (US 4-Business)—this is an alternate to the US 4 main route through town, accessing older, industrial Rutland—and follow it past banks, offices, and stores. Turn left (there's a light) at **Merchant's Row**, a small commercial district with colorful architectural details on tall stone and brick buildings that lend a stately vintage feel to the area. On Wednesday and Saturday in the summer, a bustling **farmers' market** sets up in Depot Park beside the train station and shopping plaza on Merchant's Row.

Though **Rutland** has just about 16,500 year-round residents, it is the second-largest municipality in the state, maintaining a healthy economy while reclaiming an older identity as a center for art and culture in southern Vermont.

The **Chaffee Art Center** (802-775-0356) on busy South Main Street (US 7) is home to the **Rutland Area Art Association**. The imposing Queen Ann Victorian mansion, with its arched entry, stone foundations, and soaring three-story corner tower, was built by George Thrall Chaffee and completed in 1886. Its many spacious interior rooms and nooks have served as exhibit halls for the art center since the early 1960s. The center is currently renovating and opening new spaces for exhibits and events in the stately old building and on the grounds.

The art center sponsors an **Art in the Park** event each summer, setting up tents and booths across Main Street (US 4&7) on the town green, where guests find vendors of fine art and artisan items, natural products, and food.

The town dates back to the years before Vermont became the 14th U.S. state in 1791, being chartered in 1761 by the governor of New Hampshire, Benning Wentworth. By the 1850s, Rutland had become a railroad center, with trains serving local businesses and an especially thriving marble industry. Under Vermont Marble Company's management, Rutland's marble industry became one of the world's largest. The prosperous city celebrated art, theater, and music as well, becoming known for visual and performing arts at the turn of the nineteenth to the twentieth century.

DETOUR

Detour to Vermont Marble Museum

Boasting "the world's largest marble exhibit," the **Vermont Marble Museum and Gift Shop** (802-459-2750; 52 Main Street, Proctor) has more than 100 exhibits of structural and decorative uses of marble, and has added information and demonstrations to show the industrial uses of calcium carbonate, which is ground and pulverized marble used in many products, from paint to toothpaste.

To get there, from US 4&7 in Rutland, turn right on US 4-Business. Follow through Rutland's industrial district (not scenic, but the views improve shortly), traveling about 2 miles to VT 3. Turn right and continue another 3 miles through more pleasant terrain along Otter Creek to Proctor. Turn left onto Main Street and remain on Main as it turns right to reach the museum, open daily 10 AM–5 PM daily, late May–late October. $.

Rutland's dense commercial district for 2 miles. Fill up at a choice of gas stations or roadside restaurants. You'll pass by the **Vermont State Fairgrounds**, the end-of-summer site of the **Vermont State Fair** for more than 170 years. The fairgrounds are also a popular spot for exhibitions, special events, and car and truck rallies.

At the far end of the commercial district, turn right onto scenic US 4 and leave the hustle and bustle behind to head west toward small towns, rolling green landscapes, and mountain vistas in the shadow of the Taconic Mountains to the west.

Enjoy the drive westward, with green and rolling terrain stretching into the distance on either side of the road and slowly building to slopes and valleys as you near the **Taconic Mountains**. These peaks reach halfway up the western side of Vermont, from the southern border to the Middlebury area.

Take Exit 5 off US 4 toward **Castleton**. East Hubbardton Road takes you to VT 4A westward and on to South Street in Castleton. This section of town is quaint and lovely, with tree-lined streets and stately Greek Revival homes from ages gone by, some famous for their columned architecture designs by Thomas Royal Dake and dating back to the early 1800s. Visit **Castleton University** here, or just stop and stroll, visit the school, and enjoy the ambience.

The **Birdseye Diner** (802-468-5817) at 590 Main Street is open from 7 AM to 9 PM and offers a true "diner" experience in Castleton. The structure, a 1940s Silk City Dining Car, has been serving locals and visitors alike on Main Street for 50 years, with additional seating and an outdoor patio.

From Castleton, take VT 4A through town to pick up VT 30 and head north to reach the Bomoseen area. Drive along the lake with the water on one side of the road and forested hills on the other to reach **Crystal Beach** on the shores of **Lake Bomoseen**. Turn onto Prospect Point Road to access the beach. Dine on the shores Wednesday through Monday at the **Palms at Prospect Bay** (802-671-8180), or stop at the picturesque **Lake Bomoseen Lodge and Taproom** (802-468-5251) for a meal and an overnight stay with views of the lake outside your window.

INTO THE HILLS

Staying on VT 30, head north through the Crystal Beach area into hill country, where views are bounded on the west by the blue waters of Lake Bomoseen and on the east by the forested Taconics. From **Hubbardton** on VT 30, take Monument Hill Road, a narrow, winding way through roll-

VISIT THE HUBBARDTON BATTLEFIELD VISITOR CENTER FOR INFORMATION AND GUIDED HIKES TO MANY OF THE STATE PARK'S HISTORIC BATTLE LOCATIONS

The 204-acre **Taconic Mountains Ramble State Park** in Hubbardton is a recent addition to Vermont's Department of Forests, Parks, and Recreation. Accessed via US 4 Exit 5, head north onto East Hubbardton Road (becomes Monument Hill Road), then take St. John Road to the park. To visit the park after stopping at **Hubbardton Battlefield**, head south on Monument Hill Road to St. John Road and follow to the park. The area has no phone or facilities, and camping and open fires are prohibited. The park includes trails and gardens developed by the landowner, Carson Davidson, who donated acreage to the state to be maintained for public use. The trails can be steep and rocky, including the one that leads to a **Japanese Garden**. Still under development, the area is carry-in/carry-out; no overnight stays currently allowed.

ing and forested terrain, to the **Hubbardton Battlefield State Historic Site** (802-273-2282). At the battlefield, stop in at the visitor center to learn about guided hikes replete with historical context and nature lore, activities, and events surrounding this Revolutionary War battle site. Hike to the top of Mount Zion to overlook the battlefield, green and serene below. At this site in July 1777, soldiers from the colonial town of Hubbardton and the Green Mountain Boys held off an invasion from Canada to give troops of the colonial army time to escape to fight another day. Today the grounds are peaceful and visitors gaze from this high vantage point out onto rolling landscapes to the south.

From the battlefield, head south on narrow, winding Monument Hill Road to pick up East Hubbardton Road. Follow it several miles through narrow winding valleys and between treed hillsides, with the occasional homestead or vacation cottage along the way. Make the uneventful but lovely ride back to US 4 and return to Rutland and Killington.

Best Places to Sleep

THE KILLINGTON GRAND RESORT (802-422-5001), 228 East Mountain Road, Killington. At the top of Killington Road is a 200-room resort at the base of the ski lifts. Options range from standard hotel rooms to three-bedroom, condo-style suites. Amenities include an outdoor pool and a health club. $–$$$$.

SUMMIT LODGE & RESORT (802-422-3535), 200 Summit Road, Killington. A four-season inn, the cozy, rustic lodge has two restaurants and lounges, swimming pools, and hot tubs. Laid back and comfy, many of the 44 rooms sleep up to six. $$.

THE INN AT LONG TRAIL (802-775-7181), 709 US 4, Sherburne Pass, Killington. This is the first building in New England specifically built to serve as a ski lodge. It began in 1938 as an annex to a splendid summer inn that has since burned. Designed to resemble the inside of the forest as much as possible, the interior incorporates parts of trees and boulders in amazing ways. The furnishings are largely Adirondack-style, and the fire in the large stone hearth is real. Since 1977 the inn has been owned by the McGrath family, and it caters to through-hikers on the Appalachian and Long Trails and to outdoorspeople of all sorts. The 22-foot-long bar is made from a single log, and a protruding toe of the backyard cliff can be seen in both **Rosemary's Restaurant** and **Pub McGrath's Irish Pub** (music Fri.–Sat.). Guest rooms vary from the small but cheery ($) to two-room suites with fireplace ($$–$$$), many rates varying with the seasons. All guests can access the redwood hot tub to soothe muscles after hiking or skiing.

KILLINGTON-PICO MOTOR INN (802-773-4088), 4840 US 4, Killington. On the road to Mendon, this traditional motor inn is affordable and convenient to Killington, Rutland, and beyond. Neat and tidy alongside US 4, its 30 rooms come with mini fridge, cable, and complimentary continental breakfast. $–$$.

MOUNTAIN TOP INN AND RESORT (802-483-2311), 195 Mountain Top Road, Chittenden. Luxury accommodations, spa, heated pool, gourmet dining, horseback riding, boating, and more in an unparalleled setting of natural beauty, Chittenden Reservoir, surrounded by protected Green Mountain National Forest on mountain slopes all around. $$–$$$.

RED CLOVER INN & RESTAURANT (802-775-2290), 7 Woodward Road, Mendon. Created out of an old farmhouse that dates to the mid-1800s, the inn is now fully renovated and updated to provide upscale lodging for skiers and summer visitors. The inn and adjacent carriage house offer selections including fireplaces, Jacuzzi, and two-level suits, all with private bath. $$–$$$.

LAKE BOMOSEEN LODGE (802-468-5251), 2551 VT 30N, Bomoseen. This is a good choice for a gracious overnight stay on the shore of Lake Bomoseen. Rooms, suites, condos, and cottages are available. The new owners have completely renovated the accommodations, previously known as Edgewater Lodge. From the lodge, visitors can stroll the shores of the lake or take part in water sports. $$–$$$.

Best Places to Eat

The Killington/Rutland region is replete with lodges and restaurants on US 100, US 4, and US 7 to serve the myriad travelers who flock to the region year-round. Here are a few notable choices:

KILLINGTON PEAK LODGE (800-621-6867), 4763 Killington Road, Killington). Open 10:30 AM–3 PM daily. At the top of Killington's tallest peak, the lodge sits 4,241 feet above the rolling landscape. Views through surrounding walls of glass include three mountain ranges and green forests stretching over the horizon. Reached by hike or gondola, the lodge offers burgers, chicken, pasta, steak, and more. There is also a deli and light fare. Open for ski season, but also for summer and foliage season. $$.

ROSEMARY'S RESTAURANT, THE INN AT LONG TRAIL (802-775-7181), 709 US 4, Sherburne Pass, Killington. Rosemary's offers casual fine dining in Killington near the start of several trails on the mountain, including the Long Trail and Deer Leap. Situated on a quiet parcel along US 4 at The Inn at Long Trail, it's a relaxing and rewarding end to a busy day. $$.

RED CLOVER INN & RESTAURANT (802-775-2290), 7 Woodward Road, Mendon. Open Thurs.–Mon., 5:30–9 PM. Fine dining at its Vermont best in a charming old-time setting, warm and inviting, serving local produce and meats with wild touches. $$$.

THE RUTLAND RESTAURANT (802-775-7447), 57 Merchant's Row, Rutland. Open 7 AM–8 PM daily except Sun. In the heart of Rutland's downtown, within an easy walk of the weekly farmers' market, this light-fare, casual café serves breakfast, lunch, and dinner in simple surroundings. $$.

PALMS AT PROSPECT BAY (802-671-8180), 111 Prospect Point Road, Bomoseen. Open 5–9 PM Wed.–Sun., 12–4 PM weekends for lunch. Dine in comfort on delicious traditional American fare as you enjoy views of the water and watch the sky turn to dusk. $$.

BIRDSEYE DINER (802-468-5817), 590 State Street, Castleton. Open daily 7 AM–9 PM. Offers a true "diner" experience popular with locals and visitors. Tasty cuisine is served in an authentic old Silver City Dining Car trucked in from Paterson, New Jersey, decades ago. Enjoy the vintage diner ambience and local Vermont flavors. $.

LAKE BOMOSEEN LODGE AND TAPROOM (802-468-5251), 2551 VT 30, Bomoseen. Open 4–9 PM Sun.–Thurs., 4–10 PM Fri.–Sat. A nice spot for a meal and an overnight stay on the waterfront. Enjoy big juicy burgers and a cold brew while watching boaters on Lake Bomoseen just outside the lodge. A Vermont experience to be savored. $$–$$$.

8

MIDDLEBURY/BRANDON

ESTIMATED LENGTH: 90 miles

ESTIMATED TIME: 2 to 3 days

HIGHLIGHTS: That poet Robert Frost was enamored with this area comes as no
surprise. Roads meander through areas of intense pastoral beauty, linking classic New England towns with Revolutionary War historic sites and
year-round recreational areas. The dairy farms with big red barns and
black-and-white cows that visitors associate with Vermont are here, but so
are modern sculpture gardens, craft breweries, a world-class art museum,
and restaurants that push the culinary envelope. "Take the road less traveled
by" as Frost suggested and discover the unparalleled beauty and bounty of
the southern Champlain Valley.

SIDE TRIP HIGHLIGHTS: Rolling farmland, unspoiled lake views, and postcard-pretty
villages characterize this small slice of the Champlain Valley, with strong
ties to the American Revolution and a birding hot spot at Dead Creek Wildlife
Management Area.

GETTING THERE: US 7, the main north-south route through western Vermont, provides the quickest access to Middlebury.

ON THE ROAD

Middlebury, where this route begins, is no slouch when it comes to the arts,
culture, and cuisine. It's a college town, so it has a youthful vibe, though
it's also well-rooted in the past as evidenced by its large number of beautifully preserved historic buildings, including the courthouse, **Middlebury
Inn** (802-388-4961), and the white-spired Congregational church clustered

LEFT: THE CONGREGATIONAL CHURCH OF MIDDLEBURY

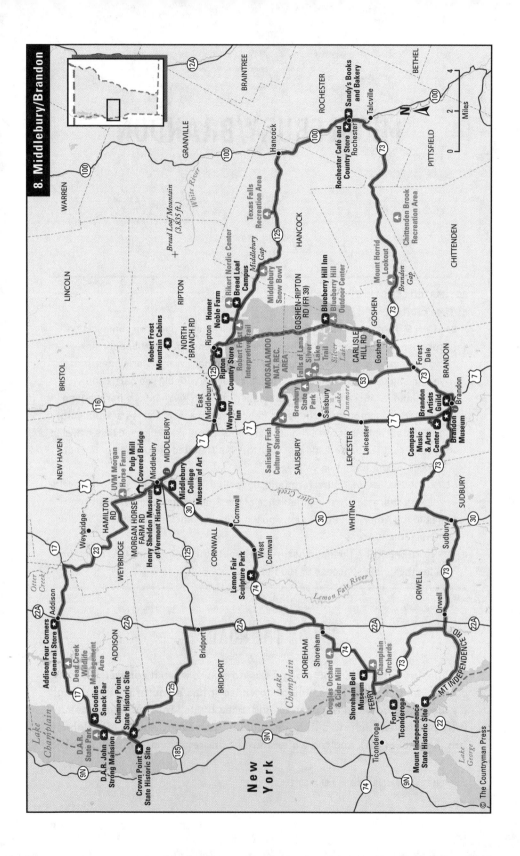

around the town green and gazebo. **Middlebury College** (802-443-5000) has several centuries-old edifices, including three known as **Old Stone Row**, which were built with locally quarried limestone. The earliest, Painter Hall, dates to 1814.

The **Henry Sheldon Museum of Vermont History** (802-388-2117) offers a good insight into what life was like here and throughout the state in the nineteenth and early twentieth centuries. Sheldon, an obsessive collector, created the museum in 1882 to display his private collections of furniture, paintings, newspapers, toys, and other items. The museum is located in the historic Judd-Harris House, an 1829 Federal-style brick building that originally was home to two wealthy marble quarry owners. Vermont's history also is preserved at the nearby **Vermont Folklife Center** (802-388–4964), a repository for audio and video recordings, photos, folk paintings, manuscripts, and other works that document life in the Green Mountain State.

That Middlebury has its own opera company, appropriately named the **Opera Company of Middlebury** (802-388-7432), may come as a surprise. The community, with a population of fewer than 9,000, also supports the arts through its **Town Hall Theater** (802-382-9222), which stages several productions and events throughout the year. The state-of-the-art venue occupies the same building as the town's original 600-seat theater built in 1884 and so named because the town offices were in the basement. Today the **Jackson Gallery**, displaying works of area artists, fills the lower level.

The acquisitions of the **Middlebury College Museum of Art** (802-443-5007) are impressive, with more than 2,500 objects—from antiquities and Renaissance paintings to Asian and contemporary art—in its permanent collection. Its 24 pieces of public art, mostly outdoor sculptures, are scattered about campus. The museum, which charges no admission, also produces six to eight temporary exhibits each year.

You can access the **Trail Around Middlebury**, known locally as TAM, from Middlebury College as well as several other points. Parking is available at most trailheads. This 18-mile running and walking trail is divided into sections, with a portion of the trails open for mountain biking. Developed by the **Middlebury Land Trust** (802-388-1007), it circumnavigates the town, weaving through residential areas, past local landmarks, and through forest preserves and tracts of conserved land.

Otter Creek cuts through the downtown area, with a dramatic 18-foot cascade that is Middlebury Falls. You can see the falls from the bridge on Main Street, but the best vantage point is from the footbridge that crosses the river below Main to the **Marble Works** (802-388-3701). Once a marble manufacturing area, it's now a small mixed-use commercial district with a number of Vermont-owned shops, restaurants, and offices. Pop into some of the shops here and around Main Street, the majority of them independently owned, before heading to Exchange Street on the northern edge of town.

MIDDLEBURY FALLS

In recent years this area has experienced a renaissance from characterless industrial park to vibrant food-and-drink hub.

A number of breweries, distilleries, and a cidery can be found here, loosely linked as the **Middlebury Tasting Trail**, which also includes a few outliers within a 5-mile radius. These places all have tasting rooms. **Otter Creek Brewing** (802-388-0727) also serves food, and the **Woodchuck Cider House** (802-385-3656) has an informative self-guided tour of its production area that includes signage about the history of Woodchuck Cidery and how cider is made.

The **Vermont Coffee Company** (802-398-2776), a local coffee roaster, also shares this mile-and-a-half stretch and has a small café where you can grab a fresh-roasted brew or espresso drink and a light lunch or breakfast sandwich. A viewing window allows customers to observe the coffee-roasting process.

There are two more stops you should make while in this area. **Maple Landmark Woodcraft** (802-388-0627), a manufacturer of wood products including toys, offers tours of its work area. **Vermont Soap** (802-388-4302), a small factory outlet selling organic soap by the pound and other natural bath and home products, has displays of vintage soap products, soap boxes, and washing machines.

For lunch options, Middlebury doesn't lack for choices. For take-out, **Costello's Market** (802-388-3385), an Italian gourmet market and deli located at **Marble Works**, is a local favorite. **The Lobby** (802-989-7463) on Bakery Lane, one of the newest additions to Middlebury's culinary scene, has an eclectic, locally sourced menu with several vegetarian options, including a black bean and quinoa burger. Several food-themed quotes are chalked on the walls, and outside dining is preferred seating at this riverside restaurant.

THE ROAD LESS TRAVELED

Head south on US 7 for about 4 miles, turning left on VT 125 through East Middlebury to Ripton Village with a stop at the old-timey **Ripton Country Store** (802-388-7328). This lovely 16-mile ribbon of tarmac, christened the Robert Frost Memorial Drive, stretches from East Middlebury to Hancock over Middlebury Gap. It rambles through shaded wooded areas, paralleling the South Branch of the Middlebury River for a spell.

Watch for the sign for the **Robert Frost Interpretive Trail**, a relatively flat 1.2-mile path that winds through woods and meadows, flush with wildflowers and a bounty of wild raspberries, huckleberries, and blueberries in summer. Appropriately placed trailside plaques showcase the former Vermont poet laureate's scenery-inspired poems. A portion of the trail is handicapped-accessible. Just past the trail's parking area, on the opposite side of the road, is the **Robert Frost Wayside Area**. Look for the unmarked dirt road adjacent to this picnic area and follow this for 0.5 mile to Frost's

RIPTON COUNTRY STORE

farm, also known as the **Homer Noble Farm**, which the poet purchased in 1940. He summered here for more than 20 years, until his death in 1963, penning several notable works, including *A Witness Tree* for which he was awarded the Pulitzer Prize for Poetry in 1943.

Now a National Historic Landmark, the property, which includes a white wood-frame farmhouse, woodshed, apple orchard, and the rustic cabin where Frost preferred to live and write, is owned by **Middlebury College**. It is not far from the college's historic **Bread Loaf** campus, a complex of nineteenth-century, sunshine-yellow buildings with green roofs and unbeatable views of the 3,835-foot Bread Loaf Mountain, part of the Green Mountain Range. The internationally acclaimed **Bread Loaf Writers' Conference** (802-443-5418) has been held each summer since the 1920s. Frost was a regular participant at the conference, which invites prominent writers to give readings and teach classes and workshops on the craft of writing fiction, nonfiction, and poetry. In winter, you can purchase a trail pass at the **Rikert Nordic Center** (802-443-2744) to snowshoe and cross-country ski on more than 35 miles of groomed trails. The **Middlebury Snow Bowl** (802-443-7669), open to the public for downhill skiing and snowboarding, is a few miles past Bread Loaf.

ON BLUEBERRY HILL

You now have a choice to make. You can backtrack on VT 125 for 2 miles to the unpaved Goshen-Ripton Road (Green Mountain National Forest Road 32), which meanders through the 15,857-acre **Moosalamoo National Recreation Area** (802-779-1731). It travels past the **Blueberry Hill Inn** (802-247-6735; see *Best Places to Sleep*) to connect with VT 73 near Forest Dale. The inn's **Blueberry Hill Outdoor Center** maintains more than 30 miles of trails for hiking, biking, trail running, and winter sports.

Or continue east on VT 125 to Hancock, stopping first at **Texas Falls Recreation Area** (802-747-6700). To get there, take a left on Green Mountain National Forest Road 39. Park at the falls observation site or at the picnic area farther up the road to view the cascading falls that rush through the glacial gorge or to walk the 1.2-mile nature trail.

In Hancock turn right on VT 100 toward Rochester, about a five-minute drive, where you can stop for lunch at the **Rochester Café and Country Store** (802-767-4302), with its old-fashioned soda fountain, or **Sandy's Books and Bakery** (802-767-4258) across the street. Tables and chairs are tucked among the bookshelves and placed out back near the garden where flowers are grown, both ornamental for table decorations and edible for salads.

Hop on VT 73 just past Rochester at Talcville, which will take you through the **Chittenden Brook Recreation Area** (802-767-4261), another Green

Mountain National Forest holding, and over Goshen Mountain through Brandon Gap to Brandon. Stop at **Mount Horrid Lookout** on the eastern side of the gap. Grab your binoculars to search for peregrine falcons nesting on the cliffs or moose feeding in the wetlands.

Brandon, which bills itself as the "Art and Soul Village of Vermont," lives up to its claim with a number of art galleries and antiques shops along

DETOUR

At Forest Dale, take VT 53 north, which hugs the eastern shore of Lake Dunmore, an area jam-packed with summer camps. The road skirts **Branbury State Park** (802-247-5925), which transitioned from a working farm to a guest house, then a summer boys' camp and private ownership before it joined the Vermont State Parks system in 1946. Although the park can get crowded on summer weekends, it's a great place to swim, rent a boat, or learn about the area's plants and wildlife at the nature center.

It's also an ideal base for hiking. Ask the ranger for directions to Ethan Allen's Cave, where the Green Mountain Boys leader hid to escape the British. It's a 1-mile hike from the trailhead at the park's campground. Or park your car here to hike to the **Falls of Lana** on the **Silver Lake Trail**. Although there's a small parking area near the trailhead, it's often full. Plan on about a 15-minute walk from the trailhead to the lower falls viewpoint, another 10 minutes to the base of the upper falls. Wear your bathing suit for a dip in one of the swimming holes.

If you want to continue to **Silver Lake**, it's another 1.6 miles past the falls. The secluded lake, also ideal for a swim, has a picnic area and 15 primitive campsites. A hotel once stood at this spot but was destroyed by fire in 1942. Part of the trail follows the old carriage road used by guests. The **Silver Lake Loop Trail** continues around the lake for another 2.5 miles, or you can return to your car the same way you came.

Continue on VT 53 to the **Salisbury Fish Culture Station** (802-352-4371), one of five fish hatcheries in the state. This facility, which began raising fish in 1931, is a brood stock station that provides up to 9 million trout eggs each year to both Vermont and federal fish hatcheries. It's listed on the National Register of Historic Places.

When you reach US 7, head south through Leicester. About a mile before you reach Brandon, pull into **Park Village** on the site of the former Brandon Training School to visit the **Compass Music and Arts Center** (802-247-4295). The venue celebrates music and the creative arts through performances, workshops, and changing exhibits. Be sure to check out the Phonograph Rooms, a permanent exhibit on the history of recorded music. A number of phonographs and record players from the 1890s through the 1980s are on display along with vintage television sets, radios, movie projectors, and tape recorders. Have lunch or a quick snack at the **SoundBite Café**.

GOURMET PROVENCE BAKERY AND WINE SHOP, BRANDON

its main drag—VT 73 and US 7—that loops through town. The **Brandon Artists Guild** (802-247-4956) was formed 20 years ago as a way to connect area artists and provide a place for them to display and sell their work. The gallery, located on Center Street (US 7), is open seven days a week.

The free **Brandon Museum** (802-247-6401), near the Baptist Church at the junction of VT 73 West and US 7, celebrates the town's history, including the legacy of native son Stephen A. Douglas, who lost to Abraham Lincoln in the 1860 presidential race. He was known as the "Little Giant" for his short stature. He was reportedly only 5 feet 4 inches tall. Interestingly, he too courted Mary Todd, who chose to marry Lincoln instead. The museum, housed in his birthplace, also addresses the anti-slavery movement in Brandon and the impact the Civil War had on the town.

The **Brandon Visitor Center** (802-247-6401) shares space with the museum in a circa-1800 building, which is on the National Register of Historic Places along with the entire downtown area. A total of 243 buildings are included on this list, among them the **Brandon Inn** (802-247-5766), quite possibly the oldest continuously operating inn in the state, and a handful of elegant homes that have been turned into B&Bs. Maps are available at the visitor center for a self-guided walking tour of Brandon's Historic District.

US 7 will take you back to Middlebury, 17 miles north, but why cut your exploring short? Instead continue on VT 73 West, which gently winds

> **M**ount Independence State Historic Site (802-948-2000), 497 Mount Independence Road, Orwell. Open Memorial Day weekend–Columbus Day, 9:30 AM–5 PM daily. This historic site is a lesson in Revolutionary War history. Several archaeological digs here have unearthed artifacts, including musket balls, gun bits, wine glasses, buttons, and even a 3,000-pound cannon that was found in Lake Champlain, all of which help tell the story of this fort built to guard against British attack from Canada. It was under construction when the Declaration of Independence was signed in 1776, and so named Mount Independence. A year later British troops invaded, led by Lt. Gen. John Burgoyne, forcing the American soldiers to retreat.
>
> Start your journey through history at the visitor center museum for a look at life at an eighteenth-century military outpost. Then head outside to explore the remains of the star-shaped fort, artillery batteries, blockhouses, barracks, hospital, and other ruins on the 6 miles of trails, many with lake vistas.

through endless stretches of rolling farmland. When you reach the T intersection, VT 73 briefly joins VT 30 as you take a left to Sudbury before splitting off again as you head into Orwell. Stay straight on Mount Independence Road for 6 miles, which will bring you to the **Mount Independence State Historic Site** (802-948-2000), considered one of the best-preserved Revolutionary War sites in the country.

After exploring the historic site, backtrack to VT 73 to VT 74 and hang a

FORT TICONDEROGA CABLE CAR FERRY DOCK

left to Larrabee's Point in Shoreham, where you can catch the **Fort Ticon-deroga Ferry** (802-897-7999), a cable car ferry to New York, to visit **Fort Ticonderoga** (518-585-2821). This beautifully restored eighteenth-century fortress played an important role in both the French and Indian War and the American Revolution. The ferry operates daily from early May through the end of October, which coincides with the fort's schedule. There are continuous crossings, about seven minutes each way, during daylight hours.

En route to the ferry, you'll pass by **Champlain Orchards** (802-897-2777), a sustainably managed orchard and u-pick operation that grows more than 100 varieties of apples, peaches, and other fruits. The orchard has apple pies and other apple products for sale, including both fresh and hard ciders, during harvest season. It is one of several orchards in Addison County where you can pick your own fruit, another nearby option being **Douglas Orchard and Cider Mill** (802-897-5043), also on VT 74.

This route will take you through Shoreham, an agricultural community with an unusual museum, the **Shoreham Bell Museum** (802-897-2780), open by chance—look for the "Open" flag—or by appointment most afternoons. The museum houses the private collection of Judith Blake. Over the years, she and her late husband Charles amassed more than 5,500 bells of all sizes, vintages, colors, and functions, many with an interesting back story. To get to the museum, which is south of the village, take a left off VT 74 on Smith Street, then left again at the third driveway. Heading east on VT 74, you'll pass **Lemon Fair Sculpture Park** (802-383-8161), a free 1-mile walking trail with more than 20 sculptures, open weekends May through late October. Continue to West Cornwall and Cornwall, where you'll head north on VT 30 to Middlebury.

There's one last place that merits a visit, and that's the **University of Vermont Morgan Horse Farm** (802-388-2011) in Weybridge, a few miles northwest of town. To get there, stay on VT 30, which becomes Main Street in Middlebury, turning left on Seymour Street. This route takes you through the **Pulp Mill Bridge**, a rare double-barreled (two-lane) covered bridge, one of only seven in the country. Built circa 1820, it's the oldest covered bridge in Vermont. As you near the farm, Seymour Street becomes Morgan Horse Farm Road.

You can tour the historic farm to learn about the Morgan horse and the man, Col. Joseph Battell, who began breeding Morgans on this property in the late 1870s. Today the farm is dedicated to preserving and improving the breed through genetic selection.

Best Places to Sleep

WAYBURY INN (802-388-4015), 457 East Main Street, East Middlebury. The inn, built as a boarding house and tavern in 1810 and later used for a stage-

UNIVERSITY OF VERMONT MORGAN HORSE FARM

coach stop, has a long tradition of welcoming travelers. Robert Frost was a frequent guest, although the inn also found fame as the fictional Stratford Inn on the 1980s TV show, *Newhart*. Each of its 13 Vermont-chic rooms has a private bath, and one, the Robert Frost Suite, has a secret. Ask innkeepers Tracey and Joe Sutton what it is. Cooked-to-order breakfast is included, and pets are welcome for an added fee. A two-night minimum stay is required on summer and fall weekends. The inn is open to the public for lunch and dinner. $$–$$$$.

ROBERT FROST MOUNTAIN CABINS (802-388-9090), 2430 North Branch Road, Ripton. These self-catering cabins on the eastern slope of Robert Frost Mountain offer privacy and full immersion in nature while still within convenient driving distance of Middlebury. The finely crafted timber-framed cabins were built from wood that owners Marty and Carol Kulczyk harvested and milled on the 112-acre property. Each of the six cabins has two bedrooms and a full kitchen, although **Bread Loaf Catering** offers home-cooked meals delivered right to the door. Two cabins are pet friendly, and Owl's Branch is handicapped-accessible. $$–$$$.

BLUEBERRY HILL INN (802-247-6735), 1245 Goshen-Ripton Road, Goshen. Innkeeper Tony Clark is the consummate host, making guests at his four-season destination inn feel like family. The inn, located in the Green Mountain National Forest, has 11 rooms, four of which are original to the 1813 home, and a separate cottage that was once a granary. Before hitting the trails, guests can fuel up with a full country breakfast, including blueberry pancakes with Vermont maple syrup or waffles with blueberries. In winter, free hot soup is served at the inn's outdoor center from 12–2 PM. There's a bottomless cookie jar, with cookies also available by mail order. Bookings can include reservations for dinner. The four-course prix fixe menu changes daily. $$–$$$$.

Best Places to Eat

FIRE & ICE RESTAURANT (802-388-7166), 26 Seymour Street, Middlebury. Open Mon.–Thurs. 5–9 PM, Fri.–Sat. 12–10 PM, Sun. 12–9 PM. Patrons will be forgiven if they think that they walked into a museum at this family-run restaurant. World War I airplane propellers share wall space with vintage snowshoes, mounted fish, and black-and-white photos. A 1920s runabout sits near the famous 55-plus-item salad bar. While known for their slow-roasted prime rib, hand cut to order, the menu also includes such choices as roast duckling and drunken pork chops. All entrées come with a self-serve bread and cheese board. For casual fare, visit the **Big Moose Pub**, also the place to linger while waiting for your table. $–$$$$.

CAFÉ PROVENCE (802-247-9997), 11 Center Street, Brandon. Open Mon.–Sat. 11:30 AM–9 PM, Sun., 10 AM–9 PM. Chef-owner Robert Barral puts his own spin on traditional French dishes at his bistro in Brandon, using local ingredients and creative plating for an unforgettable dining experience. The airy space and open kitchen add to the casual ambience. The Café Provence seafood stew is a perennial favorite, combining shrimp, scallops, mussels, and fish in a lobster-tarragon broth. Try the warm chocolate bomb or maple crème brûlée for dessert, or stop at the **Gourmet Provence Bakery and Wine Shop** (802-247-3002) for a French-style pastry or two. The shop also sells pâtés, cheeses, and wines. $–$$.

SIDE TRIP
Southern Champlain Valley
Meandering along Lake Champlain

ESTIMATED LENGTH: 36 miles

At Shoreham, go north on VT 22A to Bridport, which will take you through fertile farm country, then west on VT 125 to the **Chimney Point State Historic Site** (802-759-2412) at the foot of the Lake Champlain Bridge that links Vermont to New York.

The museum, which is housed in a 1785 tavern, provides an excellent interpretation of the people who inhabited this site as long as 9,000 years ago. Informational exhibits share the history and legacy of the early Abenakis and the first Europeans to build forts and settlements here. Displays in the taproom, believed to be the oldest on Lake Champlain, focus on the history of the building; the Barnes Family, who owned the property from 1821 to 1966; and lake transportation, including the ferries and original 1929 bridge at this location. Another exhibit describes the history of the old Chimney Point post office.

Some of the displayed artifacts were found when the 1929 bridge was replaced in 2011. You can learn more about the history and engineering of the bridge and other significant happenings at this site on the **Chimney Point History Trail**, a short outdoor walking trail with interpretive signs.

A similar trail was created on the New York side of the lake. Drive or walk across the bridge to the small parking lot on the left to access the walking trail. Close by is the **Crown Point State Historic Site** (518-597-4666), where you can explore the ruins of an eighteenth-century strategic military stronghold.

VT 17 will take you to **D.A.R. State Park** (802-759-2354) on the shores of Lake Champlain and the **D.A.R. John Strong Mansion** (802-759-2309), just past the park's entrance. The mansion, purchased by a local chapter of the Daughters of the American Revolution in 1934, belonged to John Strong. He was a Revolutionary War patriot and later a probate judge and member of the 1791 convention that adopted the U.S. Constitution and admitted Vermont to the Union as the 14th state. He built this impressive Federal-style brick mansion after his family's cabin was burned to the ground by British Loyalists in 1790. Today only the foundation of that early homestead remains; it can be seen near the picnic pavilion at the state

D.A.R. JOHN STRONG MANSION

park. Guided tours of the mansion with commentary about the family are offered on summer weekends.

There's always a line at **Goodies Snack Bar** (802-759-2276) on VT 17 in Addison, and for good reason. This local favorite, open from late spring to summer only, offers more than a dozen variations of hot dogs and hamburgers, several sides from spicy fries to poutine (fries topped with cheese curds and gravy), and creemees (what Vermonters call soft-serve ice cream), including a "Flavor of the Week."

For birders, the Vermont Fish and Wildlife Department's 2,858-acre **Dead Creek Wildlife Management Area** (802-759-2397) is Mecca, with more than 200 species reported here, including bald eagles and several species of raptors, marsh dwellers, and waterfowl. In winter, snowy owls are attracted to this area, but the most anticipated arrival is that of the tens of thousands of snow geese that congregate here every fall on their migration south. There's a public viewing area with signage on the south side of VT 17. Paddlers can put in at the small boat access area on the opposite side of the road, which is just before the viewing area if approaching from the west.

You can learn more about the Dead Creek area, its history and the species that call it home at the **Dead Creek Wildlife Management Area Visitor Center**, which opened in September 2017. Interactive displays focus on waterfowl management, upland wildlife, the role of game wardens, emerging issues, land management, and other natural science topics.

DEAD CREEK WILDLIFE MANAGEMENT AREA VISITOR CENTER

End your trip at the **Addison Four Corners General Store** (802-759-2332) at the intersection of VT 17 and VT 22A, a gem of a country store where you can buy cider doughnuts, homemade pastries, and chocolates by the pound along with Vermont clothing and the usual grocery items. But the real find is the deli. They smoke their own meats, so don't pass up the house-smoked pulled pork sandwich or the Smokehouse, a combo of smoked turkey, pepperoni, apples, and cheddar cheese smothered in BBQ sauce.

9

THE CAPITAL REGION

ESTIMATED LENGTH: 80 miles

ESTIMATED TIME: 2 to 3 days

HIGHLIGHTS: The Capital Region encompasses a handful of communities, including Montpelier, a capital city with a laid-back vibe, and Barre (pronounced "berry"), best known for its granite quarries and Hope Cemetery, arguably one of the state's prettiest cemeteries. Historic covered bridges span rivers throughout the area, with five alone in Northfield, home to Norwich University, the nation's oldest private military college. Agriculture also dominates the landscape, with a number of sugarhouses, wineries, and u-pick operations open to the public.

GETTING THERE: Take I-89 to Exit 8, and then follow Memorial Drive (US 2) a short distance to the downtown area. Take a left on Bailey Avenue and a right on State Street, where you will begin your visit at the Vermont Statehouse. From the east, take US 2 West to Montpelier or US 302 West to Barre if starting the route from there.

ON THE ROAD

When exploring the Capital Region, a logical starting point is Vermont's capital city, Montpelier. The smallest state capital in the country, it's a compact, walkable city with a population just shy of 8,000. It's an unpretentious spot—the governor doesn't even have a mansion—where back-to-the-earth types mingle with politicians and visitors on the street and in the restaurants and shops, most of which are independently owned.

The distinctive gold-domed **Statehouse** (802-828-2228), capped with a

LEFT: VERMONT STATEHOUSE

statue of Ceres, the Roman goddess of agriculture, reigns over the downtown landscape. Much of the Greek Revival building has been restored to its original 1859 appearance, including the legislative chambers, governor's office, and the Hall of Flags, where many of the 68 different flags carried by Vermont's Civil War regiments were once displayed prior to being stored for preservation. Many of the original furnishings remain, including the Senate Chamber's 30 black walnut desks and chairs used by members of the 1859 Senate.

Friends of the Vermont Statehouse offer free guided tours every half hour from July through mid-October. Or stop by the Sergeant at Arms office to pick up a free audio wand for a self-guided tour on weekdays (available in

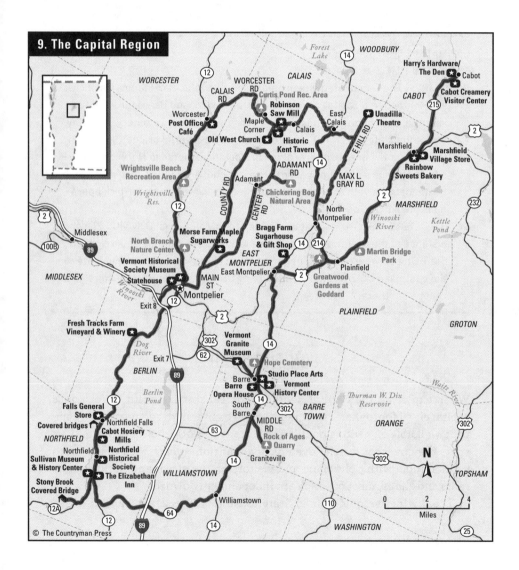

VERMONT HISTORICAL SOCIETY MUSEUM

English, French, German, and Spanish). Under the Dome Gift Shop hours correspond with tour hours.

Delve into the history of the Green Mountain State at the **Vermont Historical Society Museum** (802-828-2291) in the adjacent Pavilion Building. Its main permanent exhibit, "Freedom and Unity: One Ideal, Many Stories," takes you from the 1600s to the present, exploring everything from the arrival of the Abenakis, Vermont in wartime, agriculture, politics, and tourism to the realities of living in the state, including how the Depression, Flood of 1927, and 1918 influenza epidemic impacted communities. Admission to the museum also provides entry to the Vermont Heritage Galleries at the **Vermont History Center** (802-479-8500) in Barre.

A CAPITAL EXPERIENCE

In the Statehouse's "backyard," stretch your legs with a 20-minute uphill hike to Hubbard's Tower, a 54-foot stone observation tower in **Hubbard Park**. The 194-acre wooded property has around 7 miles of hiking and cross-country ski trails and an off-leash area for dogs. If driving, the park can be accessed via Hubbard Park Drive.

At the **U.S.S. Montpelier Museum**, located on the second floor of City

Hall, explore the history of three naval vessels named *Montpelier*. Pick up the key from the City Manager's Office (802-223-9502) during regular business hours. On weekends and evenings, ask at the **Lost Nation Theater** (802-229-0492), which has its office on the balcony of the third-floor auditorium. The theater stages more than 125 performances a year, including five main stage shows, cabarets, and special events such as the Edgar Allan Poe Spooktacular Halloween show.

For a small community, Montpelier has a large number of bookstores, art galleries, and shops. Check out **Cocoa Bean** (802-225-6670), a boutique chocolatier; **Bear Pond Books** (802-229-0774), a Montpelier institution; **Artisans Hand Craft Gallery** (802-229-9492), featuring the work of more than 100 local artisans; and **T. W. Wood Gallery** (802-262-6035), among Vermont's oldest art galleries. On Saturdays from May to October, mingle with the locals at the **Capital City Farmers Market** (802-793-8347) on State Street to shop for fresh fruits and vegetables, local meats and cheeses, maple products, and baked goods. In winter the market moves indoors, held at various locations including **Montpelier City Center** (802-229-4948).

Locally grown foods also are featured prominently on the menu at many Montpelier restaurants, including those operated by the **New England Culinary Institute** (802-223-6324), which is based here. For light fare, check out NECI's **La Brioche Bakery and Café** (802-229-0443), open daily except Sunday. **Capitol Grounds Café** (802-223-7800) is a popular gathering place for local residents to grab a bite. The café roasts its own coffee, sold under the brand name of 802 Coffee.

To head out of the city, take Main Street (a left at the end of State Street) to the rotary to pick up VT 12 North toward Worcester.

NATURE UNPLUGGED

Two miles north of downtown Montpelier on VT 12, the **North Branch Nature Center** (802-229-6206) introduces visitors to the state's flora and fauna through its exhibits, kids' activities, and citizen science programs. This 28-acre regional center of the **Vermont Institute of Natural Science** (802-359-5000) also maintains several trails, some of which connect with the East Montpelier Trails system and Hubbard Park. Leashed dogs are allowed on the trails, which are open daily.

Continuing north, you'll reach **Wrightsville Beach Recreation Area** (802-552-3471), ideal for a quick swim or picnic near the water. In Worcester you can't miss the yellow building that houses both the town's post office and the **Post Office Café** (802-225-6687). The cozy eatery offers a generous selection of doughnuts, pastries, and other baked goods, all made on

Instead of taking VT 12, go right at the rotary for 2.7 miles, following Main Street until it becomes County Road (stay left at the Y) to **Morse Farm Maple Sugarworks** (802-223-2740). At this working farm you can view a short video on maple sugaring in a woodshed theater, purchase maple and other products, and tour the sugarhouse and outdoor farm museum. Owner Burr Morse has carved several folksy figures out of wood. Walk behind the store to view the replica of the Vermont Statehouse.

CARVED WOODEN CHARACTERS AT MORSE FARM MAPLE SUGARWORKS

Continue along County Road to Bliss Pond Road, and then hang right on Fowler to Adamant Road. A quick detour on Lightening Ridge Road, so named because farmers had to lighten their wagon's load if they wanted to get up it, will take you to **Chickering Bog Natural Area** (802-229-4425) on the Calais–East Montpelier border. (The site also can be accessed from VT 14 just north of North Montpelier Pond.) The parking area is on George Road. Follow the 1-mile loop trail through the spruce, tamarack, and fir forest to the bog (misnamed, as it's actually a fen), then keep on the boardwalk to observe wetland plants, including several species of carnivorous plants.

Or stay on Adamant Road to Adamant on the shores of Sodom Pond. The hamlet's quirky **Black Fly Festival** each May is a favorite with visitors, although the town is also home to **Adamant Co-op** (802-223-5760) and the **Adamant Music School** (802-223-3347), which offers summer concerts. Center Road takes you through East Montpelier back to Montpelier, where you can pick up VT 12.

the premises, along with breakfast sandwiches, vegetarian quiche, soups, salads, and sandwiches. Just past the café, look for Worcester Town Hall, where you'll turn right on Calais Road. If you miss the turn, you'll end up at **Elmore State Park** (802-888-2982) on Lake Elmore. Heed the highway signs that caution drivers to watch out for moose.

At the point where Calais Road turns to gravel and becomes Worcester Road, continue straight. Alternatively, take Collar Hill Road on the right, which feeds into this route farther along. It's a pretty drive, especially in fall foliage season. As you near Maple Corner you'll see a sign for **Curtis Pond Recreation Area**, a great spot to launch a canoe or kayak or take a swim. At the stop sign just past the pond, you have two options. Head left on the dirt road to Woodbury, which bills itself as the "Land of Lakes and Ponds," an apt nickname as there are at least two dozen bodies of water within its borders, or our preference, a right-hand turn on County Road through Maple Corner, an unincorporated village in Calais.

The **Maple Corner Store** (802-229-4329), which shares the building with the Calais post office, offers pizza, wings, and sandwiches named for local places such as Gospel Hollow and Curtis Pond. Local musicians play at the Whammy Bar, located inside the store, several nights a week, with open mic night every Wednesday.

LESSONS IN HISTORY

Just past the store, take a left on Kent Hill Road and travel 0.7 mile to a four-way intersection. **Historic Kent Tavern**, listed on the National Register of Historic Places, will be directly ahead. The brick tavern was built by Abdiel Kent in the 1930s and is now owned by the **Vermont Historical Society**. It is open periodically for events and exhibits or by appointment (802-828-3051) from late May to mid-October.

Take Robinson Cemetery Road to the left to view the historic post-and-beam **Robinson Saw Mill** and waterfall. One of the state's only remaining water-powered sawmills, the 1803 mill is undergoing restoration by a group of dedicated volunteers. If you head past the tavern in the opposite direction for 0.8 mile you will come to the **Old West Church**, unchanged since it was erected in 1823. The door is never locked, so peek inside to see the original wooden box pews. Although the church last was open for weekly services in Civil War times, its annual Christmas Eve service is always well attended.

Back at the tavern, take a right on Kent Hill Road, following this to North Calais Road, then Moscow Wood Road to East Calais, where you will pick up VT 14. A left on Max L. Gray Road (which becomes East Hill Road) for 5 miles will bring you to **Unadilla Theater** (802-456-8968), launched by nonagenarian Bill Blachy in 1979. Cows graze in pastures behind this quirky repertory theater with dual venues for plays. Theatergoers are welcome to picnic before the performance, and a perpetual used book sale and homemade cookies fill the intermissions.

VT 14 continues south through North Montpelier, where you can catch VT 214, which meanders past **Goddard College** (802-454-8311), a private liberal arts school in Plainfield. The campus, established in the 1930s on a former gentleman's farm, is on the National Register of Historic Places for its Tudor Revival architecture and formal estate gardens designed by American landscape architect Arthur Surcliff. The public is welcome to tour the restored **Greatwood Gardens at Goddard** and take part in seasonal Tea and Tour events.

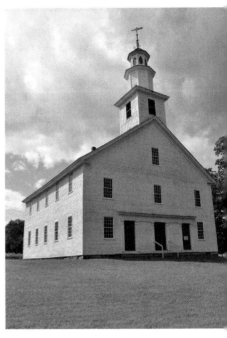

OLD WEST CHURCH, KENT'S CORNER

Just past Goddard, head east on US 2 to the village of Plainfield. Browse the extensive array of old books, vintage postcards, and other ephemera at **Country Bookshop** (802-454-8439) before popping across the street to **Positive Pie** (802-454-0133), popular with locals for its hand-tossed thin-crust pizza and large selection of craft beers.

OLD SCHOOL

Follow US 2 to East Montpelier, taking a quick jaunt north on VT 14 to **Bragg Farm Sugarhouse and Gift Shop** (802-223-5757) to sample maple syrup, maple creemees, and other maple products and watch a short video on maple sugaring. The farm is old school, preferring to gather sap with buckets—2,200 of them—instead of the more modern pipeline systems. If you call ahead during sugaring season, you may be able to arrange to accompany the sap gatherers to the sugarbush.

Reverse direction and stay on VT 14 South to Barre. Once there, park your car to explore the city's many architectural treasures on foot, starting at the **Vermont History Center** (802-479-8500), housed in the former Spaulding School. The Victorian building alone is worth a visit for its beautiful stained-glass windows and pressed tin ceilings. The center includes the

From Plainfield, continue east on US 2 to Marshfield. It's worth the detour for a stop at **Rainbow Sweets Bakery** (802-426-3531). For more than 40 years, Bill Tecosky and his wife, Trish Halloran, have prepared Engadiner nusstorte, Linzertorte, and other exquisite European sweet and savory pastries at their village location. The **Marshfield Village Store** (802-426-4321) has pizza and sandwiches. Or enjoy a generous scoop of ice cream in a waffle cone while relaxing on the front porch next to the wooden Indian and vintage Coca-Cola machine.

Take a 5-mile side trip on VT 215 to the **Cabot Creamery Visitor Center** (800-837-4261). It's a good place to stock up on cheese and other Vermont products, sample cheeses, and view a video to learn about the cheese-making process. Continue past the creamery to Cabot Village, with its inviting town green and white-steepled church. Visit **Harry's Hardware** (802-563-2291), Vermont's first hardware store with a liquor license. **The Den**, open Wednesday through Sunday, has Vermont craft beers and hard cider on tap. Its 12-foot granite-topped bar is set among the paint, tools, and fishing and hunting supplies for sale in this operating hardware store. On live music nights, the bar serves chicken wings and other appetizers from **Sarah's Country Diner** (802-563-2422), located at the back of the hardware store.

Returning to Marshfield, take US 2 to Plainfield, making a quick stop first at **Martin Bridge Park.** The park's single-lane, century-old covered bridge makes a great photo op. You can launch a canoe or kayak here, or stroll through the 44-foot-long bridge to the picnic area and trails. Picnic tables overlook the water.

Vermont Heritage Galleries, with rotating exhibits on various aspects of the state's history, and a research library. The bulk of the collection is Vermont history books and pamphlets dating from the 1770s to the present, although the library also is an excellent resource for New England genealogy information.

Barre Opera House (1899), **Aldrich Public Library** (1908), and the many magnificent sculptures and monuments scattered throughout this blue-collar community are all testaments to the skill and artistry of the early stone carver residents. Among the city's most significant sculptures is *Youth Triumphant*, designed by C. Paul Jennewein, who won a nationwide competition in 1921.

In **Dente Park** on North Main Street, a 23-foot-high statue of a sculptor holding a chisel and hammer was erected in 1985 to pay homage to Carlo Abate. The Italian craftsman opened a school around 1900 to teach design, sculpting, and other skills to workers in the granite industry. Modern-day sculptors can learn the trade at the **Stone Arts School** at the **Vermont Granite Museum** (802-476-4605).

A SHRINE TO STONECUTTERS' LIVES

Hope Cemetery (802-476-6245) on Maple Avenue on a hill high above Barre is a veritable showcase of memorial art. This is no ordinary cemetery. Every headstone and crypt is made of local granite, with many sculpted in unusual shapes or intricately carved with elaborate designs, everything from floral patterns to bas-reliefs of people, angels, and personal mementos. Among the 10,500 grave markers are a full-size armchair, a race car with the number 61, and a loving older couple dressed in nightclothes reclining in bed for all eternity.

Vermont Granite Museum (802-476-4605), 7 Jones Brothers Way, Barre. Open June–Oct., Tues.–Sat. 10 AM–4 PM. The museum, in the former Jones Brothers Granite Shed, tells the story of Vermont's granite industry through photos, vintage equipment, sculptures, and interactive exhibits on history, geology, and technology. Visitors can try their hand at freehand sculpting or create their own sandblasted or etched tiles. Through workshops at the **Stone Arts School**, students have an opportunity to work side-by-side with experienced sculptors and stone workers to learn stone-carving techniques, sandblasting, and stonewall construction.

STATUES AT THE VERMONT GRANITE MUSEUM

ELIA CORTI GRAVESTONE AT HOPE CEMETERY, BARRE

Established in 1895, the 65-acre cemetery is the final resting place for many of the stoneworkers and their families. It became tradition for these men to create their own memorials before retiring. If they passed away early, as many did from silicosis or other lung diseases before the mandate for ventilation systems in the cutting sheds was enforced in the 1930s, then a relative or co-worker would do the honors. A life-sized, lifelike figure of Elia Corti, carved from a single block of granite, marks the grave of the Italian stonecutter considered among the very best in the country in the early 1900s. He died after being accidentally shot during an argument between the anarchists and socialists at Barre's **Socialist Labor Hall** (802-331-0013), now a National Historic Landmark, in 1903.

Lesser known but equally intriguing is **Elmwood Cemetery** (802-476-6245) on Washington and Hill Streets. Many of Barre's earliest residents are buried here, including the city's first settlers, John and Rebeckah Goldsbury; its first doctor; and former Vermont governor Deane C. Davis.

Before leaving the downtown area, visit **Studio Place Arts** (802-479-7069) on North Main. This working art center gives visitors access to contemporary art galleries and the resident artists who have studios in the historic three-story building.

GRANITE CENTRAL

Head south on VT 14, turning left on Middle Road to visit the **Rock of Ages Quarry** (802-476-3119). Located in the appropriately named village of Graniteville, at nearly 600 feet deep, it is the world's largest deep-hole granite quarry. At the visitor center, view exhibits and a video on the granite industry and its history, which will make it clear why Barre is considered the Granite Capital of the World.

The only way to observe the working quarry is on a 40-minute guided tour that departs from the visitor center several times daily, except Sunday, from Memorial Day through mid-October. From the observation area you can watch steel derricks slowly hoisting gargantuan blocks of gray granite from the yawning pit, later to be cut, sculpted, sandblasted, and polished for headstones, statues, countertops, and numerous other items. Keep in mind that quarry workers have weekends and holidays off, so you won't see much activity on those days.

ROCK OF AGES QUARRY, GRANITEVILLE

The self-guided factory tour in the building adjacent to the visitor center will let you watch stonecutters and artisans at work. Many of them are descendants of the early Italian, northern European, and French Canadian immigrants who traveled here in the late nineteenth and early twentieth centuries. Facing economic hardship in their own countries, they saw Barre's then fledgling granite industry as a lifeline for a new start.

Upon exiting the building, you'll find an outdoor granite bowling lane tucked away behind the hedges. Although **Rock of Ages** planned to manufacture these for commercial bowling alleys in the 1950s, their marketing efforts were unsuccessful. Try your hand at knocking down the pins. You may find that it's not as easy as it looks. For a glimpse of some of the Barre area's abandoned quarries, head to Millstone Hill, where more than 70 miles of trails, maintained by the **Millstone Trails Association**, wind past quarry ponds, grout piles, and rusting, forgotten mining equipment. Mountain bikers are charged a nominal fee for a day-use pass. Walkers, snowshoers, and cross-country skiers can go for free.

SOCKS, SOLDIERS, AND BRIDGES

Back on VT 14 South, at Williamstown go west on VT 64 then VT 12 to Northfield Center, where a short detour on VT 12A brings you to **Stony Brook Covered Bridge**. Built in 1899, it was the last kingpost-truss covered bridge constructed on a public highway in the state. Retrace your steps and head north on VT 12 to Northfield. Although **Norwich University** (802-485-2000), founded in 1819, put it on the map, the annual sock sale at **Cabot Hosiery Mills** (802-485-6066), New England's last remaining sock mill, brings thousands of shoppers to this town of 6,200 for two weekends in November.

To reach the **Sullivan Museum and History Center** (802-485-2183) on the **Norwich University** campus, take University Drive and watch for signs for visitor parking. The museum, in a rotunda-like building, showcases the university's 200-year history. Exhibits of war memorabilia are changed out occasionally, with new temporary exhibits installed throughout the year. The university hosts a free summer concert series with guest carillonneurs from throughout the world. Following each performance, concertgoers are invited to meet the musician and go inside the bell tower for a peek at the carillon bells.

Just past the campus you'll encounter the **Northfield Historical Society** (802-485-4792) at 75 South Main Street. The building was once the home of Vermont's fifth governor, Charles Paine.

If ready for a lunch break, check out **O'Maddi's Deli and Café** (802-485-4700) on Depot Square with its locally made desserts and local art on the walls, or **Cornerstone Burger Co.** (802-485-4300) on East Street,

which has an inventive burger menu. Order the Vermonter (New England beef, cheddar cheese, smoked bacon, Granny Smith apples, and peanut butter) or the poutine burger (cheddar cheese curds, house gravy, and french fries on Angus beef) for a taste of regional fare.

Continuing north on VT 12, stop at the **Falls General Store** (802-485-4551) in Northfield Falls on the corner of Cox Brook Road. The specialty food store and café, housed in a recently renovated 1892 building, carries a number of Vermont products along with grab-and-go cuisine. Proprietors Vincent and Norma Rooney, who studied at the International Culinary Center in New York, bake their own bread for their signature sandwiches and use locally sourced ingredients whenever possible on their menu, which features grass-fed beef burgers, pizza by the slice, and salads. All bakery items, including the Italian pastries, cookies, and fruit muffins, are freshly prepared on site.

Two covered bridges are visible from the store's parking area, the first of which, the **Northfield Falls Covered Bridge**, was built in 1872. The next two bridges, located on a quarter-mile stretch of Cox Brook Road, are both queenpost-truss construction, as is a fourth bridge, the **Slaughter House Bridge**, which crosses the Dog River on Slaughter House Road nearby.

As you head back to Montpelier, cap off the day with a wine tasting at **Fresh Tracks Farm Vineyard and Winery** (802-223-1151) in Berlin, established in 2002 by Christina Castegren and her husband Kris Tootle. The farm, which grows all its own grapes for its wines and taps 1,000 maple trees for syrup and its maple dessert wine, prides itself on its sustainable agricultural practices.

Best Places to Sleep

THE INN AT MONTPELIER (802-223-2727), 147 Main Street, Montpelier. The inn, owned by John and Karel Underwood, offers accommodations in two adjacent Federal-style homes, both beautifully restored and decorated with antiques and Oriental rugs. Each of the 19 well-appointed rooms has a private bath—some also have a fireplace—and comes with a continental breakfast. A 24-hour guest pantry provides hot beverages and cookies, which can be enjoyed on the wraparound veranda at the brick Lamb-Langdon house, one of the inn's two buildings. $$–$$$.

FIREHOUSE INN (802-476-2167), 8 South Main Street, Barre. Located in the heart of the city, this boutique hotel in a restored 1904 Queen Anne–style firehouse has two 1-bedroom suites and two studio suites with firehouse memorabilia. A sign in each room describes the room's original purpose. The hotel retains much of its original character with firefighter lockers, a vintage telephone switchboard, and other artifacts. Owners Richard Beaudet and Valerie White-Beaudet also run the **Ladder 1 Grill and Pub** (see *Best Places to Eat*). $$–$$$.

THE ELIZABETHAN INN (802-552-4791), 965 South Main Street, Northfield. Convenient to Norwich University, this charming B&B with an English flair features three well-appointed guest rooms, all with private bath. Each room is named after a famous author, including the nautically themed Herman Melville Room with its king-sized bed and a copy of *Moby Dick* for bedtime reading. Hosts Tom and Rita Clifford, both artists, have filled their home with their own original art. Continental breakfast is included in the room rate, with afternoon tea available upon request. $.

Best Places to Eat

SARDUCCI'S (802-223-0229), 3 Main Street, Montpelier. Open Mon.–Thurs. 11:30 AM–9 PM, Fri.–Sat. 11:30 AM–9:30 PM, Sun. 4–9 PM. This Mediterranean-style Italian restaurant overlooking the Winooski River is renowned for its wood-fired pizzas and pasta dishes, including Linguine al Pescatore (sea scallops, mussels, and shrimp in a white-wine tomato sauce) and Ravioli di Spinaci (baked spinach ravioli in a garlic and mushroom cream sauce). Gluten-free options are available. Reservations are recommended, especially on weekends. $–$$.

KISMET (802-223-8646), 52 State Street, Montpelier. Open Wed.–Sat. 5–9 PM; brunch Sat. 8 AM–2 PM, Sun. 9 AM–2 PM. This farm-to-table restaurant pulls out all the stops when it comes to its menu and presentation. Dishes are prepared with local and organic meats and produce with a focus on in-season, fresh whole foods. The fish is regional and sustainably harvested. Check out the seasonal craft cocktails, and don't say "no" to dessert. Chef-owner Crystal Maderia is accommodating when it comes to special diets, including vegan, paleo, and gluten-free. $–$$.

LADDER 1 GRILL AND PUB (802-883-2000), 8 South Main Street, Barre. Open Tues.–Sat. 11 AM–9 PM. It's all about firefighters past and present at this casual-dress restaurant with firehouse memorabilia and photos as the decor. Many of the dishes are named in honor of local firefighters. The eclectic menu offers a range of choices, from brick-oven pizzas, calzones, and pasta to steak, seafood, and comfort food such as shepherd's pie and fish-and-chips. For smaller appetites, there are soups, hero sandwiches, and wraps. Wednesday is Mexican Night. Before dining, the over-21 crowd can head downstairs for drinks and appetizers at **Moruzzi's** (802-479-2100), a Gatsby-style lounge. Drinks are named after mobsters, and 1920s attire is encouraged. Open Wed.–Fri. 5–10 PM. $–$$.

10

THE MAD RIVER VALLEY

ESTIMATED LENGTH: 80 miles

ESTIMATED TIME TO VISIT: 1 to 3 days

HIGHLIGHTS: This magnificent valley, named for the river down its center, is best known for the expansive ski trails streaking the high mountains that form its western wall. In summer the focus shifts from skiing at expansive **Sugarbush Ski Resort** and rugged **Mad River Glen** to golf links, ridgeline hikes, and mountain biking on trails that lace the forested slopes. Swimming holes spot the **Mad River** as it tumbles down from its source high in the mountain gap, coming through the **Granville Gulf** and moving serenely along the valley floor. It's shadowed through the valley by VT 100 and VT 100B, and also by the **Mad River Path** (802-496-7284), a series of recreation paths that follow the river or cross the landscape on small bridges, winding beside working farmland or through wooded glades. Two high passes in the Green Mountains— the **Lincoln** and **Appalachian Gaps**—afford spectacular panoramas and links to the Champlain Valley to the west, while the **Roxbury Gap Road** offers a splendid overview of this valley as it heads over the Northfield range to the east. Within the valley we explore quiet roads lined with rolling meadows set against the majestic mountains above. Lodging and restaurants dot the Sugarbush Access Road and cluster around the ski resort base, but the miles of VT 100 linking the lively valley villages of **Warren** and **Waitsfield** give little hint that several thousand visitors can bed down in the valley's widely scattered lodgings. While there is plenty here to please visitors, including a full schedule of summer and fall special events, much of it is here for the enjoyment of its sophisticated outdoorsy and ecology-conscious residents, many of whom originally came here to ski.

GETTING THERE: Perhaps it's the Mad River valley's lack of direct access to an interstate highway that keeps it a bit of a summer and foliage season secret. From the south as well as the north, it's best accessed from I-89 Exit 9 in Middlesex, 13 miles northeast of Waitsfield via VT 100B and VT 100. Valley

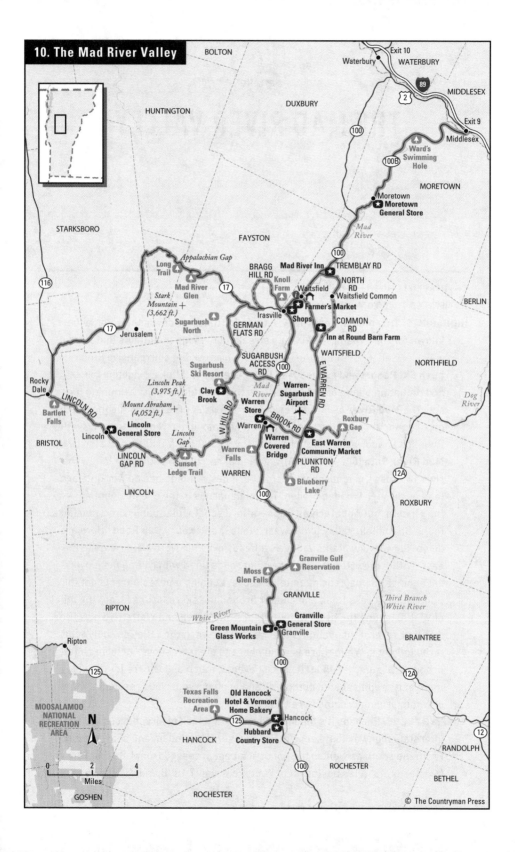

10. The Mad River Valley

BOLTON

Waterbury
Exit 10
WATERBURY

89

MIDDLESEX

2

Exit 9
Middlesex

HUNTINGTON

DUXBURY

100

100B

Ward's
Swimming
Hole

MORETOWN

Moretown
Moretown
General Store

STARKSBORO

FAYSTON

Mad River

100

116

Long
Trail

Appalachian Gap

Mad River
Glen

17

BRAGG
HILL RD

Knoll
Farm

Mad River Inn

TREMBLAY RD

NORTH
RD

Waitsfield

Waitsfield Common

BERLIN

Stark
Mountain
(3,662 ft.)

Sugarbush
North

Irasville

Farmer's Market

17

Jerusalem

GERMAN
FLATS RD

Shops

COMMON
RD

Inn at Round Barn Farm

WAITSFIELD

NORTHFIELD

Rocky
Dale

Sugarbush
Ski Resort

SUGARBUSH
ACCESS
RD

100

Lincoln Peak
(3,975 ft.)

Clay
Brook

Mad
River

E WARREN RD

Warren-
Sugarbush
Airport

Dog
River

LINCOLN RD

Mount Abraham
(4,052 ft.)

W HILL RD

Warren
Store

Warren

BROOK RD

Roxbury
Gap

Bartlett
Falls

Lincoln
General Store

Lincoln
Gap

Warren
Covered
Bridge

East Warren
Community Market

BRISTOL

Lincoln

LINCOLN
GAP RD

Sunset
Ledge Trail

Warren
Falls

PLUNKTON
RD

12A

LINCOLN

WARREN

100

Blueberry
Lake

ROXBURY

Granville Gulf
Reservation

Moss
Glen Falls

GRANVILLE

Third Branch
White River

RIPTON

White River

Green Mountain
Glass Works

Granville
General Store

Granville

BRAINTREE

Ripton

125

100

Texas Falls
Recreation
Area

Old Hancock
Hotel & Vermont
Home Bakery

MOOSALAMOO
NATIONAL
RECREATION
AREA

N

125

Hancock

12A

12

Hubbard
Country Store

HANCOCK

RANDOLPH

0   2   4
Miles

GOSHEN

ROCHESTER

ROCHESTER

100

BETHEL

© The Countryman Press

residents will tell you that the quickest access from the southeast is I-89 Exit 4 in Randolph, then 15 miles north to Roxbury on 12A and 8 more on Warren Road up over Roxbury Gap. Our drive approaches the Mad River Valley from the south on VT 100 at its junction with VT 125, which runs west over the Middlebury Gap to US 7.

ON THE ROAD

VT 100 follows the main stem of the White River north through a wide valley with open fields bordering wooded glades, some planted in hay and corn, past cows, sheep, and horses grazing in pastures, all set against the Green Mountains on the east. In the crossroads village of Hancock (population 300), marking the junction of VT 100 and VT 125, the landscape changes. The **Old Hancock Hotel and Vermont Home Bakery** (802-767-4976) here

A SMALL BARN ALONG VT 100 BETWEEN HANCOCK AND GRANVILLE

DETOUR

Detour to Texas Falls

Turn on VT 125 in Hancock, and in about 3 miles, Texas Falls Road is on the right. It leads to the **Texas Falls Recreation Area** (open 6–10 PM daily), maintained by Green Mountain National Forest. There's a small wooded park with hiking trails through the forest and a picnic area a short drive into the park where a pavilion and grills sit beside an open field for games. A walkway over Texas Brook leads to a lovely view of the falls and a gorge cut through the forest. The brook flows down to meet the waters of the Hancock Branch, eventually joining the White River.

has a weathered, frontier look. The sign on the door says it's closed Tuesdays "for a while," and the sign itself has been there for a while, but the door is usually open and breakfast, lunch, and a light dinner are served; the reasonably priced all-you-can-eat Sunday buffet brunch has a following. Upstairs rooms are also reasonably priced, and there's a small gift nook with souvenirs and new and used books good for browsing while waiting for a meal, preferably eaten at a table on the pleasant porch. Across VT 125 the **Hubbard's Country Store** (802-767-9012) is the genuine article, with fuel pumps out front, hot coffee to go, and picnic supplies to take to nearby **Texas Falls**.

Back on VT 100, continue north from Hancock, and in roughly 4 miles church and town hall spires rise around a bend and the tiny hamlet of Gran-

ALONG VT 100 BETWEEN GRANVILLE AND HANCOCK

GLASSBLOWER MICHAEL EGAN AT GREEN MOUNTAIN GLASSWORKS INVITES VISITORS TO WATCH HIM WORK OR ASK QUESTIONS ABOUT THE ART AND INDUSTRY OF HAND-BLOWN GLASS

ville appears, straggling along the road. Originally chartered in 1781, the town still only counts around 300 residents. The **Granville General Store** (802-767-4600) offers hot and cold deli items as well as groceries. A few hundred feet farther on, **Green Mountain Glass Works** (802-767-4547) is worth a stop. The multicolored glass on display comes in a spectrum of bright colors in shapes and sizes ranging from large vases to delicately designed earrings. Michael Egan can usually be found working beside his forge, heating, blowing, and shaping his decorative designs while happily talking with visitors about the process. In addition to this location, Egan's work is available in galleries around Vermont and across the country.

UP AND OVER

Beyond Granville, the landscape closes in and the hills hover high above VT 100, affording a cool, green passage through the **Granville Gulf Reservation**. The gulf is a narrow, 7-mile gap that winds up between steep slopes, its lush green forest sheltering fox, rabbits, porcupines, deer, moose, and bear. Drive slowly, and watch for a moose along the next 5 or 6 miles, its gangly body sauntering along under the leafy canopy or munching greens in a woodland marsh. The reservation itself comprises more than 1,100 acres and includes the source of the south-flowing White River, which joins other branches downstream and eventually empties into the Connecticut River. It also includes the source of the Mad River, beginning its north-flowing course to join the Winooski.

A little more than halfway up the gulf, look to the left for the frothy white waters of **Moss Glen Falls**. Here the Deer Hollow Brook tumbles over rocks from 80 feet above the road to join Alder Meadow Brook via a small pool at the side of the road. Just past the falls, a turnout offers parking so visitors can use a walkway to a close-up view of the falls. At the right time of year, fresh Vermont maple syrup may be on sale in the parking area, a favorite spot for local sugar producers to set up a stand.

VT 100 continues to climb through the gulf, deep shaded here as the forest closes in on all sides. The winding road is steep, and sheer walls lean out toward your car as you pass. Winter travel is precarious through here, but it

SWIMMING AT BLUEBERRY LAKE IN WARREN

is also beautiful, with thick, blue-white sheets of ice sheathing the rock faces at each turn in the road. At the top of the gap, the road plateaus for about 2 miles and the way opens out, with marshes here and there on either side, the most likely spot to see moose wandering the woods or standing in the water, enjoying a meal of goo. Once through the gulf, you leave Granville behind and begin your descent down the far side of the gap into the town of Warren at the southern tip of the Mad River Valley.

FOLLOW THE RIVER

About 4 miles down the hill, keep a lookout on your left for signs pointing to **Warren Falls**, the first great swimming hole along the Mad River. Parking is off the road, and a marked trail leads through the woods to swim spots in the river as it rushes downhill. Local swimmers swarm over rock cliffs, jumping 20 or more feet into deep mountain pools below. Water flows out and down through stony sluices into ponds farther on in the river, finally coming to a wide, level, pebbly area that is ideal for small children and waders. But be advised, reaching the shallow water via the wooded path requires climbing down a small rocky hill (not easy in flip-flops).

VT 100 continues its descent into the Mad River Valley, and as it levels out there's a sign on the right that directs you to Warren Village. Turn here onto Main Street and keep an eye out in 0.4 mile for a vintage 1880 covered bridge. The small village clusters around the **Pitcher Inn** (802-496-6350; $$$$) and **Warren Store** (802-496-3864). And it's soon apparent that this is no backwoods village. The white clapboard, double-porched inn looks like it has been there forever, but it dates to 1997, when it replaced a more modest village inn that was lost to fire. Each Vermont-themed guest room has been elaborately decorated by a different designer, and a formal dining room and its restaurant—**275 Main**—offers fine dining on linen-draped, candlelit tables. Warren Store (open 8 AM–7 PM in summer and fall, otherwise until 6 PM) is a beloved institution with an outstanding deli counter and bakery and a seasonal patio with tables overlooking a small waterfall in the Mad River. The upstairs boutique offers an eclectic and sophisticated mix of clothing, jewelry, hardware, and gifts. Next door, the **Parade Gallery** (802-496-5445) is a long-established and respected showcase for original art and affordable prints.

A block farther on Main Street, turn right onto Brook Road and follow its twists and turns as it becomes East Warren Road. But before it does, you might want to detour to **Blueberry Lake**.

Continue on **East Warren Road** past the Roxbury Gap Road. Near its start, note the **East Warren Community Market** (802-496-6758), housed in

Detour to Blueberry Lake

At the top of the Brook Road, turn right onto Plunkton Road and follow it to the top of the hill; it turns to hard-packed dirt and, in a few hundred feet, you'll see the access road to Blueberry Lake on your left. Drive in and park near the lake and—if it's mid- to late August and they haven't all been picked yet—you can sample the fresh blueberries, planted here when the lake was dredged from a parcel of forest and marshland by its owner in the early 1980s. Eventually it was sold to the U.S. Forest Service, which developed several hundred acres of hillside surrounding the lake into a protected area open to public use. It's now a popular boating, swimming, hiking, and biking destination available free to visitors, with trails used for hiking and mountain biking in summer and snowshoeing and cross-country skiing in winter.

BLUEBERRY LAKE AND THE NORTHFIELD RANGE

If you don't take the first access road to the water's edge, continue on Plunkton Road over the earthen dam to a second access road on the far side of the lake. Park here to walk to the small beach. Just before the dam there's a separate parking lot for people intent on spending time on marked, wooded trails.

Detour on Common Road

To explore higher up the east side of the valley, follow East Warren Road and bear right at the Y onto Common Road. This is a well-maintained dirt track leading in about 2 miles to Joslin Hill Road and **Waitsfield Common**, the town's original settlement site, set high above the present village. You pass by the **Skinner Barn** (802-496-4422) on your left, a special events and entertainment venue, and as you approach the end of the road, you'll notice the **Von Trapp Greenhouse and Nurseries** (802-496-4385), owned by members of the family made famous by *The Sound of Music*.

Cross over Joslin Hill Road and take North Road. At the intersection with Tremblay Road, turn left and drive less than a mile to reconnect with VT 100 north of Waitsfield. The **Mad River Inn** (802-496-7900) is on your right on Tremblay Road about a quarter mile before you reach VT 100. Picnic tables sit beside the road under a copse of pines at the junction with VT 100.

an old schoolhouse. It's a local destination for produce from valley farms and Vermont specialty foods, a great place to browse. This road climbs several miles, and there are pull-offs along the way with glorious views down and across the valley to the Green Mountain ridgeline. The road crests at the height of land known as **Roxbury Gap**. Turn where you can and enjoy the view on the way back down.

East Warren Road continues to wind through pastureland, past grazing horses and cows, with remarkable views up and down the valley. In a few miles, just after a dip, it veers to the left (Common Road is straight ahead; see *Detour*) and passes **The Inn at Round Barn Farm** (802-496-2276), a luxuriously refitted farmhouse inn adjoining a nineteenth-century round barn that's been preserved as a cultural center and popular wedding venue. The way into Waitsfield this way is through the one-way **Village Covered Bridge**, dating from 1833 (beware the 9.5-foot height restriction) and spanning the Mad River above a swimming hole; in summer the bridge and its walkway are a popular jump-off point for kids taking a dip.

WAITSFIELD

Cross the one-way covered bridge onto Bridge Street, the walkable heart of Waitsfield, and park where you can. There's parking on Bridge Street, in a lot directly across VT 100 from Bridge Street ahead and another just south on VT 100, hidden behind the shops and restaurants. Along Bridge Street check out the **Artisans' Gallery** (802-496-6256) with its well-selected crafted clothing, pottery, rugs, glass, and much more. **Peasant** (802-496-6856; open for dinner Thurs.–Mon.; $$) is a popular local dining spot. If it's open, you might like to look into the funky but fascinating **Madsonian Museum of Industrial Design** (802-496-6611; open Sat. and Sun. 12–4 PM; $), displaying items from toasters to automobiles.

At the corner of Bridge Street and VT 100, the Mad River Valley Chamber of Commerce maintains a volunteer-manned **Visitor Center** (802-496-3409; madrivervalley.com), well stocked with local info.

Waitsfield's many independently owned establishments, featuring antiques, furniture, quilts, wine, glass-blowing, and more, straggle along VT 100 north and south of Bridge Street. Just to the north is the **Valley Players Theater** (802-583-1674), staging live performances and dance, and across the way **Clearwater Sports** (802-496-2708) is the local source for canoe and kayak rentals. For details about the **Mad River Path** network of trails, which runs alongside the river through woodlands and by farm fields and pastures, visit the path headquarters in the historic **General Wait House** (802-496-7284; office hours are generally Mon. and Wed., 10 AM–noon; Tue. and Thu., 1–3 PM; the Wait House information center is open 24/7, including

A DAIRY FARM ON VT 100 BETWEEN WAITSFIELD AND FAYSTON

access to restrooms and trail maps) just past the Waitsfield-Fayston Volunteer Fire House on VT 100.

Turning south on VT 100 from Bridge Street, around the bend a little more than a quarter mile or so, the **Big Picture Theater and Café** (802-496-8994), right on Carrol Road, shows popular and eclectic movies and holds film festivals. It includes a café and bar that are popular all day long and as a night spot. The theater adjoins a small pond in which locals "drown" an outhouse every spring, part of a bet on when the ice will melt.

Just past the theater is the Irasville section of town where two shopping centers—**Village Square** on the left on VT 100 and the **Mad River Green Shops**, set back off the road across the street—form the practical shopping heart of Waitsfield and include supermarkets, independently owned restaurants, and shops worth shopping. From 9 AM–1 PM Saturdays, mid-May–mid-Oct., the **Waitsfield Farmers Market** sets up on the grass of the Mad River Green right on VT 100 between the two centers, packed with vendors selling local produce and wares. Musicians and other entertainers are on hand, and there are usually horse-drawn wagon rides for families.

South on VT 100 a scant thousand feet, just before its junction with VT 17, turn up **Bragg Hill Road**. Broad and breathtaking vistas on this hilly, winding road encompass the forested heights of the Northfield Ridge across the valley to the east and the Green Mountains to the west—they seem so close you feel you can reach out and touch the slopes and ski trails. As you begin to wind and climb the steep track, look on your right for **Knoll Farm** (knollfarm.org; open mid-May–mid-Oct., 8 AM–6 PM, with organic berry-picking mid-July to late August). With its big weathered barn and white farmhouse, it's a special place to stop.

The nonprofit farm is known for its regenerative farming system, growing blueberries and raising a flock of Icelandic sheep for widely distributed meat that's available here. It's also a venue for special events and workshops (there's yurt housing for groups). Weekend farm tours feature visits to the barnyard animals and demonstrations of sustainable farming practices.

From Knoll Farm, head up Bragg Hill Road as it swings to the left, taking in the valley panoramas before finally descending via Number 9 Road to VT 17; a left leads down to VT 100 in Waitsfield, while a right continues to climb toward the Appalachian Gap.

On the way to the top of the Appalachian Gap heading west toward the Champlain Valley, pass the modest base area of the **Mad River Glen**, a ski area with a large following. Its ubiquitous bumper sticker is "Ski It If You Can," and its naturally contoured trails are challenging and its snowmaking scant. This was the country's first ski area to be cooperatively owned by its skiers and the last to preserve a single chair (vintage 1948) to its summit.

Now the road winds up steep grades, switching back several times as it climbs. At the crest of the gap, parking is available with access to the **Long**

Looping the Gaps

Note: This loop, winding and unpaved in places, is unsuitable for cars with trailers, and the road between Lincoln and Warren is closed in winter.

From the crest of the **Appalachian Gap**, VT 17 spirals down past rocky outcrops and a mountain pond, descending over the course of 9 miles to the Champlain Valley floor. A turn south on VT 116 leads in 2 miles to **Rocky Dale**. Note the pullout for **Bartlett Falls**, a swimming hole with 20-foot cliffs. It's a beautiful spot by a stream with shallow falls dropping into pools. (Swimming shoes are a good idea.) Turn on the **Lincoln Gap Road**, which is unpaved in sections but leads to the little village of Lincoln, with its **Old Hotel**, (802-453-2567) and the **Lincoln General Store** (802-453-2981), described in works by best-selling author and Lincoln resident Chris Bohjalian. Continue to the crest of **Lincoln Gap**, where you'll find parking and trailhead access to the **Long Trail** south to Sunset Ledge and north to the 4,052-foot-high summit of **Mount Abraham** (this is a serious 10-mile round-trip hike). The relatively short, steepest grade of the road is closed in winter; it's 4.7 miles down a narrow, winding road to VT 100, but you can turn off halfway down onto **West Hill Road**, and traverse the mountain to reach the Sugarbush Resort base area.

Trail which, if you follow it south here for a steep 2.6 miles, leads to the top of **Stark Mountain** with panoramic views.

If you don't "Loop the Gaps," turn back from the crest of the Appalachian Gap on VT 17, and in about 4.5 miles turn right on German Flats Road, another 3.5 miles to **Sugarbush North** (formerly Mount Ellen Ski Area). Just past there, pick up the Sugarbush Access Road and turn right to **Sugarbush South** at the base of Lincoln Peak, the center of **Sugarbush Resort** (802-583-6300 or 800-537-8427). This is one of the few major New England ski resorts owned by a locally based partnership, Summit Ventures NE, LLC, headed by primary investor Win Smith. Back in the '90s, a multiresort owner proposed building a "grand resort hotel" here, but the community balked. The present 100-room **Clay Brook** condo hotel is barn red with a silo at its center, and the surrounding base area is human-scaled. The big draw here in summer is the 18-hole golf course, but there are also tennis courts, hiking trails, and a health and rec center. Kids will love the zip line behind Clay Brook, and they'll thrill to jumping on the bungee-assisted trampoline in good weather (call the **Farmhouse Rental Shop**, 802-583-6504, to be sure it's open in the event of rain).

For an exciting but relaxing adventure, take a scenic ride on the **Super Bravo Express Quad Lift** (800-537-8427; open during activity hours,

June 4–Sep. 4, Fri.–Sat. 10 AM–6 PM and Thurs., Sun. 10 AM–4 PM; call for fall season) to the top of the slopes and enjoy unparalleled views across to the Northfield Ridge and up and down the valley. You can hike up or down. It's steep in places, but the lift will take you both ways.

LEAVING THE VALLEY

Whether or not you visit **Sugarbush Resort** itself, the quickest way out of the valley, whether you are traveling north or south, is via VT 100 north to VT 100B (6 miles north of Waitsfield Village). **Moretown General Store** (802-496-6580) is a good fuel stop with pumps outside, and inside there's an exceptional hot/cold deli and tables. Back on the road, VT 100B still follows the Mad River. Just before crossing the Middlesex town line, a large parking lot on a small rise is the tip-off for **Ward's Swimming Hole**, with its small beach suitable for wading and swimming. For those of us with a little more adventure in our souls, rocks across the river tempt swimmers to jump into deeper pools there.

Beyond this spot, the road curves once or twice more and ends at the intersection of VT 100B and US 2 in Middlesex. A left here takes you back to the I-89 Exit 9 interchange on US 2, past a gas station on the right and the **Red Hen Café and Bakery** (802-223-5200), a great breakfast and lunch spot, on your left. The highway interchange to north and south is just beyond this.

Best Places to Sleep

THE PITCHER INN (802-496-6350), 275 Main Street, Warren. Luxurious and unique rooms and suites in the heart of charming Warren Village makes this a real vacation experience. One suite accepts dogs for an extra fee. Relais & Chateaux accommodations. $$$$.

INN AT THE ROUND BARN FARM (802-496-2276), 1661 East Warren Road, Waitsfield. Rooms are beautifully appointed in Colonial mode in this grand old inn. Formerly a working farm, the iconic Round Barn is on spreading grounds that invite visitors to sit a while. Gracious accommodations with excellent attention to detail. $$–$$$.

MAD RIVER INN (802-496-7900), 243 Tremblay Road, just off VT 100, Waitsfield. This lovely Victorian B&B serves up a true Vermont country experience, with antique decor and period accoutrements, feather beds (some with foam toppers), and private baths. Relax in the gracious living room, or enjoy pool, television, or games in the recreation room. Relax out-doors with pastoral views of the Valley. $–$$ nonpeak, $$ peak

CLAY BROOK AT SUGARBUSH RESORT (802-583-6300), 22 Gate House Lane, Warren. For a large hotel experience with luxury accommodations, try this foot-of-the-slopes option. Take part in resort activities during any season, or just stay for the comfort and views. $$$.

Best Places to Eat

PEASANT (802-496-6856), 40 Bridge Street, Waitsfield. Open for dinner Thurs.–Mon. 5:30 PM; reservations suggested. The à la carte menu favors Pan-European comfort food, cassoulet, and nightly pastas. Chris Alberti walked out of his World Trade Center office 20 minutes before the first plane hit on 9/11. His well-earned joie de vivre is palpable in the ambience and good food. $$–$$$.

AMERICAN FLATBREAD'S WAITSFIELD HEARTH (802-496-8856), 46 Lareau Road, Waitsfield. Open Thurs.–Mon. 5–9 PM. American Flatbread is baked on a local-stone hearth and topped with local ingredients. Salads and desserts are also made with as much local sourcing as can be had. The concept was developed by founder George Schenck in the 1980s, when he developed a hearth, itself made from local stone and materials, and baked flatbread made with nutritious local toppings. Developing his business at Lareau Farm in a barn that was a production center during the week and a restaurant on weekends, Schenck created a national brand that is produced and distributed off-site now but continues to attract foodies from around the world. The restaurant and bar in the rustic big red barn at Lareau Farm, where flatbreads are still cooked on a stone hearth, remains a favorite gath-ering spot for locals and visitors for meals and nightlife. $$.

GRACIE'S KITCHEN (802-496-9000), 4752 Main Street, Waitsfield. There's a different selection daily, with meat and vegetarian options, at this ready-to-eat buffet. Also, wraps and desserts to go. Breakfast and lunch served but no menu, just the small buffet. $–$$.

HYDE AWAY RESTAURANT (802-496-2322), 1428 Mill Brook Road, Waits-field. Open for dinner daily, 4–10 PM, this cozy and comfortable tavern and din-ing room serves pub fare and dinner entrées. Also a popular nightspot. $–$$.

LOCALFOLK SMOKEHOUSE (802-496-5623), 9 VT 17, Waitsfield. With its funky and interesting ambience, folks stop in for a bite and a brew here and stay to listen to live music or make it themselves on open-mic nights. The specialty is smoked BBQ. $$.

MIX CUPCAKERIE & KITCHEN (802-496-4944), 5123 Main Street (right beside Mehuron's Market). Gourmet pastry and catering chef Darcy Acker creates cupcakes of all sizes and flavors. Salads, sandwiches, and meals-to-go also available, and call ahead to order your dinner ready to take home when you get there. $$.

VIEW OF MOUNT MANSFIELD FROM BRYCE HILL, MIDWAY BETWEEN CAMBRIDGE AND UNDERHILL

11

MOUNT MANSFIELD LOOP

ESTIMATED LENGTH: 82 miles

ESTIMATED TIME: 1 to 3 days

HIGHLIGHTS: This loop circumnavigates Mount Mansfield, Vermont's tallest mountain. From the resort town of Stowe, **Mountain Road** (VT 108) climbs up to **Stowe Mountain Resort** and through **Smugglers' Notch**, winding down to the village of **Jeffersonville** at the northern base of the mountain, where you quickly understand why this small village in the town of Cambridge is a longtime gathering spot for artists. We drive on into **Cambridge**, circling back along bucolic byways to **Underhill State Park**, with trails up Mansfield's western slopes, on to Richmond with its **Round Church** and past **Little River State Park**, with access to camping, boating, and swimming on the Waterbury Reservoir.

Many visitors understandably get no farther than Stowe. Known as the Ski Capital of the East, the town draws more visitors in summer and fall, when the focus shifts from ski trails to golf courses, mountain bike and equestrian trails, and hiking, cultural events, and family-geared attractions. **Mountain Road**, as this stretch of VT 108 is known, is lined with shops, restaurants, and lodging, but the paralleling **Stowe Recreation Path** winds more gently up through cornfields and meadows. Mount Mansfield's ridgeline is said to resemble the profile of an upturned face; the **Mount Mansfield Toll Road**, built in the 1840s to reach a summit hotel, accesses "the Nose," while the **Gondola Sky Ride** hoists passengers to the Cliff House below "the Chin." The 4,400-foot-high summit peak, accessible from both sites, commands a view west across the Champlain Valley, north and south along the spine of the Green Mountains, and down the beautiful valley and hills to the east.

With its many shops and restaurants, as well as the state's largest concentration and range of lodging options, Stowe is an obvious pivot from which to explore the backcountry described in several of our northern Vermont drives.

E: Stowe is accessible from north and south via I-89 to Exit 10 in
. The exit feeds directly onto VT 100 on the edge of the Waterbury
strict. Coming from the north, turn left at the light at the end of
; from the south, turn right.

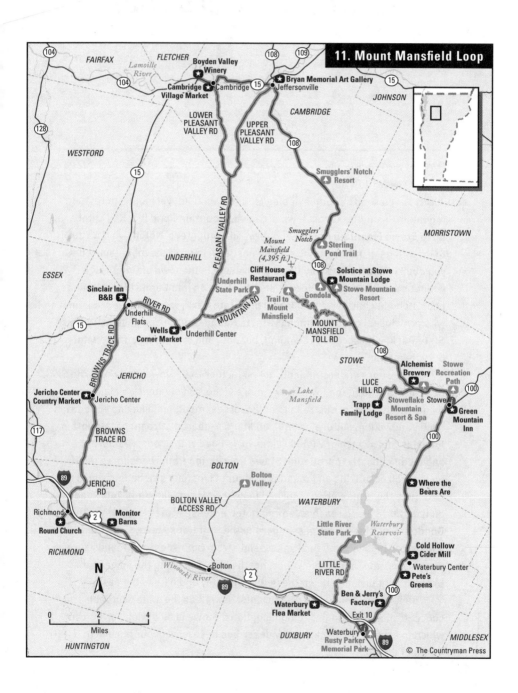

11. Mount Mansfield Loop

ON THE ROAD

The **Ben & Jerry's Factory** (802-882-2047) is just over
VT 100 in Waterbury. Traffic streams in to watch ice cream
to taste perennial favorites; half-hour tours ($) depart ever
outside playground includes a Flavor Graveyard with headstones containing
epitaphs for bygone flavors. Inquire about free movie nights.

This short stretch of VT 100 is studded with major outlets for Vermont
products, including **Lake Champlain Chocolates** and **Cabot Cheese**. That
distinctive structure is **Pete's Greens** (802-241-2400; open daily 10 AM–7 PM),
an outlet for organic produce from Pete's Craftsbury farm, as well as a source
of prepared food and Vermont cheese and meats. A bit farther on, **Sunflower
Natural Foods** (802-244-5353), a purveyor of local fare, natural foods, and
bulk herbs, is known for quality at good prices. **Cold Hollow Cider Mill**
(800-327-7537) is the original traffic stopper along this strip. Apple cider
(free samples) from their own orchards is made here the traditional way, and
the honey is from their hives of orchard-pollinating bees (you can watch the
bees). The cider doughnuts are legendary, and the Apple Core Luncheonette
features fresh-baked breads, hard cider, and local brews.

SCULPTOR AND WOOD CARVER CHARLIE O'BRIEN WORKS ON A PIECE AT WHERE THE BEARS ARE, VT 100 BETWEEN
STOWE AND WATERBURY

etour to Stowe Village

Before turning onto Mountain Road, continue through the blinking light and up Main Street in 200-year-old Stowe Village. The brick, double-porched **Green Mountain Inn** (802-253-7301) here dates to 1833 and, while much expanded, it still evokes a sense of the village's long history as a summer resort. Neighboring **Shaw's General Store** (802-253-4040) was founded in 1895 and has been in the same family for 120 years. It's a favorite of residents and visitors alike, offering outdoor gear, quirky souvenirs, and more. The few compact village streets are lined with vintage storefronts filled with places to shop and eat. The imposing brick Akeley Soldiers Memorial Building houses the **Stowe Theatre Guild** (802-253-3961), which stages live performances. Close by, the **Helen Day Art Center** (802-253-8358) shares a vintage 1861 Greek Revival building with the **Stowe Free Library**, hosting changing art exhibits well worth checking. At the heart of Main Street, the **Stowe Area Association** (802-253-7321; gostowe.com) maintains the area's prime visitor center, open Mon.–Sat. 9 AM–6 PM, Sun. 11 AM–5 PM. Inquire about **Stowe Lantern Tours**, nighttime guided walks with ghostly tales of Stowe's history and hauntings.

Continue on toward Stowe and keep an eye out on your right for a menagerie of life-sized wooden animals arranged across the grass and under the trees as you come down a hill just short of the Stowe line. This is **Where the Bears Are** (802-241-2100), an ever-changing collection of woodland creatures great and small, from life-sized fox, raccoons, and bear cubs to standing grizzlies, wolves, and maybe a 7-foot moose. The whimsical chainsaw sculptures are often created on site and visitors are welcome; there's also a shop.

At the blinking light, turn off VT 100 and up VT 108, better known for the next 18 miles as the **Mountain Road**. It climbs steadily up, looping gently at first and lined most of the way with eateries, shops and pubs, inns and lodges. Behind this road, the 5.5-mile **Stowe Recreation Path** rises even more gently, inviting walkers, joggers, and bikers along a paved path through cornfields, wildflowers, and raspberry patches. The path is accessed from Stowe Village behind the Stowe Community Church on VT 100.

A few miles along the Moutain Road, veer left at the Y on **Luce Hill Road** (it's beyond **PieCasso Pizzeria & Lounge**) and follow it up to **Trapp Family Lodge** (802-253-8511, or 800-826-7000), still owned by the family depicted in *The Sound of Music*. In winter its extensive cross-country ski trail network, ranging in elevation from 1,100 to 3,000 feet, attracts skiers from throughout the East, and in warmer weather more than 50 miles of trails attract mountain bikers of all skill levels. Bike rentals, guided tours, and lessons are available. In addition to the lodge dining room and lounge, the **Austrian Tea**

and Tap Room (open Mon.–Wed. 8 AM–2 PM; Thurs.–Sun. 8 AM–7 PM) serves light fare and mouth-watering pastries along with house brews and views of the valley and Worcester mountain range.

Stowe's must-stop for beer lovers is back down off Mountain Road. **The Alchemist** (802-882-8165) on Cottage Road (turn right just beyond Luce Hill Road), famed for its much-prized Heddy Topper Beer, is open for tours and tastings Tues.–Sat. 11 AM–7 PM.

Mountain Road earns its name as the grade steepens. Keep an eye out for the **Mount Mansfield Toll Road** (802-253-3500; $$ per car) near the Toll House Conference Center on the left. A ski trail in winter but open to cars in summer and fall, subject to weather, it winds 4.5 miles up from a visitor center all the way to a summit station just below "the Nose." (Good brakes are required, and you may have to stop on the way down to rest them.) At the top, a mile-long, moderate hike along the ridge leads to Vermont's highest peak, with views sweeping across the valley and mountain ranges to the east and over Lake Champlain to the Adirondacks on the west.

Back on Mountain Road, the **Stowe Mountain Resort** complex of lodges and town houses soon towers up on the right (802-253-3000 or 888-253-4849). Here restaurants, shops, and lodging cluster around a pedestrian plaza at the base of **Spruce Peak**. Activities range from golf to a zip line (riding from 10 feet off the ground to 180 feet up!) or a climb through the tree-

THE ROADWAY THROUGH SMUGGLERS' NOTCH WINDS AROUND BOULDERS THAT PREVENT LARGE VEHICLES AND BUSES FROM PASSING THROUGH

THE CREST OF SMUGGLERS' NOTCH PASS OFFERS MARKED PATHS AND STEEP CLIMBING THROUGH THE FOREST

tops. Weather permitting, the resort's eight-passenger **Gondola Sky Ride** (mid-June to mid-Oct., daily 9:30 AM–4 PM; $$ per person) departs from the base area across the road, gliding up to the **Cliff House Restaurant** near the top of the mountain. The hike from there to the summit is short but steep.

Mountain Road continues winding and climbing. The forest closes in and the grade grows even steeper as it enters **Smugglers' Notch**. This high pass closes during snow season for the several miles between Stowe Mountain Resort in Stowe and Smugglers' Notch Resort in Jeffersonville. Trucks and buses are not permitted any time of year, and wide vehicles may have trouble navigating the narrow passages. The paved way becomes almost single-car narrow near the crest, and massive boulders with colorful names like Elephant Head, The Hunter, and Natural Refrigerator line the shoulder. Within the notch itself, the forest opens up somewhat and cars can pull off to enjoy the wooded area and steep hiking trails. From here the Long Trail North leads in an easy mile-plus to Sterling Pond, a beautiful spot at 3,000 feet that is stocked with fish.

Beyond its crest, VT 108 winds down into the village of **Jeffersonville** at a less precipitous grade than the climb from Stowe, but only slightly so. Passengers can gaze up to the left at a soaring rock face above the notch, where climbers challenge the heights with ropes and spunk. But, given the steep, winding downward grade with the forest falling away to the left, drivers are advised to keep their eyes on the road.

Cambridge Village and Boynton Farm and Winery

From Church Street (VT 108) in Jeffersonville, drive west to the wide intersection with VT 15. A left turn leads over the **Lamoille River** toward Cambridge. Continue about 2 miles, following the winding river until the road crosses back over the Lamoille and through Cambridge Village, past the **Cambridge Village Market** (802-644-2272), another quintessential Vermont country store. Brightly painted, striped **Angelina's Pizza** (802-644-2011) captures your eye near the end of the village.

At the junction of VT 15 with VT 104, the **Boyden Valley Winery** (802-644-8151) is worth a stop. The 800-acre Boyden farm has been operated by the family for more than 100 years, first as a small dairy farm, now primarily raising beef cattle; growing organic corn, hay, and soy; and maintaining a vineyard. Restaurant menus throughout Vermont now note their use of Boyden Farm beef, and the farm's wine tasting room (open daily 10 AM–6 PM) is one of the first in the state, featuring wines that use their own grapes along with other fruits to create wines, ciders, and spirits. The barn is also a popular wedding venue. Our drive backtracks to the Cambridge Village Market on the corner of South Main Street and Lower Pleasant Valley Road. Turn right onto Lower Pleasant Valley Road and follow it past bucolic vistas as it winds along the path of the **Seymour River**, eventually joining the aptly named Upper Pleasant Valley Road and head to Underhill on Pleasant Valley Road.

PLEASANT VALLEY, VIEWED FROM BRYCE HILL SOUTH OF CAMBRIDGE HILL

Just as it seems the forested twists and turns will never end, an entire condominium town rises like an apparition beyond the trees. This is **Smugglers' Notch Resort** (800-419-4615), a family-geared destination clustered at the bottom of ski trails on 3,640-foot-high Madonna Mountain. In summer "Smuggs" features reasonably priced condo lodging with children's programs, hiking, biking, and swimming.

In a few miles VT 108 levels out in the village of Jeffersonville and you quickly realize that you are in a very different place than Stowe. **Hanley's General Store** (802-644-8881), supplying much more than the basics, marks a tricky junction of VT 108 and South VT 108; stay straight down South VT 108, Main Street. Stop in at **158 Main** (802-644-8100; open for breakfast, lunch, and dinner except Mon., closes Sun. at 2 PM) if just to breathe in the aroma of baking bread. Established in the 1950s as the Windridge Inn, this landmark eatery shares a large, high-ceilinged storefront with a bakery, and its large, locally sourced menu blends traditional Vermont comfort food with innovative options. There's also pizza upstairs.

For more than a century Jeffersonville has been a gathering spot for plein air landscape artists attracted by the luminous light and views of Mount Mansfield towering above gently rolling farm country. A little farther along Main Street, the **Bryan Memorial Art Gallery** (802-644-5100; open daily July–Columbus Day, 11 AM–5 PM, closed Christmas through the month of January) showcases traditional and contemporary Vermont landscape paintings and hosts workshops with well-known Vermont landscape artists. The nearby **Visions of Vermont Galleries** (802-644-8183; open Tues.–Sun., 11 AM–5 PM) also showcases Vermont artists.

The name "Smugglers' Notch" evokes the use of this pass as a smuggling route from Canada since the early nineteenth century, and in the 1920s, it was a well-used bootleggers' run. **Smugglers' Notch Distillery** (802-309-3077; 276 VT 108; open daily 11 AM–5 PM) claims to offer a half-dozen kinds of spirits worth smuggling, even if you don't have to.

To finish the drive from Jeffersonville, backtrack on Main Street to the intersection at Church Street (VT 108) and turn right for a scant block, then left onto **Upper Pleasant Valley Road** beside the **Village Tavern** (802-644-6765), which serves dependable, moderately priced fare and brew.

Drive south toward **Underhill**, following Upper Pleasant Valley Road about 10 miles into **Underhill Center**. Halfway there, the road descends a hill and joins Lower Pleasant Valley Road to become simply Pleasant Valley Road. This is a beautifully scenic but uneventful drive. Relax and enjoy it.

About 10 miles from Jeffersonville you'll see another **Mountain Road**, this one on your left, leading up to **Underhill State Park** (888-409-7579), a campground on the western slope of Mount Mansfield. The 2½-mile park access road turns to dirt, but steep grades are paved. There's a manned ranger station inside the gate and bathrooms nearby, but there are no showers for the limited number of campsites and lean-to sites, and nothing suitable for trailers or RVs. The park is popular for day hikes; several trails lead to the summit ridge of Mount Mansfield, where plants grow that are more commonly found on Arctic tundra. The seeds were left behind by glaciers in the Ice Age.

Pleasant Valley Road leads to Underhill Center; bear right in front of St. Thomas Catholic Church onto River Road and pass **Wells Corner Market** (802-899-2418), another small, classic country store with gas pumps out front, deli and provisions inside. Follow River Road for about 3 miles to VT 15. During leaf season, the hills on either side of River Road, replete with sugar maples on most of their slopes, are breathtaking.

At the junction with VT 15, turn left and head west for a quarter mile or so to Brown's Trace Road (a left) and on to **Jericho Center**, where the locally acclaimed **Jericho Center Country Store** (802-899-3313) is sited across from the green. There you'll find produce and fare from farms just down the road and around Vermont, as well as creemees, hot and cold sandwiches, soups, and Vermont brews (patrons are invited to fill a growler to carry home).

Drive around the green in Jericho Center and stay on Brown's Trace Road, which becomes Jericho Road, about 5 miles to the small town of **Richmond**, where the road intersects with **US 2** at a traffic light. Turn left here to return to **Waterbury**.

FARMS AND FIELDS IN THE SHADOW OF CAMEL'S HUMP MOUNTAIN, FROM US 2, RICHMOND

Leaving Richmond to head south on US 2, two historical barns, the **Monitor Barns**, are on your left across from wide-open farmland that affords an impressive view down the valley toward **Camel's Hump Mountain**. Follow US 2 to Waterbury.

On the way you'll pass the access road to **Bolton Valley**, a ski area with condo-based lodging and a sports center, pool, and events throughout the summer and fall. Five miles farther, Little River Road leads into **Little River State Park** (802-244-7103) and the **Waterbury Reservoir**, created in the mid-1930s by the Civilian Conservation Corps and the U.S. Army Corps of

The Round Church

THE ROUND CHURCH IN RICHMOND IS MAINTAINED AND MANNED FOR VISITORS BY THE RICHMOND HISTORICAL SOCIETY

At the traffic light in Richmond, marking the junction of Jericho Road and US 2, drive straight through onto Bridge Street. This is Richmond's tiny business district, including a small market on the right just before you cross over the railroad tracks. Beyond the tracks, on the edge of the grassy Volunteers Green Park, the **One Radish Eatery** (802-434-7770; closed Monday) is a popular stop for breakfast or lunch.

To reach Richmond's **Round Church and Meetinghouse** (802-434-2556; www.oldroundchurch.com), drive over the bridge that spans the **Winooski River** and you'll see the church in front of you. It's a 16-sided, two-story, white clapboard structure built between 1812 and 1814 as a meetinghouse and place of worship. The impressive building sits on a grassy parcel beside the road, with green lawns spreading out under an occasional tree. Drive onto

THE INTERIOR OF THE ROUND CHURCH INCLUDES BOXED-OFF PEWS

tiny **Round Church Road** to your left to park alongside the building and stop in to speak with a volunteer inside.

In 1812 it cost 65 Richmond residents a total of $3,000 to finance construction of the Round Church by "buying" box pews. The donors included two Methodists, five Baptists, six Christians, 23 Universalists, and 29 Congregationalists. Religious services and town meetings were regularly held there for decades. During the 1880s the building passed into the hands of the town and was used as a meetinghouse for nearly another 100 years until structural concerns put an end to that function. The structure is now a National Historic Landmark and maintained by the Richmond Historical Society, whose volunteers keep the building open for visitors as regularly as possible.

Engineers to protect Waterbury from floodwaters during extreme weather. This is Vermont's largest hand-built earthen dam.

The park offers boat access and rentals, swim beaches, and play areas. Hiking trails crisscross the area, and camping is available at 81 tent sites, 20 lean-tos, and five cabins (with access to hot showers). Also 27 remote and primitive campsites are strung along the shore of the reservoir and accessible only by boat.

If you're driving this route on a weekend from May through September, the **Waterbury Flea Market** (802-272-3158; 802-882-1919) will likely be in session. A large field on your right is the flea market's standing location on Saturday and Sunday in spring, summer, and early fall. Look for the tents and tables of vendors and stop by to see what's for sale.

Driving on US 2 beyond Little River Road, the junction of US 2 and VT 100 in Waterbury is marked by the **Crossroads Beverage & Deli** (802-244-5062), which has gas pumps outside and is also good for creemees and deli and grill selections.

Drive a little farther around the traffic circle and under the railroad trestle, past the well-restored and maintained **Old Stagecoach Inn** (802-244-5056). Stay on VT 100 as you come into the business district, driving up the hill and through the light to the town green, **Rusty Parker Memorial Park**. At the traffic light, turn left and park along the road, or continue to the foot of the park, where the **Green Mountain Coffee Café and Visitor Center** (877-879-2326) is housed in the renovated train station (train service still stops here). Stop for coffee and view the Green Mountain coffee exhibits. A well-stocked travel information center is also on site. The park, named for Craig S. "Rusty" Parker, a prominent local radio personality and longtime town selectman, is a small open space with a spreading lawn, gazebo, tree-shaded picnic area, and war memorial. The Waterbury Rotary Club maintains the grounds, a venue for town events, markets, and concerts. If you're in the area on Wednesday, Thursday, or Friday, you'll see **Roy's College Dogs**, a hot dog cart that's a longtime fixture at the top of the park. Folks know the proprietor's schedule, and they make a point of stopping for a chili dog, meat or veggie burger, Italian sausage or kielbasa snack, and a chat.

THE LARGEST HAND-BUILT EARTHEN DAM IN VERMONT HOLDS BACK THE WATERS OF WATERBURY RESERVOIR NEAR LITTLE RIVER STATE PARK

GREEN MOUNTAIN COFFEE CAFE AND VISITOR CENTER, WATERBURY

Best Places to Sleep

OLD STAGECOACH INN (802-244-5056; oldstagecoach.com), 18 North Main Street, Waterbury. The inn dates in part from 1826, but the triple-tiered porch, oak woodwork, ornate fireplaces, and stained glass were added by a millionaire from Ohio in the 1880s. Sited within walking distance of Waterbury's shops and restaurants, it offers a wide range of tastefully furnished accommodations, from guest rooms to efficiency suites. Shared spaces include a library and a bar, and a full breakfast is included in the rates. $–$$.

BEST WESTERN WATERBURY-STOWE (802-244-7822), 45 Blush Hill Road, Waterbury. A chain hotel but with local flair, a popular restaurant, and close to everything in Waterbury while convenient to Stowe. Easy access to VT 100. $$–$$$.

TRAPP FAMILY LODGE (800-826-7000), 700 Trapp Hill Road, Stowe. Offering luxurious chalet accommodations with luxurious Austrian ambiance, the inn was founded by the family made famous in *The Sound of Music*. Built high on the hillside on 2,500 acres, views of the surrounding landscape are breathtaking. Excellent food, impeccable service. $$$–$$$$.

THE GREEN MOUNTAIN INN (802-253-7301; greenmountaininn.com), 18 Main Street, Stowe. The area's most historic inn is on the National Register of Historic Places and has marked the middle of Stowe Village since the mid-nineteenth century. The 104 guest rooms in several buildings range from old-fashioned rooms to luxurious suites, apartments, and two- and three-bedroom town houses in additions that ramble out the rear of the original inn. Guests enjoy use of the heated pool and athletic club, and afternoon tea is served in the living room hung with original art. The Whip Bar and Grill (named for its collection of horse and buggy whips) offers pub and comfort food. $$–$$$.

STOWEFLAKE MOUNTAIN RESORT AND SPA (800-253-2232; stoweflake.com), 1746 Mountain Road. Accommodations range from the original motel-style rooms and bright, comfortable inn rooms to luxury suites and town houses of various sizes. The spa features a heated, jet-filled pond with a 15-foot waterfall replicating Stowe's Bingham Falls. Facilities include tennis and badminton courts plus a nine-hole golf course. Charlie B's Pub serves three meals a day. $$–$$$.

SINCLAIR INN BED & BREAKFAST (802-899-2234), 389 VT 15, Jericho. Magnificent Victorian inn with rounded peaked and domed towers, wide verandas and screened porches, and bays and gables galore. The Victorian-era "Painted Lady" sits on well-manicured grounds on VT 15 in the Underhill Flats section of Jericho. It offers six well-appointed rooms with period decor upstairs and down. Rooms have their own bathrooms with tub or shower, and a wheelchair-accessible room is on the ground floor. $$.

SMUGGLERS' NOTCH RESORT (802-644-8851; smuggs.com), 4323 VT 108 South, Smugglers' Notch. A reasonably priced, family-geared resort with 540 condominiums accommodating a total of 3,200 guests. A ski resort in winter, it maintains well-organized family programs for upward of 400 kids (ages 3–17) in warm seasons. The 1,000-acre property features heated pools, water slides, and rides. Activities include a zip line canopy tour, tennis, mini golf, canoeing and kayaking, llama treks, hikes, and fishing. Amenities include the Hearthside Deli for lunch and treats, and the Hearth & Candle for dinner. $$.

Best Places to Eat

GREEN GODDESS CAFÉ (802-253-5255), 618 South Main Street, Stowe. Just south of Stowe Village, enjoy a hot breakfast made with local ingredients, create your own sandwich, or dive into a giant bowl of salad! $–$$.

HARRISON'S RESTAURANT AND BAR (802-253-7773), 25 Main Street, Stowe. Open nightly from 4:30 PM. There's summer seating outside, and year-round the attractive downstairs pub with its stone hearth is a winner. The menu is standard—burgers and crabcakes, seafood and steaks—but everything is done with flair and service is fast and friendly. Singles feel comfortable dining at the bar. $$.

TRAPP FAMILY DINING ROOM (800-826-7000, x5733), 700 Trapp Hill. Dinner reservations are requested and the ambiance is formal, with white-clothed tables in this window-walled room where the service and food are outstanding. The menu is wide, but it would be a shame to pass up Austrian specialties like Wiener Schnitzel vom Schwein with Trapp family-raised pork loin, or desserts like apple strudel, Sachertorte, or Linzertorte. Breakfast is also served in this sunny room and it's a delight. Most dinner entrées $$$.

SOLSTICE AT STOWE MOUNTAIN LODGE (802-253-3560), 7412 Mountain Road. Open for breakfast, lunch, and dinner. The soaring space has an open kitchen and views of Spruce Peak Mountain. The menu changes with the season. Dinner reservations suggested. The Hour Glass Café offers more casual dining. Dinner $$–$$$.

158 MAIN STREET (802-644-5556; pizza 802-644-5550), 158 Main Street, Jeffersonville. Open Tues.–Sat. for breakfast, lunch, and dinner, Sun. 8 AM–2 PM. A landmark restaurant, it shares space with a bakery. Current owner Jack Foley calls his fare "innovative traditionalism." The dinner menu ranges from a Vermont turkey dinner, meat loaf, and Worcestershire shepherd's pie to Thai lettuce wraps and Filet Mignon au Bleu. Everything that can be is organic and locally sourced. Jeffersonville Pizza Depot is upstairs. $–$$.

ARVAD'S GRILL (802-244-8973), 3 South Main Street, Waterbury. A popular local place to find good food, good drink, and good company. Enjoy local fare inside or on the porch and watch Waterbury go by. $$.

PROHIBITION PIG (802-244-4120), 23 South Main Street, Waterbury. The bustling restaurant sits in the heart of Waterbury's business district. Local fare from numerous farms, food purveyors, and brewers is available daily. Smoked meats are a specialty, and their own brewery is 'round back. No reservations needed for dinner. $–$$.

AN OLD MILL AND WATER WHEEL AT SHELBURNE MUSEUM

12

BURLINGTON SOUTH

ESTIMATED LENGTH: The main loop is 49 miles. The side trip to Huntington is 21.5
miles, one way; 43 miles roundtrip. Side trip into Burlington city is 4 miles
one way, 8 miles roundtrip to start of trek.

ESTIMATED TIME: 2 to 4 days

HIGHLIGHTS: In many states, the diminutive city of Burlington rising up a gentle
hillside on the shore of Lake Champlain would be a byway in itself. But in
the rural Vermont constellation, the compact but busy Queen City serves as
a jumping-off point for our exploration of towns and hamlets to the south or
ranging eastward into forested terrain toward the Green Mountain spine of
Vermont. In Shelburne, south of Burlington, the family-friendly **Shelburne
Museum** is the major destination, with multiple historic buildings set in
landscaped lawns. Exhibit buildings showcase classic and modern art and
design, along with extensive Americana that includes the side-paddlewheel
steamboat, *Ticonderoga*, sitting out in a grassy meadow on site where
visitors can climb aboard and explore. At neighboring **Shelburne Farms**, a
splendid visitor-friendly family estate, paths lead through woods and meadows to Lake Champlain, the mansion welcomes dining and overnight guests,
and the impressive barns invite families to visit. The neighboring town of
Charlotte is home to **Mount Philo State Park**, offering some of the most visu-
ally striking views of Lake Champlain and New York State's Adirondacks. In
Ferrisburgh, visit the **Rokeby Museum**, the eighteenth-century home of the
Robinsons, a Quaker family dedicated to fostering the cause of abolition and
supporting the Underground Railroad in the years before the Emancipation
Proclamation. Driving over narrow roads past farm and forest toward the
Green Mountains in the east, discover the **Green Mountain Audubon Center** in the hills of **Huntington** close beside the Greens. The center's hiking
trails wind through woods and meadows and connect near a picturesque
pond, with more trails crossing over from the neighboring **Birds of Vermont**

Museum, where a collection of carved birds is the centerpiece of a destination dedicated to educational programs about Vermont's avian populations.

GETTING THERE: Take I-89 at Exit 14W to visit downtown Burlington, or use Exit 13 to access the US 7 corridor for towns and attractions south of the city.

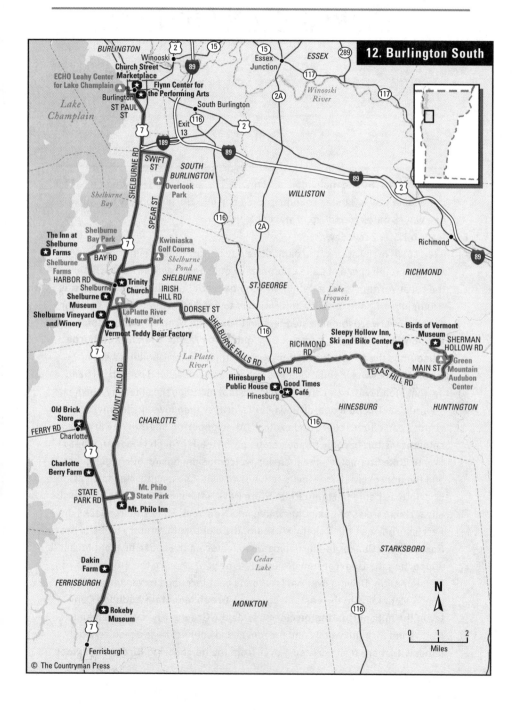

ON THE ROAD

The trip begins just off I-89 Exit 13 at a traffic light at the junction with US 7. This is a dense commercial part of the drive, known as **Shelburne Road**, and we'll drive around rather than through this section to regain the US 7 corridor farther south.

At the traffic light turn left, but keep to the far left lane heading south and turn left onto **Swift Street** at the next light (a Denny's Restaurant is on the corner). Follow Swift up the hill to **Spear Street**, where you'll turn right at the traffic light and head past contemporary houses with lake views. In about a mile you'll come to **Overlook Park** on your right.

At the start of your explorations, it's worth a moment to stop at this scenic overlook to contemplate a view and the Adirondacks rising layer upon layer on the far side of the lake. There's ample parking, a stone wall to sit on, and a picnic table. An informational marker provides background and geological information about the lake and its environs.

AT OVERLOOK PARK THE VISTA IS ACROSS ROLLING PLAINS TO LAKE CHAMPLAIN AND BEYOND TO NEW YORK'S ADIRONDACK MOUNTAINS

Burlington, Vermont's Queen City

To reach the waterfront and **Battery** and **Cherry Streets**, take **Shelburne Road** (US 7) north. Stay left after the small island in the road onto **St. Paul Street**, left on **Maple Street**, and right onto Battery Street. Proceed through lights to hotels on Battery and its intersection with Cherry Street.

While you're in Burlington, walk to the waterfront. From Battery Street, cross over and visit **ECHO Leahy Center for Lake Champlain** (802-864-1848), grab lunch at the boathouse, then walk the promenade or bike the bike path.

Another option is to turn uphill to cobbled **Church Street Marketplace**, an outdoor walking mall where shops, galleries, and restaurants line the streets, tables are out for alfresco dining, and the **Flynn Center for the Performing Arts** (802-652-4500) and **City Hall Park** are within easy reach. It's a walker's city; parking can be tough, but there's lots to do.

Continue on Spear Street over the Shelburne line where it cuts through the middle of the course at **Kwiniaska Golf Club** (802-985-3672). Members and nonmembers alike are welcome to reserve tee times at this semiprivate course with views from the fairways and the clubhouse eastward, where forests and rolling hills stretch toward Vermont's **Camel's Hump Mountain.**

KWINIASKA GOLF CLUB OFFERS VIEWS OF CAMEL'S HUMP MOUNTAIN

SHELBURNE MUSEUM AND SHELBURNE FARMS

At the stop sign just past Kwiniaska Golf Club, turn right onto Webster Road and follow about a mile, taking a sharp turn to the right and reaching US 7 at a traffic light. Turn left here to drive into Shelburne Village.

On your way into town, the **Trinity Episcopal Church** (802-985-2269) will be on your left, its sanctuary windows easily visible. These are some of the Tiffany windows that grace the church, courtesy of the Webb family, whose members also founded **Shelburne Museum** and **Shelburne Farms** and whose descendants remain active in the life of the town to this day. The central elements of the church's chapel were completed in 1886 after the congregation lost its previous building to fire. A year later, William Seward Webb and Lila Vanderbilt Webb came to town. Heirs to well-known railroad fortunes, the Webbs built a 400-acre estate on the shore of Lake Champlain. As members of the Trinity congregation, they soon began contributing to the church, financing new construction, enlarging sanctuary space, and sheathing the building in stone. They hired Louis Comfort Tiffany to create several of the stained-glass windows depicting biblical scenes for the sanctuary.

Beyond the traffic light in Shelburne Village, the **Shelburne Museum** (802-985-3346; open May 1–Dec. 30, daily 10 AM–5 PM; Jan. 2–April 30, Wed.–Sun., 10 AM–5 PM; $) stretches along the highway; an entrance is at the far side of the village. The extensive grounds include 39 buildings of varying vintage, many of them older New England structures here as architectural illustrations of a particular era, now housing historic exhibits and folk art for the museum. The collections themselves are primarily the work of Electra Havermeyer Webb, daughter-in-law of William Seward and Lila Vanderbilt Webb. Electra was interested in artifacts and folk art that reflected American culture. She collected such varied items as cigar store Indians, quilts, pottery, dolls, toys, weather vanes, and duck decoys. In 1947 she founded the Shelburne Museum to preserve and display a collection of horse-drawn carriages, eventually creating the foundation of today's museum and transporting historic buildings to the site to house her "collection of collections." The side-paddlewheel steamboat *Ticonderoga* sits landlocked on the lawn, where visitors can climb aboard to view interiors, decks, halls, crew quarters, and more. The vessel is a luxurious, early twentieth-century excursion boat that plied the waters of the lake until its retirement in 1953. The museum chronicles America's history, but programs and exhibits reflect ongoing progress in design, engineering, and the arts as well. New items are added regularly, and educational programs are integral to the museum's mission. The white-columned art gallery holds an eclectic range of exhibits, and the museum boasts fine art by masters like Rembrandt, Degas, and Manet. It has also mounted exhibits of circus posters, fiber arts and quilts, and rock 'n' roll photography. The grounds of the museum are landscaped with flower gardens, an apple orchard, and a wealth of lilac bushes that draw visitors from throughout New England each spring.

At the traffic light in the heart of the village, turn right on Harbor Road and head 1½ miles out to the Webbs' lakeshore estate, now open to the public as **Shelburne Farms** (802-985-8686). Bear right and stay on the narrow, quiet, and tree-lined road to reach the stone pillars and parking lot for Shelburne Farms. Cars are not permitted onto the estate except those with reservations at the inn, so park here and walk the trails or catch a tractor-pulled wagon to visit the barnyards and animals. A kiosk for tickets and information is beside the lot. This is a working farm and education center tasked with developing and teaching sustainable farming and land management.

While in residence in the last century, the Webbs hired architect Frederick Law Olmsted, the historic master of landscape artistry, to design the grounds of their estate. Now 400 acres of rolling meadows, forest, and pastureland touch along the shore of Lake Champlain. The estate has passed into the hands of a nonprofit organization whose mission is to use the model farm for environmental education. Its imposing mansion and barns with round turrets and expansive rooflines are breathtaking as they rise out of the wooded landscape. Many are still in use and most are open to the public. Visitors to the farms can hike miles of easy trails past meadows, pastures, grazing animals, and along the lakeshore, or to and from the intricately designed barns and the mansion. Gracious dining is available in the nineteenth-century halls of the mansion, now **The Inn at Shelburne Farms**, offering lodging and a restaurant (802-985-8686, main; 802-985-8498,

Shelburne Bay Park

The waters of Shelburne Bay offer boat access to Lake Champlain. The **Shelburne Bay Park** features a nature trail on one side of the street and boat launch and beach area on the other, just across Harbor Road and a short way up **Bay Road** from the entrance to Shelburne Farms. Visitors can approach from US 7 onto Bay Road north of Shelburne Village, but that route includes driving under a low railroad trestle. The town road department says it's deemed a two-way passage through the underpass but it could be tight for trucks and wide vehicles (overhead clearance is 11 feet). The park has a mile-long bike, hike, and recreation path used year-round. It's dog friendly; leashes required. Fishing is popular along the LaPlatte River across the road from the boat launch, or in the waters of the bay. The boat ramp is managed by the Vermont Department of Fish and Wildlife, and rules apply for putting clean boats into the lake.

inn reservations; restaurant open for breakfast 7:30–11:30 AM, dinner 5:30–9:30 PM, Sunday brunch 8 AM–1 PM; $$–$$$).

If you remain on Spear Street past Kwiniaska Golf Course, you will circumvent Shelburne village. The trees are closer to the road now. You start to see older farmhouses and pastures, terrain more like what you would expect in Vermont. Turn right on **Irish Hill Road** and head down the hill. The road changes to **Falls Road** after you cross a small bridge and enter a neighborhood of neat little houses in the southern reaches of Shelburne. Pass an access to the **LaPlatte River Nature Park** on your right next to the bridge, where walking trails follow the LaPlatte River for a short way; the parking spots here are wheelchair accessible only. Another entrance to the trail is nearby on Falls Road behind the Shelburne Supermarket in **Shelburne Shopping Park** (to get there, continue to the intersection of **Falls Road** and **Mount Philo Road**, where Falls Road turns right and passes the entrance to Shelburne Shopping Park on the way to Shelburne Village).

At the corner of Falls Road and **Mount Philo Road**, turn left onto Mount Philo Road and follow 5 miles to **Mount Philo State Park** in Charlotte. This is a quintessential Vermont drive, the road rolling and winding past working farms, with the landscape of Vermont's agricultural engine spread out to the east and Camel's Hump and Mount Mansfield on the far horizon.

Mount Philo is Vermont's oldest state park, sitting on 237 acres of forest and hillside. The original park was developed on 150 acres donated in 1927 by owner Frances Humphreys, with more acreage added later. At the top of the mile-long access road, the terrain opens up for some of the most striking and expansive views of the Champlain Valley and the Adirondacks from the 968-foot summit. The Civilian Conservation Corps developed roads, lodges, and the campground on the original parcel in the 1930s. A small lodge sits under shade trees at the summit, where open, grassy stretches invite picnics. The lodge can be rented for events, weddings, or celebrations. A restroom is close by. Seven tent sites and three lean-tos are available. For hikers, a ¾-mile trail leads from the entrance on Mount Philo Road to the top. Hikers see deer and the occasional moose during the climb and watch bird migrations and predatory raptors on the hunt. Cars can drive up, trailers are discouraged, and buses and RVs park at the bottom.

State Park Road intersects Mount Philo Road at the entrance to the state park. Take State Park Road a short stint to US 7 in Charlotte. Turn left and follow south into Ferrisburgh. **Dakin Farm** (800-993-2546), is on your right, a great "What Vermont Tastes Like" shop. It features Vermont food products of their own making and more from providers around the state. Continue down US 7 to **Rokeby Museum** (802-877-3406) on your left. The eighteenth-century farmstead and separate new museum facility are located on the site of the Robinson family farm, originally a prosperous sheep farm that was brought into service for the Underground Railroad by the Robin-

THE ENTRANCE TO MOUNT PHILO STATE PARK

son family, Quakers who made it their life's work to support abolition before the Emancipation Proclamation. Hiking trails crisscross the farmland, and old farm equipment is on display in outbuildings and the farmhouse, where original items owned by the Robinsons decorate the home and are on display. The Underground Railroad Education Center is new. *Free & Safe: The Underground Railroad in Vermont* details the work of abolitionists pre–Civil War with photographs, letters, and books. Reproductions of events detail the history of the Robinson family, the people they helped to freedom, and the life of abolitionists in the run-up to Lincoln's proclamation. Open mid-May to late-October, daily 10 AM–5 PM. See the house by guided tour only, Fri.–Mon. 11 AM–2 PM. Free admission Tues. 1–5 PM. $

Return back up US 7 north. The road opens up here and there for views of the lake, farms, and small shops that dot the level roadside, but it's mostly uneventful. Watch for long views to the east and the mountains when the town of Ferrisburgh is here and then gone (don't blink or you'll miss it). Now drive through the town of Charlotte. The **Berry Farm** (802-425-3652) on your left sells fresh fruit, jams from their own berries, and baked goods. This is also a place to pick your own strawberries, raspberries, black raspberries, blackberries, blueberries, and pumpkins, depending on the season.

Proceeding north a mile and a half, you will come to the traffic light at Ferry Road. Turn left here to drive up to the crossroad beside the **Old Brick Store** (802-425-2421) in Charlotte's tiny village center. This is a good place to stop for road food, browse the local fare, or get a deli lunch and eat in. (Straight over the hill and all the way at the end of Ferry Road, there's a landing that feeds passengers onto the small **Lake Champlain Ferries's Charlotte**, **VT–Essex**, **NY crossing** [802-864-9804] for scenic passage across the lake to Essex, New York. Fares here are paid by cash or local check only; no credit cards are accepted at this crossing. Larger ferries with more amenities regularly leave from the Burlington waterfront or farther north at Grand Isle.)

Back at US 7 headed north, continue into Shelburne. The **Vermont Teddy Bear Factory** (800-988-8277) is on your right just before you come into town. It's a popular tourist stop to see how teddy bears are made and perhaps create one of your own (tours about 30 minutes; 9 AM–6 PM daily in summer, alternate hours in fall and winter).

Stop at the **Shelburne Vineyard and Winery** (802-985-8222, open daily all year; call for various winter and summer hours). Stay for a taste or a look at winemaking. Past the winery, come to the traffic light and Shelburne

THE OLD BRICK STORE IN CHARLOTTE OFFERS TAKE-OUT OR A DELI LUNCH ON SITE

Green Mountain Audubon Center and Vermont Bird Museum

For a half-hour, cross-country trek through farm country and forested roads in the Green Mountain foothills, start at the light on US 7/Shelburne Road as you enter Shelburne Village with the museum on your left. Turn right down the hill onto Marsett Road, which becomes Falls Road, then Irish Hill Road. Continue over Spear Street to Dorset Street and turn right. These roads roll past small farms, open fields, and occasional woodsy patches on the way toward the spine of the Greens. Stay on Dorset Street half a mile and veer left on Shelburne-Hinesburg Road, which becomes Shelburne Falls Road, drive straight for almost 3 miles, then straight through the traffic light onto CVU Road. Continue straight to meet Richmond Road 0.6 mile up the hill. Go straight on Richmond Road for about a mile and a half to Texas Hill Road. Take a right onto Texas Hill Road (it is dirt, so may be difficult traveling in mud season), and follow just over 2 miles to Main Road in Huntington (it is paved). Turn left onto Main Road and follow 0.7 mile to Sherman Hollow Road.

The **Green Mountain Audubon Center** (802-434-3068; 255 Sherman Hollow Road; open Mon.–Fri. 9 AM–4 PM) invites visitors to explore the forests in the foothills and on the slopes of the Green Mountain range. The 250-acre site conducts nature study programs and provides 5 miles of hiking trails through hardwood forest, hemlock swamps, and along the Huntington River. Trails are open to the public year-round. Call for event schedules and program details.

The **Birds of Vermont Museum** (802-434-2167; 900 Sherman Hollow Road; open May–Oct., daily 10 AM–4 PM; other times of the year by appointment; $ for nonmembers) maintains 40 acres on the upper side of Sherman Hollow Road in nature trails, feed lines, and educational sites. Another 60 acres on the lower side of the road alongside the museum are being developed. A pond is upland of the museum, with trails around the pond meeting those coming up from the Audubon Center down the road. On the museum grounds are pollinator gardens and a walk-in treehouse. The focal point of the museum is a collection of lifelike wooden carvings of birds used to teach visitors about Vermont's avian community. The seeds of the collection were carved by Bob Spear, author of *Birds of Vermont*. Spear helped to found and was director of the Green Mountain Audubon Nature Center and was its director for seven years. On retirement he turned a family barn into a museum for his own carvings, collecting additional items and growing the collection to more than 500 species. The museum conducts educational programs and demonstrations. Call for details.

Village. Shelburne Museum is on your left. Drive straight through, stopping at **Harrington's of Vermont** store and café (802-434-4444), famed for their smoked meats and specialty foods. Browse the shop or pick up fresh deli fare to eat in or take out.

Follow US 7 through Shelburne Village, up the commercial/retail corridor of US 7 and past innumerable shops, restaurants, car dealerships, and motels. From here, drive into Burlington or watch for signs to I-189 back to I-89 North and South on your right.

Best Places to Sleep

There are many national inns and motels along US 7.

HILTON BURLINGTON (802-658-6500), 60 Battery Street, Burlington. Facing the waterfront with magnificent views of Lake Champlain and the Adirondacks, the hotel has gracious Hilton service throughout. The location is convenient to Church Street, attractions, theaters, and nightlife. $$$–$$$$.

COURTYARD BURLINGTON HARBOR (802-864-4700), 25 Cherry Street, Burlington. On the corner of Cherry and Battery streets, with views of Lake Champlain and the Adirondacks are spectacular. It's a short walk across to the waterfront, or turn up Cherry Street to Church Street for shopping, restaurants, theater, and more. $$–$$$$.

HOTEL VERMONT (802-651-0080), 41 Cherry Street, Burlington. Quintessentially Vermont, with five floors and 125 rooms convenient to everything Burlington and beyond, this hotel has a local feel. It's near the waterfront, within walking distance of amenities, and is a popular gathering spot for local events and dinner out. Parking has plug-ins for electric cars. $$$–$$$$.

HEART OF THE VILLAGE INN (802-985-9060), 5347 Shelburne Road, Shelburne. This stately Queen Anne–style inn has nine guest rooms furnished in antiques but with contemporary comforts, private bathrooms, fridges, USB charging outlets, and more. It's convenient to the museum, restaurants, the incomparable Flying Pig Bookstore, and the Shelburne Country Store. $$–$$$$.

INN AT SHELBURNE FARMS (802-985-8498), 1611 Harbor Road, Shelburne. This 100-room mansion is sited on a bluff overlooking Lake Champlain. The Webb family, who built the estate, continues to be involved in the nonprofit that maintains it. The family's Edwardian-era furnishings still predominate. Guests can enjoy the richly paneled game room and play the piano in the library. Guest rooms vary in size and elegance, from the luxurious master bedroom to affordable but inviting former servant rooms under the eaves with some of the best views of Lake Champlain and the Adirondacks. $$–$$$$.

MOUNT PHILO INN (802-425-3335), 27 Inn Road, Charlotte. Four crisp and attractive suites are situated beside Mount Philo State Park, with easy travel to the Middlebury area, Burlington, or small towns and attractions in the countryside. All suites include a kitchen for cook-your-own breakfasts, with provisions provided. Nick House, a spacious vacation home, is also available; call for rates. Suites $$–$$$.

ELLIOTT HOUSE (802-985-2727), 5779 Dorset Street, Shelburne. Lovely rooms in this Greek Revival converted manse all have private bathrooms. There are also landscaped gardens and a pool. $.

SLEEPY HOLLOW INN, SKI AND BIKE CENTER (802-434-2283), 427 Ski Lodge Drive, Huntington. This rustic old inn and grounds were renovated in 2000 by new owners. All rooms have private baths. Cross-country skiing is available on the grounds, as well as biking and hiking in warm weather. The views are spectacular. $–$$.

Best Places to Eat

PAULINE'S CAFÉ AND RESTAURANT (802-862-1081), 1834 Shelburne Road (US 7), South Burlington. Gourmet cuisine in warm surroundings, this restaurant-bar is popular for its eclectic, locally sourced menu and creative cuisine. Lunch: Mon.–Fri. 11:30 AM–2 PM; Dinner: Sun.–Thurs. 5–9 PM, Fri.–Sat. 4:30–9:30 PM; Brunch: Sat.–Sun. 10:30 AM–2 PM. Reservations suggested for evening. Dinner entrées $$–$$$. Wednesday is $10 burger night.

HARRINGTON'S OF VERMONT (802-985-2000), 5597 Shelburne Road, Shelburne. Across from Shelburne Museum, Harrington's sells gourmet and specialty foods and their signature meats. Grab a soup-and-sandwich lunch and bakery dessert to eat in the small but comfy café corner. Open daily until 5 PM. $$.

BARKEATERS RESTAURANT (802-985-2830), 97 Falls Road, Shelburne. This comfortable, rustic restaurant and bar is convenient to US 7, but off the beaten path on Falls Road. The varied menu features local foods. Open for lunch and dinner Tues.–Sun. $$.

RUSTIC ROOTS (802-985-9511), 195 Falls Road, Shelburne. Primarily a breakfast and lunch destination, there's also an early seating dinner on Fri. and Sat. only, 6–7:30 PM, call for reservations. Food is local and expertly prepared. Meals are $ for breakfast and lunch; dinner $–$$.

INN AT SHELBURNE FARMS (802-985-8498), 1611 Harbor Road, Shelburne. Open to the public May–late Oct. for breakfast and dinner by reservation. The dining room is elegant, the view splendid, and the menu features produce and cheese from the farm itself. $$–$$$.

OLD BRICK STORE (802-425-2421), 290 Ferry Road, Charlotte. Park beside the store or on the road and stop in to browse. A good place for road food, or pick up a deli lunch and eat in. $.

HINESBURGH PUBLIC HOUSE (802-482-5500), 10516 VT 116, Hinesburg. This popular spot offers genteel dining on locally sourced farm-to-table fare. The small but eclectic menu caters to vegan, vegetarian, and gluten-free diners. Open Mon.–Thurs. 4–9 PM, Fri.–Sat. 3–9 PM, Sunday 4–8 PM. $$–$$$.

GOOD TIMES CAFÉ (802-482-4444), 10805 VT 116, Hinesburg. Soup, salad, hot sandwiches, and gourmet pizza with a Cajun twist are just some of the offerings on this interesting menu. Great for lunch or dinner, Tues.–Sun. 12–8:30 PM; take-out orders until 9 PM. $.

13

CHAMPLAIN ISLANDS

ESTIMATED LENGTH: 48 miles

ESTIMATED TIME: 1 to 2 days

HIGHLIGHTS: Stunning lake views framed by classic summer camps. Apple orchards bursting with ripe, red fruit. Fossils and the first European settlement in Vermont. These are the things that shape the character of the Champlain Islands. Mosey along US 2, the main artery that slices through the islands, with stops at antiques shops, farm stands, art galleries, and museums. Then scoot down the backroads to discover what other surprises await.

GETTING THERE: Take I-89 to Exit 17, and then follow US 2 about 5 miles to Sand Bar State Park, where this route begins. Alternatively, you can start at the northern end, crossing over the Rouses Point Bridge into Alburgh from Rouses Point, New York, to pick up US 2, or west on US 7 from Swanton to VT 78, then proceed through East Alburgh to US 2.

ON THE ROAD

There's an air of timeless tranquility about the Champlain Islands, an archipelago composed of three main islands—South Hero, North Hero, and Isle La Motte—that hopscotch across Lake Champlain in northwestern Vermont. The Alburgh Peninsula that stretches down from Quebec is part of this grouping, as are a handful of offshore islands accessible only by boat.

The chain of islands, connected by bridges and causeways, is a mere 30 miles long and only 4 miles across at the widest point. Yet they're chockablock with places to visit and things to do, especially in the warmer months. If planning a visit, keep in mind that many places are only open seasonally,

LEFT: TURTLE CROSSING SIGN IN SOUTH HERO

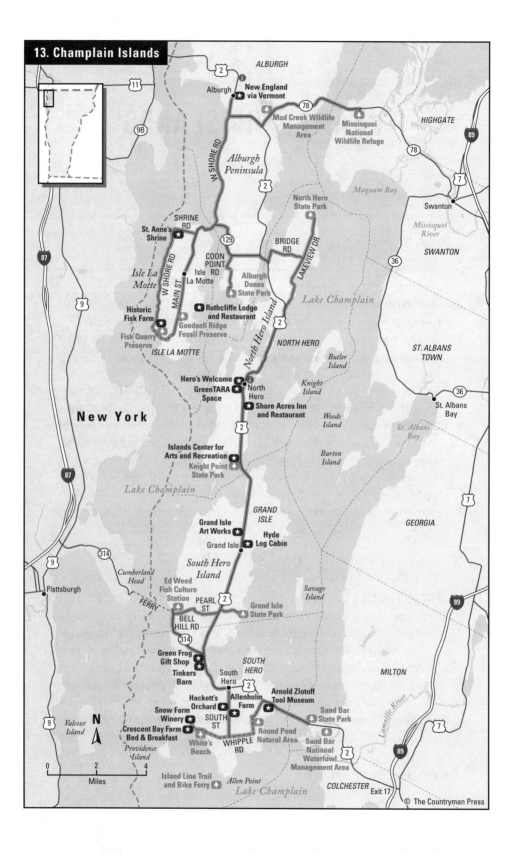

ALBURGH

New England
via Vermont

Alburgh

Mud Creek Wildlife
Management
Area

Missisquoi
National
Wildlife Refuge

HIGHGATE

*Alburgh
Peninsula*

Maquam Bay

Swanton

SHRINE
RD

St. Anne's
Shrine

*Missisquoi
River*

COON
POINT
RD

BRIDGE
RD

SWANTON

*Isle La
Motte*

Isle
La Motte

Alburgh
Dunes
State Park

Lake Champlain

Ruthcliffe Lodge
and Restaurant

LAKEVIEW DR

North Hero
State Park

Historic
Fisk Farm

Goodsell Ridge
Fossil Preserve

Fisk Quarry
Preserve

ISLE LA MOTTE

*Butler
Island*

ST. ALBANS
TOWN

New York

Hero's Welcome
GreenTARA
Space

North
Hero

Shore Acres Inn
and Restaurant

NORTH HERO

*Knight
Island*

St. Albans
Bay

*Woods
Island*

*St. Albans
Bay*

Lake Champlain

Islands Center for
Arts and Recreation

Knight Point
State Park

*Burton
Island*

GRAND
ISLE

GEORGIA

Grand Isle
Art Works

Hyde
Log Cabin

Grand Isle

*South Hero
Island*

*Cumberland
Head*

Ed Weed
Fish Culture
Station

PEARL
ST

Plattsburgh

FERRY

BELL
HILL RD

Grand Isle
State Park

*Savage
Island*

MILTON

Green Frog
Gift Shop

Tinkers
Barn

*SOUTH
HERO*

South
Hero

Arnold Zlotoff
Tool Museum

Hackett's
Orchard

Allenholm
Farm

Snow Farm
Winery

SOUTH
ST

Sand Bar
State Park

Crescent Bay Farm
Bed & Breakfast

White's
Beach

WHIPPLE
RD

Round Pond
Natural Area

Sand Bar
National
Waterfowl
Management
Area

*Valcour
Island*

N

*Providence
Island*

Island Line Trail
and Bike Ferry

Allen Point

Lake Champlain

COLCHESTER

Exit 17

0   2   4
Miles

© The Countryman Press

generally from Memorial Day through fall foliage season, with some closing by Labor Day.

As you approach the entrance to **Sand Bar State Park** (802-893-2825), check for ospreys nesting in the trees and on platforms in the marshy areas, part of the 1,560-acre **Sand Bar National Waterfowl Management Area**. Established in 1920, this is excellent habitat for muskrats, beavers, and several species of reptiles and amphibians, as well as a pit stop for migratory birds that follow the Atlantic Flyway in spring and fall. The state park, popular with families for its long sand beach, shallow water, and extensive picnic area, began as a Civilian Conservation Corps project. Under this public work relief program, a cadre of young men developed the park in the early 1930s, including the construction of a stone bathhouse that is still in use today. Although unofficially considered part of the Champlain Islands, the park's address is the town of Milton. A swim or picnic here is the perfect way to kick off your exploration of the islands. The park also has paddleboards and other watercraft for rent.

As you leave the park, turn right to cross the **Sandbar Causeway** to South Hero, which is both the name of the island and the chain's southernmost town. According to legend, South Hero and North Hero were named for two Vermont Revolutionary War heroes, brothers Ethan and Ira Allen. South

YOUNG SWIMMERS AT SAND BAR STATE PARK

Hero has a second community on its northern end, Grand Isle, which was known as Middle Hero until 1810.

A pull-off area about halfway across provides a good vantage point to take in the view, although this won't be your only opportunity to enjoy spectacular lake vistas. The Lake Champlain Inland Sea and the Green Mountains are off to your right, Malletts Bay and the Adirondacks in the distance on your left. As you travel through the islands, you are never far from water, a good reason to keep your binoculars handy. In addition to boats and abundant waterfowl, you just might spot Champ, Lake Champlain's elusive Loch Ness Monster.

FIRST OF TWO HEROES

At the causeway's terminus, after the sign for South Hero, is **Apple Island Resort** (802-372-3800), a lively RV campground with seasonal sites, a marina, golf course, and the **Apple Island General Store** (802-372-3733). Stop here to pick up lunch at the deli—the sandwiches are big enough to share—or coffee and a homemade pastry. The store also carries basic grocery items and supplies for anglers and campers.

The **Arnold Zlotoff Tool Museum**, located on the grounds of the resort, showcases one man's passion for understanding how early carpenters, joiners, coopers, and other craftspeople created and used tools. Zlotoff, a New York City industrial arts teacher, assembled this impressive collection of more than 3,000 tools, dating from the colonial period to the early twentieth century, over a 40-year period. The museum, housed in an old barn, is open Saturdays from Memorial Day to Columbus Day.

Before you reach South Hero Village, take a left on Landon Road. About a half mile down this road is the **Landon Community Trail**, developed by the **South Hero Land Trust** (802-372-3786) in collaboration with the Lake Champlain Land Trust and the original owners of the Landon Farm. This kid-friendly loop trail meanders through the woods, which burst with wildflowers in the spring.

For a longer walk, turn left just past the community trail to the **Round Pond Natural Area** on East Shore Road. The area is 0.2 mile after the turn. Look for the orange gate that marks the entrance and park along the road. The trails wind through meadows and forests to the lake where, depending on water level, you may be able to walk along the shoreline. East Shore Road continues past the **Good Hope Farm** (802-372-4087), which offers a therapeutic riding program, to Whipple Road, which becomes West Shore Drive after crossing South Street.

White's Beach is a nice place to take a break, with its grills, volleyball net, and public access to the lake. Just north of this area you will see hundreds of vibrantly colored birdhouses attached to trees that ring a swampy area where fiberglass dinosaurs roam. The project was started by Jay Purvis more than two decades ago as a means of attracting tree swallows to control mosquitoes on his property. Birdhouses are for sale at his house on the corner of West Shore and Lakeview. Stop by to read the sign that tells the story behind the birdhouses.

Continuing along this road with its expansive lake views, you'll soon reach **Snow Farm Winery** (802-372-9463). In addition to its tasting room, where you can sample wines with names such as Snow White and Naked Mermaid, the winery displays the work of various artists. It hosts a popular weekly summer concert series, held rain or shine. Concertgoers may bring their own picnic dinner or purchase food, wine, and Vermont craft beer from on-site vendors. When the weather turns colder, **Snow Farm** offers its Winter Wine Down Music Series, which combines good food with local music.

While you could follow West Shore Road north to Grand Isle, if you do you will miss out on all that South Hero has to offer travelers along US 2. So backtrack to South Street and watch out for bicyclists, as this road is the most direct route from the **Local Motion's Island Line Bike Ferry** land-

South Hero's Stone Castles

Among South Hero's quirky attractions are its miniature stone castles. Watch for these when touring the south end of South Hero, especially along West Shore Road. All of these castles are on private land, so no trespassing allowed, although some are visible from the road, including one at **Crescent Bay Farm Bed & Breakfast** (see *Best Places to Sleep*) located farther along this road.

These elaborately detailed castles of local fieldstone, some with glazed windows, towers with conical roofs, and drawbridges, were created by Harry Barber from the 1920s to the '60s. Originally, some had electricity or running water in the moat. He also built water fountains, planters, and other garden structures.

So who was this craftsman and how did he end up in the islands?

The story goes that after being injured in a work accident and receiving a substantial settlement from the government, Barber set off from his native Switzerland, intending to hop a freighter to South America. Instead he ended up in the islands, where a local lass offered the hungry wanderer some food. She helped him find work on a farm on nearby Providence Island. Their relationship grew, and he later married her and settled on South Hero. The castles he lovingly built are modeled after Swiss castles and pay homage to his homeland.

COLORFUL BIRDHOUSES AND DINOSAURS IN SOUTH HERO

ing (802-861-2700) to US 2. The ferry, which operates from mid-June to mid-October, transports cyclists across the 200-foot "cut" where the Rutland Railroad swing bridge once operated to enable trains to cross the lake from Colchester to South Hero. The gentle terrain of the islands and low-traffic backroads make this the perfect destination for biking. With the ferry, it is possible to bike to South Hero from Burlington, Vermont's largest city, on the 14-mile **Island Rail Trail**.

A IS FOR APPLES

When you first turn on South Street, if you head right you'll reach the ferry landing at Allen Point. A left toward the village takes you past two pick-your-own apple orchards, a fun family outing in the fall when the apples ripen. The first, **Allenholm Farm** (802-372-5566), has a long agricultural history, as owner and seventh-generation farmer Ray Allen's family first settled here in 1870.

The shop's shelves overflow with Vermont products, including maple syrup, cheese, applesauce, dried apples, jellies, and sweet apple cider. Outside at the petting paddock, meet Willie and Sassafrass, the donkeys, or visit with the goats, horses, and other animals. Be sure to bring a pocket full of quarters for the feed dispensers.

You can rent a bike here, although the big attraction is picking apples. On weekends you can take a tractor-driven wagon ride to the orchard.

From Memorial Day through Columbus Day, the **Accidental Farmer Café**, an outdoor eatery set against a backdrop of apple orchards, operates at Allenholm. Food is locally sourced, including the grass-fed beef from Grand Isle's **Canamak Farms** (802-372-8258) that's on the daily menu and featured on Burger Night every Friday. Top off your meal with a maple creemee or buy a fresh-baked pie made with farm-grown fruit to enjoy later.

At nearby **Hackett's Orchard** (802-372-4848) you can pick up a six-pack of cider doughnuts—plain or cinnamon sugar, your choice—and a gallon of cold, fresh-pressed apple cider. Apple picking usually begins after Labor Day and includes a wagon ride to and from the orchard. Its small farm shop carries apple products, honey, cookbooks, and other items. Both Hackett's and Allenholm also sell berries in season.

At the end of South Street near the intersection with US 2, the **Island Craft Shop** (802-372-3945), an artisan cooperative, has the work of several local artists for sale. **Seb's Snack Bar** on the corner offers ice cream, creemees, and the usual summer fast food fare. The attached shop specializes in Vermont gift items. Or stop by **Wally's Place Bagels and Deli** (802-372-4666), a short jaunt to the right on US 2, for one of their breakfast or lunch sandwiches on bagels or homemade artisan bread.

Head north again on US 2 through the village to **Tinkers Barn** (802-372-4754), which has been in business for more than 40 years. Hats of every size, shape, and color; aprons; glassware; buttons; books; knickknacks; fishing gear; and other vintage items fill the two floors and front porch of the classic red New England barn.

DETOUR

Past Keeler Bay, look for signs for VT 314 (Ferry Road). Just after the turn, you'll see the **Green Frog Gifts & Clothing Shop** (802-372-5031), which has been in business at this location for 40 years. You can't miss it, as Croker, a 400-pound, 6-foot-tall green frog, sits outside. Stop in to say hello to owners Stan and Nancy Wood and to purchase Vermont clothing and products.

Before the ferry dock at Gordon's Landing, turn right onto Fish Hatchery Road to explore the interactive exhibits and view several species of freshwater fish in the aquariums and hatchery at the **Ed Weed Fish Culture Station** (802-372-3171). Admission is free and tours are self-guided.

A one-way trip on the **Grand Isle-Cumberland Head Ferry** to Plattsburgh, New York, takes 14 minutes. This year-round car ferry operates daily around the clock. The fares are cash-only, but there's an ATM on the dock.

Continue past the ferry dock north on West Shore Road to Bell Hill Road, then right on Pearl Street to return to US 2. Take a left toward **Grand Isle State Park** (802-372-4300), one of the most visited Vermont state parks.

One of Grand Isle's main attractions is **Hyde Log Cabin** (802-372-5440), purportedly the oldest original log cabin in New England and possibly the United States. Pioneer settler and Revolutionary War veteran Jedediah Hyde Jr. built the one-room cabin in 1783, and today visitors can experience how the early settlers in this area lived. Adjacent to the cabin, which was moved to this location in 1946, is the **Block Schoolhouse**, originally known as District #4 Schoolhouse. The 1814 building, also once used as a church and community gathering place, was constructed with foot-thick, square-hewn logs with a lime and sand mortar.

Just past the school and cabin, **Grand Isle Art Works** (802-378-4591), a gallery and café serving lunch and brunch in a late eighteenth-century farmhouse, features the work of more than 70 local and regional artisans. Continuing on, you will come to the drawbridge, the only one in the state, which connects the two Hero Islands and brings you to **Knight Point State Park** (802-372-8389). In summer, **Islands Center for Arts and Recreation** (802-372-4174) schedules weekly concerts and other special events at this park, including performances of the world-famous Herrmann's Royal Lipizzan Stallions.

HYDE LOG CABIN, GRAND ISLE

North Hero's newest art gallery, **GreenTARA Space** (802-355-2150), combines art exhibits with a coffee bar in a refurbished nineteenth-century church. Studio space is available for working artists and researchers, and for the public there are occasional bird walks and talks, workshops, and music programs. **Hero's Welcome** (802-372-4161), an island institution, stocks everything you didn't know you needed. One-of-a-kind kitchen items and sundries share shelf space with books, maps and charts, clothing, children's games, and specialty foods. Stop at the deli to order one of their custom sandwiches, many named for Vermont historical figures, to eat at the dockside picnic area across the street. The white clapboard building has a long history as a general store. It was built around 1900 by John Tudhope and was run by generations of his family for the next nine decades.

As you drive north, veer off US 2 to the right on Lakeview Drive and continue straight to **North Hero State Park** (802-372-8727). It's no longer staffed, and no fee is charged to visit this day-use only park. The park road winds through wooded areas to a shale beach on Maquam Bay where you can swim or picnic. Don't enter the roped-off beach area, as this is restricted to protect several species of turtles that nest here, including the threatened spiny softshell turtle. Return to US 2 by retracing your route or via a shortcut on Bridge Road that will bring you to the bridge to the Alburgh Peninsula.

After crossing the bridge, turn onto VT 129 at **God's Little Brown Church** and take a left on Coon Point Road. When you get to the Y, stay left for **Alburgh Dunes State Park** (802-796-4170). In addition to having one of the longest beaches on Lake Champlain, this park is noteworthy for its glacier-created sand dunes, large black spruce bog, and two rare post-glacial era plant species: the beach pea and Champlain beach grass. After enjoying a dip in the cool lake waters, pack up your beach chair and cooler and head back to VT 129 (turn left to stay on Coon Point Road). Take a left when you hit the main route and follow this to Isle La Motte, a left across the causeway.

WHERE HISTORY WAS MADE

You could say that the island is a page out of the history books, for several significant events happened on this 16.7-square-mile piece of land. A good place to start exploring is at **St. Anne's Shrine** (802-928-3362), a 13-acre spiritual site with an open-sided chapel for daily Mass and private devotion, as well as grottoes and the Stations of the Cross. The visitor center has a bookstore, gift shop, and history room where you can learn about the shrine's heritage and view artifacts and information about the **Chazy Fossil Reef**. To get there, turn right onto Shrine Road, go about a mile, then turn left onto St. Anne's Road. This spot has historical significance, as it's believed that explorer Samuel de Champlain first set foot here in 1609. The granite statue of Champlain and his Native American guide, sculpted at Montreal's Expo 67 in the Vermont Pavilion, commemorates the event.

This is also the site of Vermont's oldest European settlement and the first Mass celebrated in the area. Captain Pierre La Motte, for whom the island is named, built Fort St. Anne here in 1666 for defense against the native tribes. Before the Rouses Point Bridge was built, the Chazy Landing Ferry linked New York and Vermont. Will Sweet began this ferry service here in 1905, the first gas-powered ferry on the lake, and operated it until 1937.

Go left as you leave the shrine onto West Shore Road, which travels along the lake with views of New York State. **Historic Fisk Farm** (802-928-3364) is the setting for free summer Sunday afternoon concerts that owner Linda Fitch bills as

ST. ANNE'S SHRINE, ISLE LA MOTTE

tea, art, and music served in the garden and barn. A selection of cakes and beverages is available for purchase during the concerts, with rotating art exhibits in a historic barn. Two lodgings may be rented on a weekly basis, including a late eighteenth-century stone cottage. In 1901 Vice President Theodore Roosevelt was in town to speak at the Vermont Fish and Game League meeting. While at the farm as an invited guest of Lt. Gov. Nelson Fisk, word came that President William McKinley had been shot.

Just down the road is **Fisk Quarry Preserve** (802-862-4150), where you can search for gastropods, cephalopods, and other marine fossils in the rocks. The property was designated as a National Natural Landmark in 2009.

Continuing your drive, at the first intersection stay left on Main Street to **Hall Home Place** (802-928-3091). This family-run operation produces ice cider, hard cider, and apple wine. Stop in for a tasting or to have lunch at the seasonal café in the renovated carriage barn that's attached to the main stone house, which was built in 1828 from locally quarried stone. Another example of local architecture with island-quarried stones is the **Isle La**

Motte Historical Society (802-928-3077), open July and August only, on the corner of Main Street and Quarry Road. The museum includes three buildings, among them an 1840 schoolhouse with exhibits on quarrying and local history, and a schoolroom circa the late 1800s.

The floors in the **Vermont Statehouse** in Montpelier have tiles of black marble quarried on this island, many containing fossils. Other local marble made its way to New York City, where it was used for the Brooklyn Bridge and Radio City Music Hall.

Quarry Road will lead you to the 81-acre **Ira and Thomas LaBombard Goodsell Ridge Fossil Preserve**, the oldest fossilized coral reef in the world. Stop by the visitor center to learn about the history and geology of the reef before following the Walk Through Time trail. Descriptive panels along the meadows and cedar forests map out a timeline of the earth's evolution. Search for fossils in the outcroppings of the 480-million-year-old reef. Get back on Main Street and continue north until you reach VT 129. Cross the causeway and go left on West Shore Road straight into Alburgh. The north-ernmost town of the Champlain Islands, it was home to the first intercon-

ISLE LA MOTTE HISTORICAL SOCIETY

INTERCONTINENTAL BALLISTIC MISSILE SITE IN ALBURGH

tinental ballistic missile site east of the Mississippi River, built in the early 1960s by the U.S. Air Force.

Don't miss the **New England via Vermont** store (802-796-3665) on Milk Street, just off North Main. Although primarily a gift shop specializing in Vermont products and souvenirs, its back rooms are a treasure trove of local and Vermont history. The Room of Curiosities displays rocks and minerals,

DETOUR

The **Missisquoi National Wildlife Refuge** (802-868-4781) in Swanton has a number of trails that wind through wetlands, marshes, and upland forests, making this an ideal destination for hikers, photographers, and birders. Access to the refuge is free. To get here, take US 2 south from Alburgh to VT 78. You'll pass by **Mud Creek Wildlife Management Area**, another excellent birding spot. Turn left on Tabor Road for 0.25 mile to reach the headquarters, where you can pick up a trail map and bird checklist.

Follow the Old Railroad Passage Trail to Maquam Bay, a 3-mile round-trip. It passes through Maquam Bog, where pitch pine, the threatened Virginia chain fern, and other rare plant species live. The Stephen J. Young Marsh Trail is a 1.25-mile loop around a wetland with observation platforms to observe water birds. Boaters can launch from Louie's Landing or, seasonally, from Mac's Bend. If you continue heading east on VT 78, you will end up in the town of Swanton.

fossilized teeth, driftwood art, and a miniature sugarhouse. The impressive Civil War Museum contains memorabilia, artifacts, ephemera, and photos depicting life as a soldier and on the home front during this era, with many items from owner Margaret Theoret's own family.

Best Places to Sleep

CRESCENT BAY FARM BED & BREAKFAST (802-324-5563), 153 West Shore Road, South Hero. Open May–Oct., off-season by prior arrangement only. This farmhouse B&B, a working farm with livestock and a maple sugaring operation, has four comfortable guest rooms decorated in country style, three with en suite bathrooms. Ask to stay in the Winery Room, which has views of Mount Mansfield, Vermont's highest peak, and the vineyard at **Snow Farm Winery**, also owned by innkeepers Dave and Julie Lane. Guests have access to a private beach. A full breakfast is included in the rate. $$.

SHORE ACRES INN AND RESTAURANT (802-372-8722), 237 Shore Acres Drive, North Hero. Open Apr.–early Dec. This family-run inn has accommodated guests since 1951. Each of its 23 rooms overlooks Lake Champlain and is furnished with beautiful Vermont-made furniture and art by Vermont and New Hampshire artists. Guests are spoiled for choice when it comes to activities, which include tennis, kayaking, and lawn games. There's also a private beach and nine-hole practice golf course. A complimentary continental breakfast is provided in the off-season. The Lake Champlain Room, open to the public, serves dinner. (See *Best Places to Eat*.) $$–$$$.

RUTHCLIFFE LODGE AND RESTAURANT (802-928-3200), 1002 Quarry Road, Isle La Motte. "Secluded" best describes this island hideaway, named for innkeeper Mark Infante's mother, Ruth, and now run by Mark and his wife, Kathy. It's been in the family since 1957 and has six lake-view rooms, each with a private bath and Vermont-marble veranda. The rooms have hand-stenciled walls, wicker chairs, and other homey touches. A full breakfast is included. Guests may dine at the restaurant, which features Italian American cuisine. Kayaks, canoes, and bicycles are available to rent. $$.

Best Places to Eat

COOK SISTERS CAFÉ AND CATERING (802-372-0101), 308 US 2, South Hero. Open Mon.–Sat.; call ahead for hours. Brunch is served on Saturday. This intimate 18-seat restaurant, named for chef-owner Christine Mack's mother and aunts, earns rave reviews from its customers for its service and reasonably priced food, which caters to down-home tastes. Grilled chicken sandwiches and turkey burgers are on the menu along with a beet and white bean burger. Gluten-free options are available upon request. $.

BLUE PADDLE BISTRO (802-372-4814), 316 US 2, South Hero. Open Tues.–Sun. 5–9 PM (although hours may vary by season). The artsy decor of this well-established restaurant in the village center pairs nicely with its inventive cuisine, with each dish artfully presented. The menu offers a diverse selection of entrées for meat and seafood lovers, but options for vegetarians are limited. Chef Phoebe Bright, co-owner with Mandy Hotchkiss, taps into what's available locally for the daily specials. The bistro also offers burgers and other lighter "bar fare," along with a number of signature cocktails, seasonal craft beers, and an extensive wine list. $$–$$$.

SHORE ACRES INN AND RESTAURANT (802-372-8722), 237 Shore Acres Drive, North Hero. Open Apr.–Dec., hours and days vary by season. Dinner here comes with a spectacular view of the lake and mountains. Consider arriving early to enjoy a drink on the lawn before you are seated in the Lake Champlain Room. The varied menu includes such exquisite fare as maple bourbon–brined pork tenderloin and the Shore Acres Signature Apple Island Chicken. Chef Dan Rainville often incorporates produce and meats from local farms in his menu. For smaller appetites, the restaurant offers bistro plates. Reservations are recommended, especially in summer and fall foliage season. $$–$$$.

14

NORTHWEST CORNER

ESTIMATED LENGTH: 95 miles

ESTIMATED TIME: 2 to 3 days

HIGHLIGHTS: The scenery along much of this route is so bucolic that you may feel as if you've wandered into a picture postcard. It's a working landscape with barns, grazing herds (mostly Holsteins), endless meadows, and, of course, quaint covered bridges. This is Vermont farm country. But it's also where some major historical events took place, including the northernmost Civil War engagement and the birth of a U.S. president. The region has a burgeoning art scene, with an increasing number of galleries and an artists' cooperative in St. Albans, where this route begins, and an outdoor sculpture park in Enosburg Falls. A rail trail cuts through the area, providing an alternate way to experience the region.

GETTING THERE: From I-89 take Exit 19. If arriving from New York State via the Champlain Islands, follow US 2 to VT 78 into Swanton, then south on either US 7 or I-89 to St. Albans.

ON THE ROAD

To call St. Albans up-and-coming does it an injustice. It has arrived. In recent years it has revitalized its downtown, attracting new restaurants, shops, and the **14th Star Brewing Company** (802-528-5988), a veteran-owned craft brewery. But it's not one to shrug off its past. In fact, the **St. Albans Museum** (802-527-7933), the perfect place to get acquainted with "Rail City," is among the best local historical society museums in the state. Located on the top end of Taylor Park in the heart of downtown, it provides an excellent introduc-

LEFT: DOWNTOWN ST. ALBANS

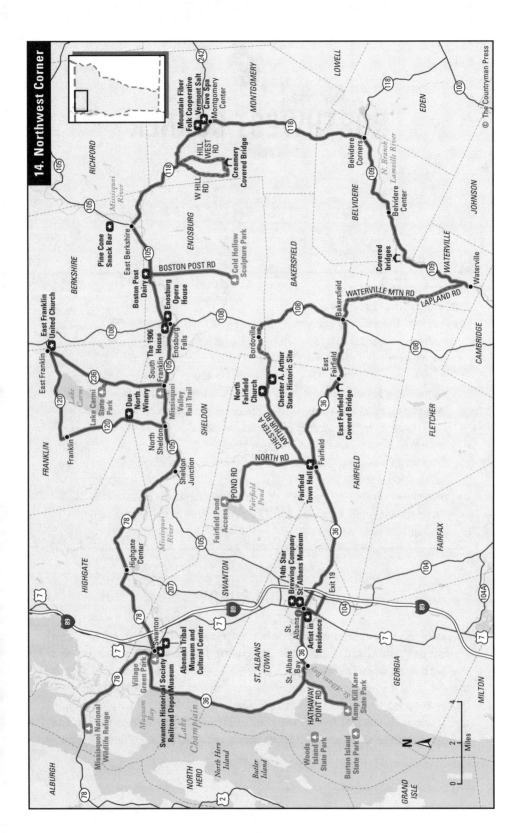

ALBURGH

RICHFORD

LOWELL

EDEN

100

118

Mountain Fiber
Folk Cooperative ★
Vermont Salt
Cave Spa ★
Montgomery
Center

242

MONTGOMERY

105

Missisquoi River

W HILL
HILL WEST
RD RD
Creamery
Covered Bridge

118

Belvidere
Corners

109

N. Branch
Lamoille River

105

Pine Cone
Snack Bar ★

East Berkshire

118

BERKSHIRE

105

East Berkshire

BOSTON POST RD

Cold Hollow
Sculpture Park

ENOSBURG

BAKERSFIELD

BELVIDERE

Belvidere
Center

JOHNSON

East Franklin
United Church ★

East Franklin

Boston Post
Dairy ★

Enosburg
Opera House ★

Covered
bridges

WATERVILLE

Waterville

109

BOSTON POST RD

108

108

WATERVILLE MTN RD

LAPLAND RD

109

South The 1906
Franklin House ★

Enosburg
Falls

Bakersfield

108

120

Lake
Carmi

105

108

CAMBRIDGE

FRANKLIN

Lake Carmi ◄
State Park

Due ★
North
Winery

236

120

Missisquoi
Valley
Rail Trail

SHELDON

North
Sheldon

Sheldon
Junction

North
Fairfield
Church ★

Bordoville

Chester A.
Arthur State
Historic Site ★

East
Fairfield

East Fairfield
Covered Bridge

36

FLETCHER

Franklin

105

POND RD

NORTH RD

CHESTER A. ARTHUR RD

Fairfield

FAIRFIELD

78

Highgate
Center

Missisquoi
River

Fairfield Pond
Access ◄

Fairfield
Pond

Fairfield
Town Hall ★

36

HIGHGATE

105

FAIRFAX

104

207

SWANTON

14th Star
Brewing Company ★
St. Albans Museum ★

36

89

89

Exit 19

104A

78

7

89

Swanton

Abenaki Tribal
Museum and
Cultural Center ★

St.
Albans

Artist in
Residence ★

104

7

7

Village
Green Park

Swanton Historical Society
Railroad Depot Museum ★

ST. ALBANS
TOWN

St. Albans
Bay

36

GEORGIA

MILTON

78

Missisquoi National
Wildlife Refuge

Maquam
Bay

Lake Champlain

St. Albans Bay

HATHAWAY POINT RD

Woods ◄
Island
State Park

Kamp Kill Kare
State Park

Burton Island ◄
State Park

NORTH
HERO

North Hero
Island

Butler
Island

N

GRAND
ISLE

Miles

0   2   4

2

© The Countryman Press

tion to the area's history, including the famous Confederate Raid of 1864, where 22 Confederate soldiers crossed the border from Canada, intending to rob the banks and burn down the community in a surprise attack.

One of the museum's knowledgeable volunteers will act as your personal guide as you explore two floors of the former Franklin County Grammar School, in use from 1861 to 1969. Or you can opt for a self-paced look around. Exhibits focus on Abenaki archaeology, military history, civic organizations, and rural medicine, including the real-life medical miracle of Phineas Gage. The railroad construction foreman survived a blasting accident where an iron rod pierced his skull.

A schoolroom on the upper level honors Louella Kittell, who taught seventh grade in this building for 41 years. The museum also recognizes longtime big band leader Sterling Weed, who lived until 104, and some of the now-shuttered local businesses, including the drive-in theater and a longtime barbershop. The Railroad Room, set up like a waiting room, complete with a ticket seller's office and telegraph equipment, explores the community's heyday as a booming railroad hub.

LOUELLA KITTELL'S CLASSROOM AT THE ST. ALBANS HISTORICAL SOCIETY

As you exit the museum, walk through **Taylor Park**, named for Holloway Taylor, an early settler who deeded this land to the town. The fountain was a gift from former Vermont governor John Gregory Smith in 1887. Known locally as "the ladies," this three-tiered sculpture features pensive maidens, cherubs, and a water sprite. From mid-May through October, the park hosts a weekly farmers' market.

STROLLING DOWN MAIN STREET

Main Street, which flanks the park, has a number of interesting shops and eateries. There's also the **Artist in Residence** (802-528-5222), a cooperative gallery showcasing the work of more than 40 area artists, among them painters, sculptors, jewelry designers, weavers, and wood turners. Monthly

DETOUR

Hathaway Point Road, a left off VT 36 after the bridge, takes you along St. Albans Bay's western edge to **Kamp Kill Kare State Park** (802-524-6021) on St. Albans Point. It's a day-use park with a great swimming beach and an interesting history. You can catch the ferry to **Burton Island State Park** (802-524-6353) from here.

Originally the land was farmed, but in the 1870s the St. Albans Boating and Fishing Club, a group of prominent local businessmen, bought the land. The Rocky Point House, a lakeshore resort hotel, opened for its first summer season in May 1894. The property later changed hands again to become a boys' summer camp in 1912. In 1967, the year after the camp closed, the Vermont State Parks system bought the 17-acre property to provide support services for its campground on the 253-acre Burton Island. Although many of the camp buildings were demolished, the three-story hotel was not, and today it contains a museum with informational displays on the property's history. A monument on the grounds, placed there in 1946 by the Kamp Kill Kare Alumni Association, honors former campers who perished in World War II.

The ferry to Burton Island runs several times daily in summer, a 10-minute crossing. Kayak and canoe rentals are available at **Kamp Kill Kare**, if you prefer to paddle. The state park on the island has lean-tos and tent sites, including a small remote tent-camping area, along with hiking trails, a nature center and museum, and the **Burton Island Bistro** (802-524-2212), which serves breakfast and lunch on weekdays. Day use is permitted. **Woods Island State Park** (802-524-6353), which offers primitive camping, is on a neighboring island, but you will need your own boat to get there.

After exploring these parks, return to VT 36 to continue north about 13 miles to Swanton.

receptions highlight three or four artists, affording them an opportunity to demonstrate or discuss their art.

Take a break at the **Traveled Cup** (802-524-2037), known for its home-made soups, sandwiches, and smoothies, or the **Catalyst Coffee Bar** (802-393-9808), specializing in syphon-brewed coffee and sweet and savory bites from **Red House Sweets** (802-782-7124), which shares its space. **As the Crow Flies** (802-524-2800) sells Vermont cheeses, specialty foods, wines, and kitchen products. Or check out the **Eloquent Page** (802-527-7243), which has a broad selection of used and collectible books—35,000 and counting—both fiction and nonfiction, including hard-to-find and unusual books. Consider visiting St. Albans in April for the three-day **Vermont Maple Festival** (802-524-5800), or in early December, when local farmers string colorful lights on their tractors for a nighttime holiday parade through the center of town.

Start exploring Vermont's northwest corner by heading west on VT 36 (Lake Street off Main) to St. Albans Bay, stopping along the way at **Hoss's Dogg House** (802-527-1373), which serves locally made burgers, hand-cut fries, hot dogs with house-made Michigan sauce, and other classic snack bar foods made from fresh and local ingredients. Its creemees are prepared with milk from local dairies.

VT 36 follows Lake Champlain's Maquam Bay and has good views of Butler Island and the Champlain Islands. As the road pulls away from the lake, look for Lanier Road on the left. The **Maquam Wildlife Management Area** is just across the road. Park near the gate and walk south on an old logging road. While today the area is open to the public for recreational use, in the early 1900s this was the site of Hotel Champlain, which had its own adjacent 700-acre stock farm for food. Guests would arrive via the Champlain Transportation Company's steamer, the *Maquam*, which traveled daily between Plattsburgh, New York, and Swanton, or by a rail excursion line from town. President William McKinley was the hotel's most famous guest, summering here one year. Part of the rail bed and the hotel site remain.

ALL ABOARD

As you approach Swanton, take a right on South River Street to visit the **Swanton Historical Society Railroad Depot Museum** (802-868-5436), open seasonally. The museum, which has an extensive collection of local railroad memorabilia and an operating model train, is housed in a restored 1890s train depot that was relocated here to save it from demolition. The building has a ticket agent's office and separate waiting rooms for men and women. Outside you can visit a 1937 Missisquoi Bay Bridge tollhouse and a 1910 Central Vermont Railway caboose, and view the foundation of a roundhouse.

Across from the museum, a restored 1902 Pennsylvania truss bridge marks the start of a 1-mile walking path, the first section of the 93-mile **Lamoille Valley Rail Trail** (802-229-0005). The recreational trail will extend from Swanton to St. Johnsbury when completed.

Head back the way you came, crossing over Lake Street (VT 36), and then take a slight left onto North River Street (VT 78) for 0.5 mile. Turn onto Brooklyn Street to get to **Maple City Candy** (802-868-5400). All of its maple products—maple sugar candy, fudge, maple cream, maple drops, and more—are made on site using pure maple syrup purchased from area farms. They also sell maple syrup and Vermont souvenirs, and in summer operate a creemee stand offering—what else?—maple creemees!

If you drive past the store for another 5.5 miles on VT 78 West, you will reach the **Missisquoi National Wildlife Refuge** (802-868-4781) on Tabor Road, a great place for hiking, recreational fishing, and wildlife watching. Its location on the Atlantic Flyway also makes it an ideal place to go birding, especially if you want to spot waterfowl. The great blue heron rookery on

SWANTON HISTORICAL SOCIETY RAILROAD DEPOT MUSEUM

Swanton's Royal Swans

BETTY AND SAM, SWANTON'S SWANS

Like many celebrities, Swanton's two most famous residents go by just their first names: Betty and Sam. They have posh digs with a pond in a prime location in the center of town where they welcome visitors daily.

Betty and Sam are Swanton's royal swans.

Although the common belief is that Swanton is a contraction of "Swan Town," in actuality the town was named for British naval officer and war hero William Swanton. The swans represent a link to the country of his birth and forge a relationship between the two countries.

The original pair of mute swans was a gift from Queen Elizabeth II to celebrate Swanton's bicentennial in 1963. They arrived in style, flown here by Trans-Canada Airlines from the Norfolk Naturalist Trust of Hickling Broad in Norfolk, England, which includes the village of Swanton Abbot. The townspeople named them Betty for the queen and Sam for Uncle Sam.

All the swans' successors are still referred to as Betty and Sam although they are not from the same lineage. From May through September they reside at **Village Green Park** on a small pond, enclosed by a black wrought-iron fence. Their house, complete with two white Corinthian columns, is modeled after the century-old Swanton Library that overlooks the green. They spend the winter at Missisquoi Valley Union High School in Swanton, where they share quarters with the school's flock of laying hens and are cared for by students in the Agricultural Sciences and Technology Department.

Shad Island, part of the 6,729-acre refuge, is the largest in Vermont. Retrace your route to town, turning left on VT 78 East (Merchants Row). As you hang right onto Grand Avenue, you'll pass the **Village Green Park** where the royal swans reside.

You can visit the **Abenaki Tribal Museum and Cultural Center** (802-868-

DETOUR

Leave VT 105 in North Sheldon, heading north on VT 120. At the 2-mile mark, look for the sign for **Due North Winery** (802-285-2053) on Skunks Misery Road. The winery typically is open Sunday afternoons for free tastings. On other days call ahead to see if you can stop by. Although essentially a one-man operation, owner and vintner Erich Marn is quite accommodating when it comes to visitors. He planted his first vines in 2008 and began selling wine four years later.

Continuing on, you will drive by several farms and have great views of Lake Carmi, the fourth-largest natural lake in the state, and Jay Peak in the dis-

tance. When you reach a four-way intersection 0.2 mile past the **Franklin United Church** (802-285-6425) and war memorial, stay to the right (VT 120/Lake Street). You will pass through more open agricultural land before you get to the north end of Lake Carmi.

The fishing access here is probably the best place for photos of the lake. Stop, take a few, and admire the vistas. Once you're back on the road, stay to the left at the Y. Mill Pond will be on your right. Take a sharp right onto VT 236. (A farm sits on this corner.) If you are interested in churches and historic church cemeteries, instead of turning you could stay on VT 120 for another 0.2 mile to the **East Franklin United Church** (802-285-6420).

FRANKLIN UNITED CHURCH

Once on VT 236, travel south for about 3.5 miles to **Lake Carmi State Park** (802-933-8383), which has more campsites than any other Vermont state park. It's a great day-use park for its swimming beaches, boat rentals, nature center, and bog boardwalk. The 140-acre black spruce–tamarack bog is unusual because of its size. In another few miles you are back on VT 105. This 15-mile route is a fun one to do by bike. You can leave your car at the parking lot for the **Missisquoi Valley Rail Trail** on Kane Road, which is on the other side of VT 105, directly opposite VT 120.

2559) to view its collection of artifacts, including clothing, tools, ceremonial headdresses, handwoven baskets, and other craftwork. Exhibits focus on the history of the Abenakis, including the fur trade and their traditions. Open weekdays, it's located in the headquarters of the **Missisquoi Abenaki Tribal Council** (802-868-6255) at 100 Grand Avenue.

Return to **Village Green Park** and make a right onto VT 78 (First Street). Drive through Highgate Center to Sheldon Junction, where you can pick up VT 105 to head east toward Enosburg Falls. The **Missisquoi Valley Rail Trail** (802-524-5958), a 26.4-mile recreational path from St. Albans to Richford, parallels VT 105 for several miles, crossing the road in places.

DRIVING THROUGH DAIRYLAND

Enosburg Falls, the next town on your route, is the self-proclaimed Dairy Capital of Vermont, hosting an annual **Vermont Dairy Festival** the first weekend in June. Although dairying has always been big in this area, the town can thank the arrival of the Central Vermont Railroad and Dr. Burney James Kendall, a graduate of the University of Vermont's Medical College, for its early prosperity.

The doctor came up with a cure for spavin, a joint ailment affecting horses. He founded the Dr. B. J. Kendall Company in town in the early 1880s to manufacture this and other patent medicines, making his company the largest employer in the area at that time. In 1892 he donated the money to build the **Enosburg Opera House** (802-933-6171) on Depot Street. The Victorian-style building, still in use as a cultural center, is on the National Register of Historic Places.

Visit the **Enosburgh Historical Society Museum**, housed in the former freight depot, to learn more about Kendall and his cures, local agriculture, the railroad, and other facets of the town's history. A caboose, which sits on a nearby siding, is open for viewing during museum hours.

Continue out of town to the **Boston Post Dairy** (802-933-2749), a family-run business with a cheese-making facility and retail store selling their award-winning farmstead cheeses, goat milk soaps, maple products, and baked goods. A viewing window provides an up-close look at how cheese is made. Just past the store, detour off VT 105 onto Boston Post Road for 4.3 miles to **Cold Hollow Sculpture Park** (512-333-2119). There is no charge to visit the 35-acre park designed by metal sculptor David Stromeyer to display his massive modern abstract sculptures. Hay fields and meadows serve as a backdrop for more than 50 sculptures, each strategically placed to integrate it with the landscape that inspired the piece. Walking trails are cut through the fields, and a map is provided. Throughout the season, which runs from late June to early October, Stromeyer teams up with other creative artists to offer "walking conversations" for the public to discuss his conceptual visions of selected works.

Return to VT 105 to continue to East Berkshire. Ask the locals where they eat, and the answer will be the **Pine Cone Snack Bar** (802-933-6630). It's been open seasonally at the same location for more than 40 years. There's dining inside or out and a miniature golf course and llamas for kids.

BACKROADS AND BRIDGES

VT 118 will take you through **Montgomery Center**, a lovely Vermont village, about 9 miles from **Jay Peak Ski Resort** (802-988-2611). Shop at **Mountain Fiber Folk Cooperative** (802-326-2092) for hats, scarves, rugs, and other products made from natural fibers. Or relax at the **Vermont Salt Cave Spa and Halotherapy Center** (802-326-2283), which offers salt cave therapy in a chamber constructed of Polish pink rock salt.

Montgomery is Vermont's Covered Bridge Capital. As late as the 1940s, it had an astounding 13 covered bridges; today there are only six, all within a

COLD HOLLOW SCULPTURE PARK, ENOSBURG FALLS

few-mile radius. Five of the bridges are along VT 118. To view the Creamery Bridge you will need to take Hill West Road to Creamery Bridge Road and take a right. Loop back on West Hill Road (yes, these are two different roads) to get back to where you began on Main Street.

Follow VT 118 to Belvidere Corners, then stay right for VT 109 to Waterville. Although there's not much to see along this 6-mile stretch, the scenery is beautiful and you will find five more covered bridges, all of which cross the North Branch of the Lamoille River. You'll have to wander off the main route to see them, so it's best to stop and ask for directions. In Waterville turn right on Lapland Road, which becomes Waterville Mountain Road, to Bakersfield. Portions of this route are unpaved. In Bakersfield, you have a choice of going west on VT 36 back to St. Albans or heading north on VT 108 to the **Chester A. Arthur State Historic Site** (802-933-8362).

If you prefer to skip this detour, VT 36 will take you through East Fairfield, where you can take a look at the **East Fairfield Covered Bridge** (left on Bridge Street), a queenpost-truss bridge built in 1865 and listed on the National Register of Historic Places. You also could head north on North Road to Pond Road to Fairfield Pond. A beach and fishing access is located at the water's northern end. This side trip is perfect for soaking up the fall colors. Follow this route to the pond, then continue on Sheldon Woods Road

---

DETOUR

Everyone knows the story of "Silent Cal," the Plymouth Notch native who made it to the White House. But what about the other Vermont-born president? Chester Alan Arthur, son of a Baptist minister from Fairfield, also served, becoming president in September 1881 after the untimely death of James Garfield.

To get to the **Chester A. Arthur State Historic Site** (802-933-8362), take VT 108 north to Bordoville Road. Go left, and then left again on Chester A. Arthur Road. You also can access the site from VT 105, just west of Enosburg Falls, although that route is slightly longer.

The cheery yellow two-room house is a reconstruction of the parsonage where Arthur's family moved when he was one year old. Pictorial exhibits tell the story of his life and political career.

The president was dubbed "Elegant Arthur," as he was always impeccably dressed, often changing his outfits several times a day. It is rumored that as an adult he never wore the same pair of pants twice. He brought his fastidiousness to the White House, insisting that the entire interior be remodeled before he moved in. Items from previous administrations were sold at public auction. Near the building is a monument, dedicated by Robert Todd Lincoln in 1903, that marks the spot where it's believed the cottage where he was

(continued on next page)

CHESTER A. ARTHUR STATE HISTORIC SITE

born in 1829 stood. Fairfield Center School students designed and built the President Chester A. Arthur Walking Trail in 2002, including the boardwalks and bridges on this woodsy nature trail. The trailhead is near the picnic area behind the monument.

After visiting the historic site, continue along this two-lane country road to **North Fairfield Church**. This church sits on the site where the Reverend William Arthur, his father, preached. It was built around 1840 to replace an earlier church and was never modernized. In fact, it still has no electricity. It's open to the public when the historic site is open, weekends from July through mid-October. Keep on this road, and at the T turn left on North Street for 1 mile to VT 36, then head west to St. Albans. Can't get enough of President Arthur? The **Fairfield Town Hall** (802-827-3261) at 25 North Street also has a small museum dedicated to the 21st president, open weekdays.

to East Sheldon Road to Enosburg Falls, cutting back to VT 36 on Boston Post Road to return to St. Albans.

Best Places to Sleep

BACK INN TIME (802-527-5116), 68 Fairfield Street, St. Albans. Wealthy merchant Victor Atwood spared no expense when he built his Victorian manor house on Fairfield Street in 1858. It was spacious—the kind of place where he and his wife Charlotte could entertain guests—and also close to the city center. Innkeepers Ron and KarenMarie Peltier have created that same sense of place in their beautifully restored inn, replete with period furnishings. The purple granite fireplace in the dining room is original to the house. They have five guest rooms with private baths, including two rooms with fireplaces, plus a self-catering apartment. Breakfast, featuring fresh, local ingredients, is included for guests booking rooms. Picnic basket lunches may be ordered, and dinner is by reservation. The inn also hosts

WELCOME TO FAIRFIELD

"Music & More" nights in its restored Carriage Barn, featuring live music and local foods. Inquire when making reservations. $$–$$$.

THE 1906 HOUSE (802-933-3030), 27 Main Street, Enosburg Falls. When Jennifer Neville Bright bought this aging property, originally the home of Moses Perley, a dry goods store owner and a partner in the Dr. B. J. Kendall Company, it needed more than just a little tender loving care. It required a complete overhaul, inside and out, but the result is a stunning Main Street inn with a relaxed ambience. The Colonial Revival house with a porte cochere has six rooms, some with shared bath, and all with original hardwood floors. Rates include a full breakfast. Jennifer also owns the four-room **Tabor House Inn** (802-868-7575) in West Swanton that overlooks Maquam Bay. $$.

PHINEAS SWANN BED AND BREAKFAST (802-326-4306), 195 Main Street, Montgomery Center. That this inn has "gone to the dogs" is an understatement. Unlike some inns that claim to be pet friendly, then tack on hefty fees and restrictions if you bring your pet, this venue treats dogs as pampered guests. Innkeepers Darren and Lynne Drevik welcome dogs to stay in the six luxury suites in the Carriage House and River House. The Main House, which has three individually designed rooms, is a dog-free zone for the comfort of guests who may be allergic. If visiting in winter, ask about the Pet Perfect Ski Package, which includes lodging, breakfast, Jay Peak Resort lift tickets, doggie treat bag, and dog-walking services while you're on the slopes. $$–$$$$.

Best Places to Eat

ONE FEDERAL RESTAURANT & LOUNGE (802-524-0330), 1 Federal Street, St. Albans. Open Sun.–Thurs. 11 AM–9 PM, Fri.–Sat. 11 AM–10 PM. Housed in the historic St. Albans Foundry and Implement Co. factory, the restaurant serves classic American fare with a Vermont twist. Chef Marcus Hamblett sources ingredients from area farms as much as possible. House specialties include frickles—deep-fried pickle slices with ranch dipping sauce—and the Vermonter burger, an Angus beef patty topped with Cabot cheddar, Granny Smith apples, bacon, and a drizzle of maple syrup. Other popular menu choices include the Vermont Surf 'n Turf—slow-roasted prime rib and maple-bacon sea scallops—and comfort foods such as the butternut ravioli and smoked pork shoulder. Kids eat free on Tuesdays with the purchase of an adult entrée. $$–$$$.

THE INN RESTAURANT (802-326-4391), 241 Main Street, Montgomery Center. Open Thurs.–Sun. 5–9 PM. An inviting atmosphere with food and drink inspired by farm-fresh ingredients adds up to an exceptional dining experience at this out-of-the way location. Seasonal menus are inventive, often with an international flair. Entrées may range from coconut red curry shrimp and Asian noodle bowl to a pan-seared beef rib eye. Seating is by the fireside or in the livelier tavern. Owners Nick Barletta and Scott Pasfield also run **The INN**, originally a late nineteenth-century timber baron's house, which has 11 tasteful but distinctively different rooms, including a dog-friendly room with a balcony. $$–$$$.

15

NORTHEAST KINGDOM

ESTIMATED LENGTH: 98 miles

ESTIMATED TIME: 2 to 4 days

HIGHLIGHTS: Given its exceptional rural beauty and relative isolation, the 2,000-square-mile northeastern corner of Vermont has come to be known as the Northeast Kingdom.

Our route runs through high, gently rolling fields with views of distant mountains and woods spotted with big ponds and lakes, most notably fjord-like **Lake Willoughby**. Everywhere there's a sense of discovery: One minute it's a 946-pound stuffed moose by the post office boxes in a general store, next it's a barn filled with the **Bread and Puppet Theater's** huge and haunting creations. At a hilltop dirt crossroads, a four-story granite dormitory built in 1836 is now the **Old Stone House Museum**. Roads that tunnel beneath double rows of maples may lead to farms selling their own prize-winning cheese and world-class beer. The gateway to this route is St. Johnsbury, home two Victorian-era time capsules: the **Fairbanks Museum and Planetarium** and the **St. Johnsbury Athenaeum**. As a change from driving, there's sculling at the **Craftsbury Outdoor Center** or mountain biking on the **Kingdom Trails** on and around **Burke Mountain**.

GETTING THERE: Despite its back-and-beyond feel, the Northeast Kingdom is more quickly and easily accessible from points southeast than much of Vermont. I-93 puts St. Johnsbury within three hours of Boston via dramatic Franconia Pass in New Hampshire's White Mountains. The **Vermont Welcome Center** (I-93 in Waterford; open daily 7 AM–7 PM) offers WiFi, but there's also a pay phone, a clue to the area's sketchy coverage. I-93 ends at I-91; heading north, the first exits (19 and 20) are for St. Johnsbury; our drive begins with I-91 Exit 21.

LEFT: STONE HOUSE MUSEUM, BROWNINGTON CENTER ORLEANS COUNTY HISTORICAL SOCIETY

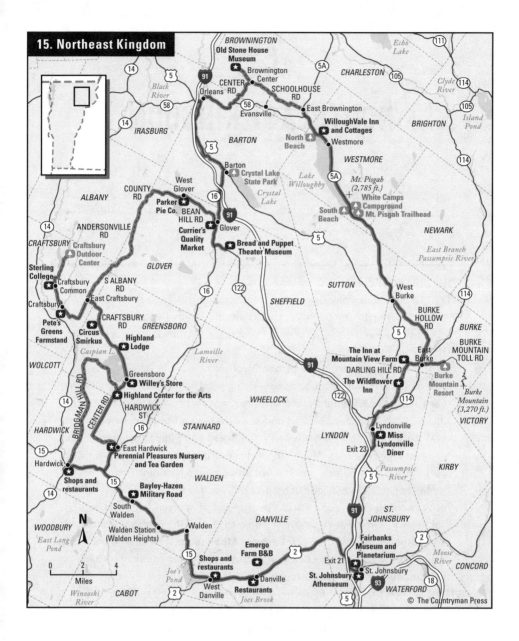

OFF THE ROAD

Almost immediately you sense the need to downshift mentally and look around.

From I-91, US 2 climbs so steeply for 7 miles that the White Mountains appear in the rearview mirror. The traffic light in Danville Village is the last for a long while. Turn right at the light to stop for lunch at **Bentley's Bakery**

& Café (802-864-3385) or for dinner at the **Creamery Restaurant** (802-684-3616). At nearby **Emergo Farm B&B** (802-684-2215), a working dairy farm that's been in the family for six generations, Lori Webster welcomes guests to stay the night or longer.

US 2 runs on to West Danville and by **Joe's Pond**. Named for a Native American beloved by early settlers, this pond is said to empty eventually into Long Island Sound, while water from Molly's Pond (a mile south and named for Joe's wife) ends up in the Gulf of St. Lawrence. Just before the junction of US 2 and VT 15, there are pondside picnic tables and a small beach. **Hastings Store** (802-684-398), across the road, is known for its daily-made doughnuts and blueberry cake. In the adjoining **Joe's Pond Craft Shop** (802-684-2192; open May–Dec.), owner Deborah Stresing weaves her rag rugs between serving customers. At **Three Ponds** (802-227-3300; open Thurs.–Mon. for breakfast and lunch), the menu ranges from corned beef hash to falafels.

HASTINGS GENERAL STORE, WEST DANVILLE

Turn off US 2 onto VT 15 and settle back for the 13-mile drive to Hardwick. It's a beautiful ride, especially beyond Walden Station, the crossroads at which our route begins to shadow the **Bayley-Hazen Military Road** (see sidebar).

Hardwick's block-long commercial center serves a wide rural area and is a logical road food stop. Options range from veggie and seriously healthy fare in the tiny café upstairs at the **Buffalo Mountain Food Co-op** (802-472-3800) to from-scratch buttermilk doughnuts and cream pies along with daily soups and specials at **Connie's Kitchen** (802-472-8800). **Positive Pie** (802-471-7126) features specialty pizzas and local brews, but there's a full menu. We usually try for reliable diner food in one of the booths overlooking the

The **Bayley-Hazen Military Road** was conceived as an invasion route from the Connecticut River to Canada, and George Washington ordered construction to begin in 1772. Given military reversals, its progress was sporadic, but more than 50 miles were eventually completed before it became obvious that the road could just as easily serve as an invasion route *from* as *to* Canada. A flop as a military effort, the Bayley-Hazen served significantly as a settler's route after the Revolution, and today it remains a popular mountain-biking route.

THE LAMOILLE RIVER CUTS THROUGH THE TOWN OF HARDWICK

Lamoille River at the **Village Restaurant** (802-472-5701; breakfast all day from 6 AM and good diner fare until 8 PM). Don't miss the **Galaxy Bookshop** (802-472-5533), with its mural of Hardwick Main Street, a large children's book section, and selections by Vermont writers.

HEART OF THE KINGDOM

From Hardwick it's a tough choice between two beautiful byways north to Greensboro. The longer, most scenic route begins on North Main Street, which turns to dirt in a half mile as Bridgman Hill Road. It runs through high farmland with fields filled with wheat and wildflowers, seemingly stretching to some of the highest of the Green Mountains. In less than a half-dozen miles, **Caspian Lake** appears in the distance. Turn right on Lake View Road, which turns into Lake Shore Road; a small memorial marks the site of the blockhouse that once stood along this stretch of the Bayley-Hazen Military Road. In 1781 two young scouts—Constant Bliss and Moses Sleeper—were

DETOUR

Follow signs from East Hardwick to **Perennial Pleasures Nursery and Tea Garden** (802-472-5104), known for its traditional English Cream Tea, served with scones, cakes, savories, and fresh cream (open Memorial Day–Labor Day, 12–4 daily except Mon.; $–$$). The brick Federal-era house is set in a 3-acre nursery of perennial plants and flowers (open May–mid-Sept., 10–5), a destination for serious gardeners. A shop features summer hats and gardening tools. From here follow Hardwick Farms Road 1.5 miles to Center Road, then north to Breezy Avenue in Greensboro Village.

killed here. (Their memory is also commemorated in the names of nationally distributed cheese produced by Greensboro-based Jasper Hill.) Turn left on Breezy Avenue into Greensboro Village.

The shorter, more well-used route from Walden to Greensboro Village begins at the junction of VT 15 with VT 16 south of the village of Hardwick. Turn north on VT 16, and in less than a mile take a left into the village of **East Hardwick** and follow Hardwick Street an unusually straight 1.6 miles (this is an original stretch of the Bayley-Hazen Military Road) into Greensboro Village.

GREENSBORO

Greensboro's year-round population (770) triples in summer thanks to a tightly knit, high-brow, low-key cottage colony founded in the 1890s on **Caspian Lake**. The lake isn't visible from the middle of the village, but its public beach is right there around the corner. The long-established **Miller's Thumb Gallery** (802-533-2045; open daily May–Oct.), with a select mix of artwork and craftsmanship, is housed in an old gristmill; its raceway is still visible through a window in the floor. The heart of the village is **Willey's Store** (802-533-2621), one of Vermont's most beloved and extensive general stores. It's good for groceries, local produce, meat, hardware, and toys, and its dairy section is a prime outlet for **Jasper Hill Cheese**. Upstairs the surprisingly wide selection of clothing and footwear has recently acquired a more sophisticated look and a wine-tasting corner, a clue to the village's rising profile.

For more than 30 years Greensboro has been home to Circus Smirkus (smirkus.org), with two campuses and dual roles: a summer camp geared to all ages and abilities, and a highly professional touring troupe with summer performances here and throughout New England. A more recent draw is **Hill Farmstead Brewery** (802-533-7450), pronounced the world's best beer in 2013 by the industry-respected website ratebeer.com. The small-batch

UPSTAIRS IN WILLEY'S STORE, GREENVILLE

brews are available in bottles and growlers at a farm that belonged to brewmaster Shaun Hill's grandfather. It's a few miles up a dirt road from the village, open Wed.–Sun. 12–5 PM; see hillfarmstead.com for current beers, special events, and directions.

Greensboro's most recent attraction is the year-round **Highland Center for the Arts** (802-533-2000; highlandartsvt.org), opened in 2017 thanks to a $14 million gift from a Caspian Lake summer resident. The complex includes an art gallery, a 250-seat state-of-the-art theater, smaller performance spaces (films are shown Wednesday evenings), and the glass-walled **Hardwick Street Café** (802-433-9399; open Tues.–Sat. for lunch and dinner, Sun. brunch). Despite a façade partly modeled on Shakespeare's Globe Theater, the center fits unobtrusively into its site south of the village.

CRAFTSBURY

From Greensboro, Craftsbury Road runs on into the heart of this glorious high country, through East Craftsbury with its Presbyterian Church (a number of area families came here from Scotland in the early nineteenth century), and on a couple more miles into the village of Craftsbury. Keep an eye out for **Pete's Greens** farm stand (open May–Oct., daily 8 AM–8 PM), with its roof-sprouting salad greens. Pete Johnson is known as one of the

STILLMEADOW GARDENS, A FORMER DAIRY FARM BETWEEN CRAFTSBURY AND ALBANY

people who has helped redefine the meaning of agriculture in Vermont. It can snow here in May, but over the past 20 years, Johnson has established a major year-round organic farming operation, producing 100 varieties of vegetables, with numerous outlets and CSA deliveries as far as Brooklyn. In addition to stellar produce, this self-service farm stand stocks eggs, raw honey, locally grown grains, and more.

Up the road at **Craftsbury General Store** (802-586-2440), Emily Maclure also features local produce, along with local beers, freshly made sushi from Hardwick, house-made specialty pizzas, locally sourced salads, sandwiches, and deli staples.

The road climbs another mile to hilltop **Craftsbury Common**, arguably the proudest village in the Kingdom. Many of its Federal-era homes now house environmentally geared Sterling College. Facing the outsized common itself is Craftsbury Academy, founded in 1829 and operating ever since as the town's public high school.

Unlike most North Country pioneers, town founder Ebenezer Crafts was university educated (Yale, class of 1740). Due to Revolutionary War debts, he was forced to sell his tavern in Sturbridge, Massachusetts (the still-popular Publick House), eventually guiding his family and 150 neighbors along the Bayley-Hazen Military Road to this site. Check out the imposing portraits of Ebenezer and his son Samuel in the **Craftsbury Public Library** (802-586-9683) at the far end of the common (turn by the church). It's a comfortable oasis with WiFi and porch rockers overlooking the mountains.

In winter most visitors who come this far are headed for the **Craftsbury Outdoor Center** (802-586-7767; 535 Lost Nation Road), one of New England's most extensive and dependably snow-covered places to cross-country ski. In summer and fall the center is best known for its sculling sessions on adjacent Hosmer Pond; it also hosts Road Scholar and running programs, housing and feeding some 90 guests per day.

DIRT ROADS GALORE

Hard-packed dirt farm roads meander off in all directions across this high, open plateau, and the best way not to get lost (although that's rewarding too) is to return to the crossroads in East Craftsbury and, instead of turning right for Greensboro, continue north (straight) up the dirt South Albany Road. Veer right on Andersonville Road, which turns into County Road, running on for 5 miles to the crossroads village of West Glover, where **Parker Pie Co.** (802-525-3366; open daily except Sun. for lunch and dinner) is a destination for visitors from throughout the area. From East Craftsbury you might follow signs to local enterprises like **Stillmeadow Gardens** (open May–July; call ahead: 802-775-6713), a former dairy farm that has been in the Urie family since 1833 and is known for Betty Urie's hanging flower baskets and healthy

CURRIER'S QUALITY MARKET, GLOVER

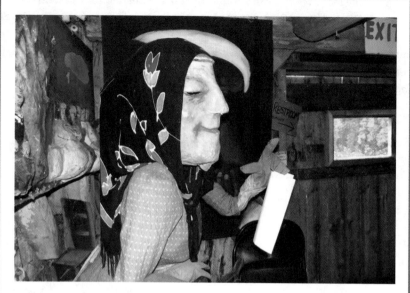

BREAD & PUPPET THEATER MUSEUM, GLOVER

Travel south down VT 16 for a mile and turn east on VT 122 for another mile or so to the **Bread and Puppet Theater Museum** (802-525-3031; open mid-June–Oct., 10 AM–6 PM). This doesn't look like much from outside, but the weathered old dairy barn houses a collection of some of the biggest puppets in the world: huge and haunting puppet dwarfs, giants, devils, and other fantastic figures of good and evil (warning: these might be scary for young children). In July and Aug., performances are staged Friday evenings (7:30 PM) in the timber-frame theater and Sunday afternoons (3 PM) in the natural outdoor amphitheater.

plantings. At nearby **Bonnieview Farm** (call ahead: 802-755-6878), Neil Urie produces outstanding cheeses from unpasteurized sheep's and cow's milk. The better to savor the beauty and deep down peace of this area, consider spending the night at **Rodgers Country Inn** (802-525-6677), a former dairy farm on our suggested route that's been in Jim Rodgers' family since the early 1800s. Nancy Rodgers directs guests to swimming holes and other local secrets and serves dinner on request.

From West Glover Village, Bean Hill Road runs downhill to VT 16 and the village of Glover, with **Currier's Quality Market** (802-525-8822) at its center. Stop in to see the 946-pound stuffed moose and the many formerly live animals lurking in the aisles and hanging from the rafters of this old-style emporium. In addition to staples and a good deli counter with hot specials, this is a major sporting goods store, selling fishing and hunting licenses and stocking extensive gear.

From Glover Village, follow VT 16 north. The entrance to I-91 presents a choice between two ways to Orleans: Either a quick 6 miles up the interstate or up VT 16 to Barton and on up US 5. If it's a good day for a swim, opt for Barton and **Crystal Lake State Park** (802-525-6205) east of town off VT 16. It offers shaded picnic tables, lifeguards, a bathhouse, a large swath of grass, and a small sand beach on this well-named lake.

THE OLD STONE HOUSE MUSEUM

However you get there, don't miss the Kingdom's most distinctive building, a 30-room, four-story, granite school dormitory completed in 1836 by Alexander Twilight, believed to be America's first African American graduate of an American college (Middlebury) and the first to serve in a state legislature (the Vermont House of Representatives).

From Brownington Center, follow Schoolhouse Road 4.4 miles to its junc-

Old Stone House Museum (802-754-2022; open May 15–Oct. 15, Wed.–Sun. 11 AM–5 PM) is posted on VT 58, less than a mile east of Orleans. Follow Center Road to Brownington Historic District, a hilltop scattering of early nineteenth-century buildings set on 60 acres of farmland along maple-lined dirt roads. This village is far smaller and stiller today than it was in 1829, when Alexander Twilight arrived to assume his duties as Congregational minister and schoolmaster. The Orleans County Grammar School had just opened and, to compete with Craftsbury Academy for students from area towns, Twilight suggested building a dormitory to house them. Lacking support from school trustees, it's still a mystery how he managed to build this stone Athenian Hall. Eventually the town center shifted downhill to its present location, and in 1917, the Orleans County Historical Society saved this building from demolition. The museum now encompasses several surrounding buildings and offers a glimpse of the vitality and inventiveness of the early nineteenth century in this far rural corner of New England.

In 2016 the Grammar School building, which has served as an active Grange Hall since the 1870s, was moved—with the help of 23 teams of oxen—a third of a mile up the road from its original location. In 2017 more than a dozen murals by Rufus Porter, one of the era's premier itinerant artists, were installed in Athenian Hall. **Old Stone House Day** (second Sunday in August) represents one of the Kingdom's biggest annual events, but it's on quiet days that we find this hilltop cluster most appealing. Don't miss the view from the **observatory tower on Prospect Hill**. Check the website for year-round special events and workshops. Guided tours begin at the Alexander Twilight House.

tion with VT 5A in East Brownington. For a paved option, turn on Hunt Hill Road in Brownington; it quickly rejoins VT 58; turn east to VT 5A.

LAKE WILLOUGHBY

Turn south (right) on VT 5A for the first stunning views of Lake Willoughby, wedged between Mounts Pisgah and Hor, each more than 2,500 feet high, together forming dramatic Willoughby Gap. In the nineteenth century this fjord-like lake was home to competing hotels and excursion boats. More than 300 feet deep in places, it's said to harbor a prehistoric sea monster named "Willy", but today all is quiet. On a sunny, midsummer day, North Beach (parking is near the junction of VT 5A and VT 16) can be almost empty, except for the seagulls that mysteriously frequent it. South Beach, some 5 miles down VT 5A, is smaller but busier; White Caps Campground across the road rents canoes and kayaks. The trailhead for a steep but relatively short climb up to a view from Mount Pisgah begins on VT 5A, less than a mile south of the lake. Continue on VT 5A to West Burke and on US 5 another 4 miles to East Burke.

BURKE MOUNTAIN AREA AND KINGDOM TRAILS

Entering the village of East Burke, you barely notice the road up Burke Mountain, but the effects of this lone mountain, towering 3,200 feet above sea level, are evidenced by the places to stay, eat, and shop here at its feet. A longtime ski area with a respectable vertical and excellent terrain, **Burke Mountain Resort** (skiburke.com) remains low-key and the village remains tiny. It's as busy in summer and fall as in winter, thanks to **Kingdom Trails** (802-626-7037), a nonprofit association that accesses over 100 miles of trails through woods and fields and up the mountain. **Burke Mountain Resort** (802-626-7300) also maintains lift-assisted trails within its **Burke Bike Park**. Recognized as one of the country's most varied and extensive mountain-biking trail networks, East Burke attracts a noticeable number of families as well as jocks.

Theoretically you can drive the 2.5-mile Auto Road, constructed by the Civilian Conservation Corps in the 1930s, to the **Burke Mountain summit**, but, having done it, we don't recommend the stress on your brakes on the way down, even in lowest gear. We much prefer the ride along maple-lined, dirt **Darling Hill Road** along a ridge lined with homes and farms that were once all owned by Elmer Darling, an East Burke native who became co-owner and manager of the Fifth Avenue Hotel in New York City. In the 1880s Darling acquired the old farms along this road, building the brick cream-

VIEW FROM THE NORTHERN SHORE OF WILLOUGHBY LAKE, WESTMORE

ery (to furnish his hotel with cheese and milk) and handsome barns that are now the **Inn at Mountain View Farm** (802-626-9924). Another former farm, the **Wildflower Inn** (802-626-8310), offers access to a beautiful stretch of the Kingdom Trails and rentals from a full-service bike shop. The terrace at the inn's **Juniper's Restaurant** commands a glorious view.

Back down on hardtop, follow signs for **Lyndonville** and continue down its broad main streets, laid out in the 1860s by the Passumpsic River Railroad Co. Note the brick Darling Hotel (now elderly housing) and, in the commercial lineup south of the village, the iconic **Miss Lyndonville Diner** (802-626-9890; open 5 AM–8 PM). Exit 23 of I-91 is a mile south.

We strongly urge a stop in **St. Johnsbury** (I-91 Exit 21), the shire town of Caledonia County and the largest community (population 7,600) in the Northeast Kingdom. Its late nineteenth century prosperity as a rail junction and industrial and commercial center is evidenced in the brick buildings along Railroad Street and the gracious homes and public buildings up on Main Street. Don't miss the **Fairbanks Museum** and the **St. Johnsbury Athenaeum** (see sidebar). Whether you begin or end this route in "St. J," the road food stop here is **Anthony's Diner** (802-748-3613; open 6:30 AM–8 PM). Regulars gather around the counter, and there are specials at every meal.

Fairbanks Museum and Planetarium (802-748-2372; open daily 9 AM–5 PM; admission $; planetarium shows on weekends). Franklin Fairbanks wished this museum to be "the people's school." The Fairbanks family's wealth came manufacturing their world-famous scale, and they traveled the world, collecting much of what's displayed in this wonderful Victorian-style "Cabinet of Curiosities." Opened in 1891, this is said to be the country's oldest science education museum, and it is the state's only public planetarium.

The main hall is capped by a 30-foot-high, barrel-vaulted ceiling, its floor lined with Victorian-style cabinets displaying thousands of stuffed animals: from mice to a vintage 1898 moose, from bats to bears (including a superb polar bear), birds galore (from hummingbirds to passenger pigeons), reptiles,

DRAWING IN THE GALLERY FAIRBANKS MUSEUM

fish, and insect nests. Franklin Fairbanks was passionate about nature, and the collection represents most native species of mammals and birds, a total of 3,000 specimens. An extensive and varied geologic collection started by Franklin is also displayed, along with a living exhibit of local wildflowers in bloom. The balcony, which circles the entire hall level, is lined with historical displays depicting local nineteenth-century life and exhibits drawn from a 5,000-piece collection representing most of the world's far corners—Malaysia, the Orient, the Middle East, and Africa—assembled by the Fairbanks family and their friends. An interactive Exploration Station invites hands-on discovery. The **planetarium** presents the current night sky as it appears in the Northeast Kingdom. The museum is also a U.S. weather observation station, and its daily "Eye on the Sky" forecasts are a fixture of Vermont Public Radio.

St. Johnsbury Athenaeum (802-748-8291); 1171 Main Street, open Mon., Wed., Fri. 10 AM–5:30 PM; Tues.–Thurs. 2–7 PM; Sat. 10 AM–3 PM. In the 1870s Horace Fairbanks personally selected the original 9,000 leather-bound books for the library and the gallery paintings by Hudson River School artists, including Albert Bierstadt, whose large rendition of the *Domes of the Yosemite* is the centerpiece. Natural light through an arched skylight enhances the effect of looking into the Yosemite Valley. Art gallery admission $.

Best Places to Sleep

Listed as they appear along the route

EMERGO FARM B&B (802-684-2215 or 888-383-1185), 261 Webster Hill, Danville. Just north of the village, this is a handsome, sixth-generation working dairy farm with 200 head of cattle, set on 230 acres with panoramic views. Lori Webster offers guests a tastefully furnished, upstairs front room (private bath) and a one-bedroom apartment with full kitchen and sitting room. $.

HIGHLAND LODGE (803-533-2566), 1608 Craftsbury Road, Greensboro. This rambling inn is a beloved local icon, set on 230 acres on Barr Hill, high above Caspian Lake but with a beach and lake access. The "lodge" moniker is misleading, dating to a developer's failed 1920s plan to build 70 cottages around it; 10 survive. At this writing breakfast is served only to inn guests (cottages are self-catering), but the bar is open to the public. In winter 35 km of well-maintained cross-country ski trails continue to be a big draw. $ for inn rooms, $$ for cottages.

RODGERS COUNTRY INN (802-525-6677 or 800-729-1704), 582 Rodgers Road, West Glover. Not far from Shadow Lake (good for swimming and fishing), this is a comfortable old farmhouse (shared bath) with plenty of space to unwind, and its peaceful setting beckons guests out for a walk down to the beaver pond or a bike ride along miles of hard-packed farm roads. A full breakfast, served at the dining room table, is included in the rate. Inquire about a rental cottage. $.

WILLOUGHVALE INN AND COTTAGES (802-525-4123 or 800-594-9102), 793 VT 5A, Westmore. This contemporary inn overlooks Lake Willoughby, and three of its housekeeping cottages are sited right on the lake. There's a dock for swimming, boating, and paddling. A taproom offers light dinners; continental breakfast is included in the rates. $–$$ for rooms, $$–$$$ for cottages.

THE VILLAGE INN OF EAST BURKE (802-626-3161), 606 VT 114, East Burke. Chris and Karri Willy's comfortable, affordable B&B is a find. There's a fully equipped guest kitchen, inviting shared spaces, a weatherproofed hot tub, a locked bike storage room, and extensive brookside gardens. Rooms (private baths) vary widely and include two apartments. A full breakfast is included in the rates. $ per couple per night plus $25 per extra person.

THE WILDFLOWER INN (802-626-8310 or 800-627-8310), 2059 Darling Hill Road. Under more than 30 years' ownership by Jim and Mary O'Reilly, the inn has grown from nineteenth-century farmhouse to include several buildings, all set high on a ridge with views across surrounding hills and valleys. There is direct access to a standout stretch of Kingdom Trails, and a full-service bike shop offers rentals. The pool and Juniper's Restaurant, its outdoor terrace, and SpokeEasy Lounge all command the amazing view. B&B $$–$$$.

BURKE MOUNTAIN HOTEL AND CONFERENCE CENTER (802-626-7400 or 866-977-4820), 2559 Mountain Road, East Burke. New in 2016, this four-floor, two-wing, 116-room ski lodge is sited almost midway up the mountain, commanding a distant view of Willoughby Gap. The one-, two-, and three-bedroom units come with kitchens and eating areas, most with balconies. Amenities include a restaurant. Rates spike and fall depending on the day and season. $$.

Best Places to Eat

PARKER PIE CO. (802-525-3366), 161 County Road, West Glover Village. Open except Mon. 11 AM–9 PM; until 10 PM Fri.–Sat. This foodie destination in the back of the Lake Parker Country Store features locally crafted beers and a dazzling array of thin-crust pizzas, cooked on stone with locally sourced toppings ranging from veggies and cheeses to smoked sausage and bacon. Local greens, sandwiches, and nachos are also available. Inquire about live music.

FOGGY GOGGLE OSTERIA (802-417-3500), 66 Belden Hill Road, East Burke. Open Thurs.–Mon. 4–9 PM. The white farmhouse is hidden behind the village and apart from the larger parking area. An "Osteria," co-owner Sara Miles explains, is a simple, roadside Italian restaurant; fare runs from burgers and pizza to Pollo al Rustica plus pad Thai and beef tenderloin. We can vouch for the quality and ambience.

INDEX